Friedman argues that an affordable path to the transcendental ideals of the welfare state is open by way of the increasing rationalization of law. Such law not only specifies the ethical principles and practical contingencies underlying redistribution, but it also formally closes the scope of sovereign responsibility at any one juncture in a nation's history. These closures, albeit temporary, are crucial to the preservation of a nation's resource base without which the legitimation of social rights grinds to a halt.

Kathi V. Friedman, now living in Washington, D.C., has taught sociology at Tulane University. She has also worked as a sociologist for the Human Resources Planning Institute and the Battelle Human Affairs Research Centers in Seattle, Washington.

LEGITIMATION OF SOCIAL RIGHTS

AND THE WESTERN WELFARE STATE

Legitimation of Social Rights and the Western Welfare State

A Weberian Perspective

by Kathi V. Friedman

The University of North Carolina Press Chapel Hill

© 1981 The University of North Carolina Press

Library of Congress Cataloging in Publication Data

Friedman, Kathi V   1943–
   Legitimation of social rights and the western
welfare state.

   Bibliography: p.
   Includes index.
   1. Welfare state—Addresses, essays, lectures.
2. Weber, Max, 1864–1920—Addresses, essays,
lectures.   3. Social policy—Addresses, essays,
lectures.   4. United States—Social policy—
Addresses, essays, lectures.   I. Title.
HN17.F74   361.6′5   80-29600
ISBN 0-8078-1480-6

FOR MICHAEL

CONTENTS

FIGURES

ACKNOWLEDGMENTS

WITHOUT THE inestimable encouragement given me by Duncan MacRae, Jr., the occasion for these acknowledgments would not likely have arisen. More than any other individual he provided the professional criticism, patience, and interest that reinforced my belief in the worth of the task I had taken upon myself. For these qualities, I thank him.

T. Anthony Jones, Paul F. Kress, Gerhard E. Lenski, Marvin E. Olsen, Guenther Roth, and Everett K. Wilson also provided constructive comment on earlier drafts, or portions thereof, of this work. Variously they helped me attend to distinctions and subtleties regarding natural law, the Marxist tradition, Weber's writings, and other areas where far more expertise was needed than I had at the time of writing. Marvin Olsen suggested the phrase "legitimation of social rights," and for this I am especially grateful because it helped crystallize my thinking at a crucial juncture during the writing of the manuscript.

I cannot miss this chance to express a note of thanks to the general collectivity of scholars whom I have never met, but whose works made mine possible. Their enthusiasm for their material was contagious, and it was an issue raised by Andrew Hacker in *The End of the American Era* (1972) that stirred my intellectual curiosity and eventually led to the present examination of the Western welfare state and its controversies. Hacker wrote:

> While government is held responsible for social order, it is not permitted to tax accordingly. . . . The question therefore arises whether Americans actually want their government to better conditions. Considering the degree to which the public holds it accountable for the shortcomings of society, one might conclude that the American people do so desire official initiatives. But . . . America has become an ungovernable nation whose inhabitants refuse to regard themselves as citizens of a social order

in which the authority of government plays a principal role."
[pp. 141–42]

Was this description accurate? And if so, how could such a state of affairs be resolved, if at all? These questions intrigued me, and this work is a response to issues raised from the late 1960s to the present regarding the welfare state. Theodore J. Lowi, for example, wrote that "governmental effort on a scale unknown in the Western world seems to offend more beneficiaries than it ingratiates" (1969:xiv). I considered this a real paradox, and my attempt to unravel it led back to the natural law tradition in Western rule.

Appropriately, then, I would also like to acknowledge the welfare state itself. Because the topic treated herein deals with the value of social insurance as a safety net for those times in a citizen's life when unforeseen events interrupt income, this is an especially pertinent acknowledgment to make: for at one interval during the writing of this manuscript I became a beneficiary of Title III of the U.S. Social Security Act—I collected unemployment insurance. Without it, the normal anxieties that attend the writing of a lengthy work could only have been aggravated.

Special thanks are due Michael Micklin, who made his personal library available to me, precluding the necessity of my having to check *Economy and Society* and other indispensable texts out of institutional libraries for years at a time. He also listened to many impromptu lectures on the welfare state which I delivered at unpredictable intervals.

Lewis Bateman and Sandra Eisdorfer of The University of North Carolina Press, as well as Trudie Calvert, who copyedited the manuscript, together made my first attempt at publishing a book a reinforcing experience, and I hope to be involved in other such enterprises. I thank them for their confidence in my work.

Finally, for the pleasure of seeing the manuscript professionally typed, these ideas gaining credibility in their aesthetic page arrangements, I thank Jan Logan, who typed the manuscript as if it were her own.

Kathi V. Friedman

Part 1

Chapter 1

INTRODUCTION: THE CONTROVERSIAL

WESTERN WELFARE STATE

WHAT ARE THE FACTORS that prompt the redistribution of national wealth in contemporary Western nations? What underlying societal values make various methods and degrees of redistribution acceptable to populaces? These questions stand at the center of this inquiry into the Western welfare state.

In Western nations (Great Britain, the countries of Scandinavia and Western Europe, the United States, Canada, Australia, and New Zealand), the welfare state has come into its own since World War II, Great Britain having provided the prototype for the other Western regimes. The welfare state is one in which government assumes responsibility for guaranteeing citizens minimum standards of living in terms of income maintenance, health and nutrition, education, and housing. Though governments throughout time have protected their subjects or citizens in various ways, the welfare state as a distinctive analytic configuration with an accompanying rationale did not emerge until after the war.

I shall compare the welfare state with the nineteenth-century liberal state, which also had a distinctive analytic configuration sustaining a set of accepted political tenets. The tenets underlying liberal rule proscribed government intervention into the play of market forces. It was assumed that a "free" market optimized not only the productive function of the economy, but also the allocative function, that is, the distribution of goods and services. By contrast, the welfare state's very existence denies this assumption: it is the unique purview of the welfare state to offset adverse effects of market distributions upon citizens' lives. This rejection of a fundamental assumption of liberal rule has always implied problematic legitimacy for welfare regimes in Western nations, the more so when social legislation was just emerging. On what grounds and by what justifications, therefore, do these regimes redistribute the societal surplus? Part I will be addressed to this query.

In replying to this question, Part I provides a theoretical rationale that explains the legitimacy of the Western welfare state. By any definition of "legitimacy" (see below), it is clear that the welfare state has been accepted by Western rulers and populaces alike, albeit ambivalently. How did the welfare state emerge and grow to its present dimensions in the shadow of the West's laissez-faire political heritage? Nineteenth-century thinking, in its considerable diversity, contained many fears regarding the direct assumption of responsibility by the state for the well-being of individuals in society. There were fears of political oppression through omnipotent government bureaucracy, of the possible stymieing of needed institutional change, of the destruction of the dignity and moral fiber of individuals, and of the ruination of the productive economy. The birth of the welfare state from such an apparently hostile ambient is a fact requiring explanation. Equally in need of explanation are the conditions that provide the welfare state with varying degrees of legitimacy today.

To explain the emergence, legitimacy, and imminent expansion of Western welfare regimes, I shall draw upon and refine concepts articulated during the 1920s by Max Weber, in his sociology of domination. I shall explicate Weber's notions of "administration" and "adjudication" as two fundamentally different modes of exercising authority. Weber uses these two constructs as a shorthand method of referring to antithetical modes of rulership, although empirically, rulership entails mixtures of the two principles. Following Weber, therefore, I will indicate how these represent poles of a continuum: the one pole refers to rulership essentially gratuitous in nature, the other allows for the development of the status of citizenship and provides for the possibility of a varied content of citizen rights. Administration is the rule of persons by persons; adjudication is the rule of law. Law is capable of undergoing rationalization; therefore the quality of rulership under law varies as the law grows more rational. Accordingly, I will show the relationship of Weber's notions of the formal and substantive rationalization of law to the continuing emergence and legitimation of citizenship rights. Social rights, the distinctive type of right associated with the welfare state, represents the most elaborate and recent aspect of citizenship, the other two aspects being, as Thomas H. Marshall (1963) has indicated, civil and political rights.

Setting forth this argument will entail a treatment of the natural law antecedents of "right rule" (that is, the exercise of legitimate authority) in the West. In treating Weber's construct, rational authority, I shall link its grounds for legitimacy to the natural law tradition, as did Weber. In expanding upon Weber's work, I shall reconcile the apparent incongruity between the assumptions that legitimize the authority of nineteenth-century liberal and twentieth-century welfare regimes. This will be accomplished by showing the analytic continuity of legitimating principles of rule from the democratic revolutions to the present. Briefly, the unifying thread underlying "right rule" in the West is the notion of the sovereign as the impartial respecter of the dignity of all persons, a fundamental natural law tenet. The welfare state is but the most sophisticated of a series of successive approximations of this ideal throughout Western history. Thus, Part I is concerned with the emergence of the welfare state as a construct, as a concrete reality, and as a sociopolitical phenomenon based within a framework of justification in continuity with long accepted tenets of legitimate rulership in the Western tradition.

Part II addresses the prime paradox of the contemporary Western welfare state. That paradox is that in order to transmute the ideal of the social right into the concrete reality of the goods and services that raise the citizen's standard of living, the welfare state, that high-water mark of the adjudicative mode of rule, needs administration. Administration is an indispensable arm of the welfare state because social rights, unlike civil and political rights, require complex programs, policies, procedures of implementation, coordination, eligibility criteria, and so forth to be usable by the citizen. Whereas Part I emphasizes the formal and substantive rationalization of law in addressing the sources of legitimacy for the idea of the social right, Part II returns to the implications for the contemporary welfare state of the differences Weber ascribes to each of "administration" and "adjudication."

Administration, primevally considered, refers to rulership in which all three government functions (executive, legislative, judicial) are merged and rule is personal (Weber, 1968:645).[1] The patriarchal household is prototypical. Weber's adjudicative mode of rule, by contrast, refers to rulership in which the judicial function is separated out from the other two: rather, there exists the idea of a general norm or law that can be applied to the individual case (Weber, 1968:654). Contingent upon the degree of rationality of the law of the political order in question, adjudication can range from "primitive" to "rationalized." In the ideal case, "adjudication," "the adjudicative principle," or "the adjudicative mode of rule" (I use these terms interchangeably) refers to rule by law that has undergone rationalization.

Rule is, accordingly, impartial and impersonal. It is this set of connections that forms the framework for this Weberian-based analysis of the Western welfare state in terms of administration, adjudication, and the formal and substantive rationalization of law.

The welfare state is a sociopolitical phenomenon that postdates Weber's writings (although, to be sure, he anticipated it: 1968:856–59, 870, 882–89), and accordingly, I have gone considerably beyond Weber in the application of these constructs to empirical events. Weber dealt with the construct "administration" in two separate senses; I have shown how these two usages are related, and I have advanced an explanation of the meaning of this relationship for the development and legitimation of social rights. Weber spoke of "administration" both as the primeval form of domination[2] and as the organization of roles for task implementation, as in "bureaucratic administration." To be sure, every domination (*Herrschaft*) needs an administrative staff to carry out commands; in turn, every administration needs domination, that is, a definitive source of authority whose commands it carries out (Bendix, 1962:292). But dominations as well as administrative staffs vary in the degree of their commitment to the rule of law. In Part II (Chapter 7), I show that it is both the character (irrational or rational) and objectives (private, personalized versus public, impersonalized) of the rules and regulations promulgated by administrative officials that differentiate administration as domination (rulership in which all three functions are merged) from administration as organization (role organization for task implementation). This distinction makes a great difference in the manner in which benefits are dispensed by state to citizen and the accompanying effects of such dispensations upon citizenship rights.

Weber uses the term "reglements" or "reglementations" to refer to the type of regulation used by the administrative staffs of patrimonial rulers. Strictly speaking, the "reglementation" issues from the patrimonial ruler and instructs his officials in how to settle disputes among subjects or otherwise administer the affairs of the realm (Weber, 1968: 664, 1006–1110).[3] The "offices" originate in the household of the ruler: domination is by administration. Conversely, administration is domination. Moreover, any benefits enjoyed by subjects as a by-product of the reglementations promulgated by patrimonial officialdom are purely gratuitous. That is, no "right" exists to them (Weber, 1968:644).

By contrast, once rules and regulations begin to undergo a process of rationalization, and once the purposes toward which they are oriented become more and more impersonal (not just the private purposes of the ruler), then "administration" successively becomes organization in the sense Weber meant when speaking of "bureaucratic administration" or "bureaucracy." Administration that is organization may become associated with domination (that is, the authoritarian power of command), if it is established by a political unit (such as an executive or legislative branch of a regime) to achieve objectives that are not only impersonal, but public.

Thus, administration that is domination orients itself toward "subjects." Administration that is organization orients itself toward "clients." But administration that is organization and also associated with domination orients itself toward "clients," who, in the modern state, are also "citizens." These distinctions foreshadow one of the major lines of my argument throughout Part II: in the degree that Western regimes have assisted citizens in ways approximating administration as domination, authoritarian (actually, "patronizing" or "feudal") implications have attached to the aid given. The legitimacy of government assistance suffered, as did the personal rights and integrity of those assisted. By contrast, in the degree that Western regimes have assisted citizens in ways approximating administration as organization, libertarian implications have attached to the aid given.[4] The legitimacy of government assistance has been reinforced (though not without other problems, which I shall also discuss), as have the personal rights and integrity of those enjoying the benefits of the welfare state.

A host of related issues enter into the general relationships noted above, and I will elaborate briefly upon them. First, I mentioned that the rules and regulations of administrative staffs may undergo rationalization. When Weber speaks broadly of the "formal and substantive rationalization of the law," he is referring to the civil or the statute law.[5] Its character can be ranked on a continuum ranging from law that is formally or substantively irrational to law that is rational both formally and substantively (Weber, 1968:653–58). The regulations of administrative units can also be ranked on a continuum from irrational to rational. Contemporary scholars (Selznick, 1969; Jowell, 1975) use two specifying concepts, "legalization" and "judicialization," as measures for movement along this continuum.[6] "Legalization" refers to the degree to which an agency will use definite rules and standards when its staff is making its determinations involving a case. "Judicialization" refers to the degree to which the determination made by the staff is open to appeal.

Accordingly, the reglementation would be the ideal typical irrational regulation. Because it is the expediently issued word of the patrimonial ruler to his staff, it is characterized by the lowest levels of legalization and judicialization that can be expected to be found within the realm of administration. By contrast, today's administrative agencies or units associated with Western regimes make and apply rules and regulations characterized by much higher degrees of legalization and judicialization—they use rules that are far more rationalized than the reglementation that is their analytic progenitor. The authoritative promulgations of today's administrative agencies, that is, the rules they apply in dealing with the public,[7] are known by the label of "administrative law" (Landis, 1966; Shapiro, 1968).[8] Thus, the reglementation and rationalized administrative law[9] represent two poles of a continuum of directives made and applied by administrative staffs throughout Western history.

It should be clear by now that if there are two major continua (the rationalization of the civil or statute law and the rationalization of reglementative-administrative law[10]) that bear upon the rights of modern citizens and the ways the state dispenses assistance, one major aspect of this analysis has to be the relationship of these two continua to one another. Indeed, it has not been until modern times that these two continua have differentiated themselves from one another, thereby necessitating a consideration of their relationship: "These conceptual distinctions are necessarily remote from the nature of pre-bureaucratic, especially from patrimonial and feudal, structures of authority" (Weber, 1968:998). For,

> there was once a situation in which such a distinction was not
> made at all. Such was the case when all law, all jurisdictions, and
> particularly all powers of exercising authority were personal privi-
> leges, such as, especially, the "prerogatives" of the head of the
> state. In that case the authority to judge, or to call a person into
> military service, or to require obedience in some other respect was
> a vested right in exactly the same way as the authority to use a
> piece of land. . . . It was a kind of political authority which was
> not essentially different from that of the head of a household, or
> a landlord, or a master of serfs. Such a state of affairs has never
> existed as a complete system, but, in so far as it did exist, every-

thing which we legally characterize as falling within the sphere of
"public law" constituted the subject matter of the private rights
of individual power-holders and was in this respect in no way different from a "right" in private law. [Weber, 1968:643–44]

By contrast, "it was left to the complete depersonalization of administrative management by bureaucracy and the rational systematization
of law to realize the separation of the public and the private sphere
fully and in principle" (Weber, 1968:998).

What this means for the present analysis is that during the time
when law was reglementation,[11] when no private rights existed for subjects, all favors or benefits subjects enjoyed were gratuities. Through
the continuing development of the adjudicative principle, however,
approximations of civil law emerged and guaranteed the rights of
subjects and, finally, of citizens (this is the subject of Chapter 2). At
first these rights were narrow in scope and unequal in content (particularized); after the democratic revolutions they were wider in scope and
equal in content (generalized). Thus, the formal and substantive rationalization of the civil or statute law can produce benefits that are
"rights" just as the issuance of a reglementation can produce benefits
that are only "gratuities." This leaves open the question of what to
label the benefit a modern citizen enjoys when that benefit is the
outcome of the making and application of rationalized administrative
law. I have labeled that category of benefit the "entitlement," and I
fully describe its meaning and relationship to gratuities on the one
hand, and the social right to benefits, on the other, in Chapters 7–10
of Part II.

To recapitulate, if the modern Western welfare state assumes responsibility to redistribute the societal surplus according to a set of
principles (humanitarian, ethical, and so forth), it can hardly accomplish the monumental task of redistribution to the millions directly
through the passage of statutes. Rather, statutes give legal form to
abstract principles underlying redistribution and then delegate to administrative apparatuses the multifarious tasks associated with actually making the transfers.[12] This fact opens up a whole new set of
relationships between citizen and sovereign in the modern state, which
is also a *welfare* state. I, the citizen, stand in a "legally relevant"
(Weber's term) relationship to sovereign political authority not only in
terms of civil or statute law, but I, the claimant, client, or applicant
stand in a newly emerged legally relevant relationship to sovereign

political authority as represented by the redistributive administrative agency, and this relationship is governed by administrative law. A question and its corollary arise: what is the relationship between "regular" (civil or statute) law and administrative law—particularly that aspect of it dealing with the redistributions of the welfare state? What is the relationship between claimant and citizen in the welfare state?

In asking these questions, I am but one of many, as will be shown in Part II. My analysis of these issues, in abbreviated form, will cover the following territory. First, as Weber has emphasized, without law there can be no rights: a right emerges from the existence of law only because the one claiming the right can appeal to have the law applied to his case (Weber, 1968:653–54, 666–68). The prospect of appeal to the law is therefore the sine qua non of a right. Accordingly, if my right as a claimant vis-à-vis the redistributive administrative agency is to exist at all, then the prospect of appeal must be open to me. One might be tempted to think that "judicialization," the process by which the law made and applied by administrative agencies is made amenable to appeal, would solve this problem. Such is not entirely the case: judicialization refers to the subjecting of the application of the agency's rules and regulations to appeal within the agency. The technical term for this is "administrative adjudication." A subunit of the agency's staff reviews the claims that arise between the agency and its clients. The staff then makes the determinations regarding those claims.

This arrangement becomes tenuous from the point of view of the legitimacy of the redistributions made in the name of the welfare state because, by a strange coincidence of history, I, the claimant, stand in an empirical relationship analytically similar, but not identical, to a subject vis-à-vis patrimonial administration. This similarity makes the legitimacy of the redistributions, at certain junctures, problematic. Namely, the modern redistributive administrative agency, with (we presume) all the best of intentions, is now coincidentally in a position to exercise legislative (through its powers of sublegislation), executive (through its mission of implementation of programs), and judicial (through its procedures of administrative adjudication) authority over me, completely within the purview of administrative law and, by implication, outside the purview of the regular civil or statute law and the regular court system. This is entirely "legal." Modern agencies have delegated authority to sublegislate, to implement, and to adjudicate claims that arise between themselves and their clients. In certain cases the agency's decision is, by statute, to be considered final, that is, not open to appeal outside the agency. Even when statute does not close the possibility of appeal to the regular court system, other obstacles have arisen effectively separating the citizen from the institution that has regularly guarded his personal rights in the Western political tradition. Thus, the similarity of circumstance of today's recipient of the redistributions made by administrative agencies and yesterday's recipient of patrimonial favors is not superficial: both have found that in order to receive the benefit they had to conform their behavior to the values of those who made the regulations. I hasten to add that this is far less true today than it was in earlier decades of this century: I illustrate this point by treating events in the United States from the Progressive Era to the present (Chapter 8). In any case, the exercise over the contemporary citizen of a conjunction of legislative, executive, and judicial authority within the ambit of administration has created legitimation problems for the redistributional activities of the Western welfare state.

Though I use the United States as my most heavily documented example (for the federal structure of the U.S. government, as well as the unique role of its court system, throw the issues into sharp relief), the basic issue of guarding citizenship rights in an era when more and more of the citizen's dealings are with agencies that relate to him through administrative law is characteristic of all the Western welfare states (Reich, 1966; Wheeler, 1965; Street, 1975; Mashaw et al., 1978). Harvey Wheeler has written that the need for an "equilibrating counterweight" for the individual citizen has always arisen wherever administrative functions have become "large and complicated" (1965: 14). Thus, the reason judicialization and, hence, administrative adjudication, cannot alone safeguard individual rights in the era of the welfare state is that administrative staffs may be subject to bias in their decisions because they also perform legislative and executive functions. Such bias may be either "institutional bias—the influence of the pressures of the work load, administrative inertia, and conventional wisdom on decision making" or it may be "policy bias—the policy predilections that may result from the dominance of certain interests in the administrative process, the peculiar preferences of hierarchical superiors, or the attitudes of influential members" of legislatures or the executive (Mashaw et al., 1978:150). Of the two kinds of bias mentioned by Jerry L. Mashaw and his colleagues, "policy bias" is the one that more closely approximates those attributes of premodern rulership that are the objects of invidious comparison here: particularized values reflected through administrative discretion. For the legitimacy of the redistributional activities that today join citizen to agency in a legally relevant relationship, this means that "if a reviewing tribunal is to serve the admittedly important legitimizing function often ascribed to judicial review, it must be independent from the bureaucratic perspective" (Mashaw et al., 1978:150). The literature is in unanimous agreement on this point. Of equal strength is the consensus that a quick solution of this dilemma is not in sight.

Part of the dilemma lies in the stark fact that administrative adjudication is as indispensable to the modern redistributional state as is the need for administration itself. The administrative adjudication of claims between agencies and clients numbers in hundreds of thousands of cases per year throughout Western regimes. Moreover, the literature indicates that the overwhelming majority of such claims are settled to the satisfaction of those on both sides of the gavel (Woll, 1963; Shapiro, 1968; Street, 1975; Mashaw et al., 1978). The problems regarding the legitimate use of the state's authority over the citizen arise within what is still, empirically and analytically, a twilight zone: what are the contingencies that surround the application of the civil or statute law to the citizen's case in protection of his "social rights" once his claim to an "entitlement" has been denied through the application of administrative law and the channels of administrative adjudication?[13] We know that sheer volume of cases alone precludes a wholesale transfer of such appeals into the regular court system; thus an alternative solution must be constructed by Western redistributional regimes.

A solution is not ready to hand partly because the constitutions and other documents that together provide for the rule of law in Western regimes were formulated long before the advent of the welfare state. Therefore, it is not surprising that the legal systems of these regimes are institutionally far better equipped to handle civil and political rights cases than social rights cases. As mentioned, social rights differ from the other types of rights in that social rights require administrative apparatuses to make them usable to the citizen.[14] Social rights, accordingly, present altogether new problems for modern rulership, but perhaps particularly for the judicial branch of rule. When Wheeler (1965:12) states that there is a need to "bestow formal recognition upon the vast system of administrative law" that has evolved, "endowing it with appropriate controls and fitting it into the legal order," he refers to the three traditional branches of government.

My argument, therefore, emphasizes the need to synchronize the phenomenon of administrative adjudication with the regular processes of adjudication that long have protected individual rights in the West. Such synchronization requires institution building to create three important linkages that, in turn, would enhance the legitimacy of the redistributions made in the name of the Western welfare state. The connections that need better institutional articulation than now exist in the West are (1) entitlements (the "best" that an agency can give a client) with rights (the "best" that a regular court of law can give a citizen); (2) redistributions (the costly benefits received by some at the expense of others) with rationales that justify them in the eyes of taxpayers, beneficiaries, politicians, and civil servants; (3) the authority of administrative agencies over clients with the authority of the three traditional branches of government over citizens in the modern state. In sum, much of the legitimation controversy that surrounds social transfers can be related to the incomplete articulation of administrative law with "the rule of law" from which the legitimacy of authority exercised in the modern Western state derives.

Accordingly, in Chapter 2, I distinguish between administration and adjudication and in Chapter 3, pursue the meaning of the adjudicative principle by outlining the natural law antecedents of the rule of law, that is, Weber's third type of legitimate authority. Chapter 4 is an explication of the meaning of the formal and substantive rationalization of law, and Chapter 5 a compilation of historical evidence to show how law was becoming rationalized in the direction of social rights in the West before World War II. In Chapter 6, I treat the emergence of the welfare state in postwar Britain. Part I ends on the note that the ideal of the social right had joined civil and political rights as a legitimate component of modern citizenship.

Part II opens with a depiction of the dilemmas posed for the welfare state by the inherent nature of administration (Chapter 7). Chapter 8 illustrates the issues raised in Chapter 7 with the case of the United States, in which a large array of welfare state dilemmas flourish. Some are general to Western regimes as an analytic type; others are unique to the United States. Chapter 9 contains an account of the progressive jurisprudential recognition of the U.S. welfare state and hints at the problems raised by "judicial legislation," treated in Chapter 10. The effects of court decisions upon the costs of social benefits, as well as upon the court's own legitimacy, are crucial issues in the United States today. Nevertheless, the connection between the costs of social rights and their legitimacy is general to all welfare regimes, a point to which I return in the final chapter. Chapter 11 is an analysis of diverse regime types throughout history against a matrix formed by the administrative and adjudicative principles, on the one hand, and the degree of rationalization of law (civil or statute and administrative), on the other. In Chapter 11 the Western welfare state finds its historical "place."

The Western Welfare State

Scholars have tended to dichotomize analyses of the welfare state's activities into those of the Western nations (Great Britain, the countries of Scandinavia and Western Europe, the United States, Canada, Australia, and New Zealand) and those of the Soviet bloc (the U.S.S.R. and the countries of Eastern Europe). Whether tacit or explicit, this division characterizes general analyses as well as empirical studies of welfare activities undertaken by national units (Burns, 1956, 1977; Jones, 1958; Titmuss, 1969, 1974; Myrdal, 1969, 1972; Briggs, 1961; Rimlinger, 1961, 1971; Viner, 1963; Cutright, 1965; Wilensky and Lebeaux, 1965; Girvetz, 1968; Pryor, 1968; Jenkins, 1969; Steiner, 1971; Hancock and Sjoberg, 1972; Marshall, 1963, 1972; Mishra, 1973; Rein and Heclo, 1973; Heclo, 1974; Israel, 1974; Heidenheimer, Heclo, and Adams, 1975; Rowley and Peacock, 1975; Wilensky, 1975, 1976; George and Wilding, 1976; Grey, 1976; Janowitz, 1976; Furniss and Tilton, 1977; Zald, 1965, 1977; Scandinavian Sociological Association, 1978; Huber, 1978; Leichter, 1979; Aaron, 1980; Flora and Heidenheimer, 1980; Meenaghan and Washington, 1980; Schaar, 1980; Stein, 1980).

Within the Western nations protection of the citizen has followed variable formats including the Bismarckian pattern in which benefits have been tied primarily to occupational status, the Beveridge or British pattern in which benefits are associated with citizenship, and a demogrant pattern based upon categories of risk (Huber, 1978:112–13; see also Wilensky, 1975). The Western experience has been characterized by considerable diversity, but, nonetheless, cultural values surrounding the uses of authority differ drastically between nations in the Western tradition, on the one hand, and the U.S.S.R. and, of course, the Orient, on the other. Indeed, Max Weber's sociologies of religion and domination have both explicated the East-West distinction in depth (see Bendix, 1962). It has been only in the West that there was a strong, if brief, history of political liberalism proscribing government interference into the immediate material circumstances of individual citizens (Briggs, 1961; Bendix, 1977; Wolfe, 1977). This history has conditioned the specific controversies that have arisen in Western nations regarding the emergence and growth of the welfare state. Thus, in order to limit the scope of this inquiry into welfare statism, primarily those criticisms, controversies, and questions of legitimation regarding the welfare state in Western nations considered together as an analytic type will be addressed here.

Welfare statism is the twentieth century's response to the demand of citizens—however articulated—for material protection from contingencies that are beyond their privately organized capacity to avoid (Reich, 1966; King, 1973; Jones, 1978; Weed, 1979). Wars and economic depressions have been prime catalysts for citizen expectations that government must assume responsibility for the effects of such events upon the lives of individuals in society.[15] The welfare state rests upon a societal surplus[16] that can be reallocated among the citizenry according to explicit, formalized criteria (Janowitz, 1976:10). In quantitative terms, the Western welfare state typically devotes at least 8 to 10 percent of its gross national product (GNP) to welfare; this includes all public expenditures for health, education, income maintenance, deferred income, and funds for community development, including housing allocations (Janowitz, 1976:2; see also Milius, 1979). Specifically, the Western welfare state modifies the play of market forces in these ways, as stated by Asa Briggs: (1) it guarantees individuals and families a minimum income regardless of the market value of their work or property; (2) it narrows the extent of insecurity of citizens by enabling them to meet certain social contingencies (such as sickness, old age, temporary disability, unemployment) that might otherwise lead the normal individual or family into a crisis; (3) it ensures that all citizens without distinction of status or class are offered a specified minimum standard in relation to a certain agreed range of social services (1961:228).

Harold L. Wilensky (1975:1) emphasizes that these guarantees by the state are legal rights, not charity. It is clear from the contemporary literature that the welfare state guarantees the citizen the "social rights" elaborated by Thomas H. Marshall in his classic chapter in *Sociology at the Crossroads* (1963), "Citizenship and Social Class." Though Marshall does not use the term "welfare state" as such, his description of the content of social rights is at one with the specific commodities and services offered by today's welfare regimes. Marshall speaks of the social rights of citizenship as including a spectrum of rights from that of "a modicum of economic welfare and security to the right to a share to the full in the social heritage and to live the life of a civilized being according to the standards prevailing in the society" (1963:74).

Legitimacy and Legitimation

In addressing the processes by which social rights are achieving legitimation in Western nations, I inevitably treat the degrees of legitimacy that accrue to regimes that make such transfers. In using the terms "legitimacy" and "legitimation," I am in step with a diverse literature[17] that implies that legitimacy inheres in a relationship of congruence between two sets of politically relevant variables. That is, the degree of legitimacy enjoyed by a regime[18] rests upon a congruous relationship between (1) political principles and political practices, and (2) the rulers and the ruled. Definitiveness regarding the elusive concept "legitimacy" has not been achieved, yet the phenomenon is most commonly analyzed in terms of these two broad sets of variables.

For example, perceived discrepancies between "theory" (political principles, values, ideals, valued objectives, and the like) and "practice" produce a sense of inappropriateness that undermines the image of the legitimate use of authority in a regime. Similarly, if rulers and ruled hold discrepant views with regard to either the principles or the practices guiding the exercise of authority, again "legitimation dilemmas" may be spoken of. Severe discrepancies or incongruities thought by analysts to imply eventual political conflict or some other form of outcome self-defeating for regime stability and effectiveness are referred to as sources of "legitimation crises." Certainly Karl Marx's analysis of the flaws of capitalist society illustrates this approach to addressing the bases of legitimate rulership. Finally, not only may rulers and ruled hold discrepant views vis-à-vis one another with regard to the principles of rulership or the actual practices in implementing the rulership, but there may also be "within category" variation.[19] If this variation is too great, competing principles, practices, elites, subjects, or citizens may each or all deteriorate into conflicting principles, practices, elites, subjects, or citizens. This is where analyses of legitimacy become peppered with references to the circulation of elites, revolution, political turmoil, political alienation, and the like.

Accordingly, in both Parts I and II, I treat the legitimation of social rights—and the legitimacy of the Western welfare state—with a view to the reconciling of incongruities or paradoxes. In Part I, I analyze events (wars, economic depressions) and processes (the formal and substantive rationalization of law) by which a congruity of principles was achieved between nineteenth- and twentieth-century presuppositions regarding the elements of legitimate rulership in the West. I show how policy makers were able to make new practices (those of positive government) consistent with eighteenth- and nineteenth-century values. I examine how the value of individualism (each for himself) became reconciled to humanitarianism (all for one, one for all) through post–World War II ideals of unity and universalism that justified the emergence of the welfare state. In Part II, I address the paradox that the antithetical principles of administration and adjudication are nevertheless complementary processes when it comes to lending tangible content to the abstract, and therefore intangible, social rights of citizenship. Therefore, I treat the incongruities between the rule of law and the requisites of administration that must be resolved if the Western welfare state is to achieve, retain, and enhance its legitimacy as it makes redistributions.

By the same token I assert that incongruity stands at the heart of the legitimation controversies of the Western welfare state. In sum, it may be argued that it is the quality of congruity, real or apparent, among politically relevant variables that characterizes an order that, in Weber's words, "enjoys the prestige of being considered binding, or, as it may be expressed, of 'legitimacy' " (1968:31).

Controversies Surrounding the Western Welfare State

That a government would redistribute the society's goods and services so that, in effect, the poor have more and the affluent have less is by no means the usual course that history has taken (see Lenski, 1966). Such redistribution is rare and thus requires explanation, the more so in that much controversy surrounds the entire notion of the use of state authority to make social transfers. Following are some of the major criticisms that have beset, and still attend, the continuing metamorphosis of the liberal into the welfare state in Western nations.

Destruction of Individual Dignity and Moral Fiber. State assistance to allow the individual to attain a higher standard of living than the individual could achieve simply through his own efforts divests him of his dignity and weakens his character. This particular critique of the welfare state had its origins among Reformation intellectuals (Heclo, 1974:48–50 passim). These intellectuals were reacting against the relief of "God's poor" undertaken by medieval parishes as a Christian duty. Emphasis in medieval days was upon the giver (Fraser, 1973). With the establishment in the sixteenth century of state churches in Britain and Sweden, however, care of the poor shifted from the Catholic church to the state.

The state, in turn, was heavily concerned with maintaining social order. Therefore, poor relief regulations came to be directed toward controlling vagrancy and begging, especially among the able-bodied. Hugh Heclo writes: "It is perhaps not too much of an exaggeration to say that a key motivating force behind the Protestant ethic and its emphasis on duty, work, and self-support was a reaction against indiscriminate charity of previous Church social policy. Henceforth, poverty could be considered a disgrace and sign of reluctance to work; attention would focus on aiding only those who were 'deserving'" (1974:48). This attitude permeated poor law policy in Britain and Sweden for the next three hundred years (Heclo, 1974:50). It is an idea deeply entrenched in that part of the Western political tradition that conditions the relationship of the state to the poor.[20]

Preclusion of Institutional Change. Government dispensation of wealth, whether through cash or services in kind, may simply forestall genuine structural change in the conditions under which wealth is generated and allocated in the society in the first place. This is the Marxist critique that sees the welfare state as "drawing the fangs of the revolutionary tiger" by offering just enough to pacify the classes who should be demanding a restructuring of the society (Wilensky, 1975: 109; Scandinavian Sociological Association, 1978).[21]

Political Oppression. Some fear that the welfare state may become politically oppressive through its administration of an omnipotent bureaucracy. It may make citizens into dependents whose behavior can then be manipulated by the rulers of the state. This foreboding regarding the welfare state springs from several sources and with good reason. Much of the present work is, in fact, addressed to an analysis of these sources and their relationship to the ways redistributions have been made in Western regimes, including the ways they are made today.

Invidious comparison with events in the U.S.S.R. or, more generally, the Eastern European welfare state as an analytic type, fuels contemporary Western fears that "bureaucracy" can metastasize to a point where the entire society feels its blight: "Numbing bureaucracy, not terror, makes the strongest impression on a current traveler through the Soviet Union. It's not unknown in the West. But ours is petty, and in some places still fiercely resisted, in comparison with Soviet society. There is a bureaucracy of food, shelter, clothing, tractors, words, mountain climbing and terror" (Scates, 1980). In Chapter 11, I pursue the theme of omnipresent administration in the Soviet bloc, where, indeed, there is a strong concern for citizen well-being, but where the health of the worker is likened by Gaston V. Rimlinger (1971:255) to the maintenance of capital.

Economic Ruin. The dual misgiving persists that the state will either bankrupt itself through overcommitting the treasury to social welfare or that the spirit of individual enterprise will be stifled by too many social programs that siphon off tax dollars from the populace (Girvetz, 1968; Wilensky, 1975; Friedman, 1980). This criticism of the welfare state is treated at any number of junctures throughout Chapters 6–11. It is an important criticism and one that must be met with the appropriate institutions if the welfare state is to wear the mantle of legitimacy while making redistributions.

Societal Fragmentation. Demands for government action on behalf of various categories of citizens may well be incompatible. Ergo, the more responsibility assumed by the state, according to this criticism, the more the state will be held accountable for meeting conflicting demands. This fear is implicitly conditioned by the previous criticism. That is, if resources were unlimited, the government could meet multifarious citizen demands, including those now mutually exclusive because of scarce resources. But, because resources are limited, choices have to be made. Choices by the sovereign, in turn, imply potential conflict or, at the very least, societal fragmentation into an infinite regress of competitors for government munificence (Bell, 1973).

This criticism is worth examining in more detail because it parallels and thus reinforces some points I will be making. I argue for the crucial connection between the generalized content of the citizenship right protected by law adjudicable by unbiased authority and the legitimate use of sovereign authority to redistribute what the society has produced. In Part I, I show that legitimate authority over Western populaces has hinged more and more upon the impartiality of the sovereign toward the ruled. The increasing impersonality of the law has been an adjunct to its impartiality. The democratic revolutions were a quantum leap in the direction of striking down personalized, particularized law.[22] They established the standard of generality as the measure of the sovereign's legitimacy in relating to individuals in society. Personal favors and individually struck bargains between rulers and ruled went "out."[23] Equality of citizenship status and uniformity of content of citizenship rights came "in."

Arguing from separate points of view and considering different subject matters, both Lowi (1969, 1979) and Daniel Bell (1973) have noted with dismay that a particularized citizen-sovereign relationship has been coming back "in" in the United States. The government has been attempting to enhance citizen quality of life through an essentially particularistic orientation toward defined societal aggregates. Lowi uses the term "interest-group liberalism" to describe this phenomenon, Bell, "quota representation." Both authors point out that until the 1930s the holders of "rights" against the U.S. federal government were either the states or citizens. Lowi refers to this phase of U.S. history as characterized by "the rule of law." The depression, however, precipitated a situation in which the U.S. government began to create and invoke particularistic criteria as bases for its legally relevant relationships to individuals in society. Rather than relating to citizens solely in terms of their citizen status, the government began to relate to people in terms of their respective statuses as members of "functional groups" (Bell, 1973:438). That is, with the establishment of the cabinet departments of commerce, labor, and agriculture, representing business, labor, and farmers, respectively, U.S. political authority began to orient itself toward its citizens on a particularistic, that is, a partial basis (Lowi, 1969:115ff.).

Lowi (1969:101–56 passim) goes on to analyze the corporatist or feudal character of the arrangement that drew portions of the private sector into legally relevant relationships with the executive branch of the U.S. sovereign through the establishment of these cabinet-level departments. He elaborates the ways this absorption of private society into the ambit of administration compromises the principle of the rule of law. He next shows how this practice, admittedly an emergency response to the crises of the depression, has gained ascendancy as a routine way for the sovereign to reach out and form legally relevant relationships with the U.S. citizen. Lowi labels this "interest-group liberalism." Interest-group liberalism is the government's post-1930s method of trying to treat U.S. citizens fairly and impartially. The government encourages the formation of interest groups oriented around an endless regress of interests so that no one will be left out and to avoid being unfair. Once the body politic has organized itself into a series of particularized aggregates, the bargaining can begin. Citizens, from the vantage point of their interest groups, bargain with agencies within the executive branch for a better share of the pie. The "pie" may be either the rules and regulations through which the agency will relate to the interest in question or the policies the agency will adopt that will affect the material position of that interest group relative to other members of the body politic.

Ironically, the rule of law, the most effective tool ever fashioned by human societies so that their regimes may achieve justice, impartiality, and fairness, is the first casualty of this approach. Legally relevant relationships shift out of the ambit of legislation and adjudication and into the ambit of administration. The rules agreed upon by interest groups and agencies are not legislative rules, but administrative ones. Not only are the rules arrived at partially, that is, with the "input" of those interests they will affect, but these rules are not even amenable to adjudication in the regular courts of law. Lowi calls this "policy without law" (1969:125–56). He points out that law has a self-correcting character by way of its amenability to court review. Of policy this is not true, and therein lies the radical difference between them.

As a consequence of this approach, the government, attempting to reach out "universally" to those within its purview, ends up by encouraging the very particularism and fragmentation of the body politic that marked prerevolutionary rule.[24] For example, George H. Sabine writes that "the abolition of feudalism meant that the [French] revolutionist . . . intended to sweep away this whole cumbersome and irritating complex of status. . . . [His] ideal was to destroy every status except one—namely, citizenship in the state, which by becoming universal would cease to be invidious (1952:462). Lowi has noted that, by contrast, the tendency in the United States has been in a direction that attempts to "destroy privilege by universalizing it" (1969:292). Lowi likens this to the situation in which it would be possible for everyone to get his traffic ticket fixed so that no one would be at a disadvantage. Only "the law" would suffer, but not for long, for this practice would eventually dissolve altogether the institution of law.

Thus, whereas the French Revolution "put at the center of modern politics the concept of equal national citizenship and as its counterpart the concept of the sovereign national state, supreme over every other form of social organization" (Sabine, 1952:462), interest-group liberalism reverses all of this. For the sovereign national state it substitutes the executive agency, for equal national citizenship it substitutes the interest group, for the commonweal it substitutes the notion that "it will all even out in the end," and for an effective and well-coordinated legal order unified under the rule of law it substitutes in Bell's (1973: 435) word, an impending "ataxia."

Bell's analysis[25] is in agreement with Lowi's in the degree that both emphasize the dangers to the modern state of compromising the rule of law and the citizenship status. Bell (1973:461ff., 438) notes that during the 1960s and 1970s "quota representation" according to biological traits (sex, color, age) or culturally acquired traits (religious affiliation, ethnicity) became a new basis of the legally relevant relationship between citizen and sovereign. To achieve equity among citizens, the government has attempted to locate, seriatim, sources of inequity and then to compensate for them.[26] Here Bell argues that "the claim for group rights stands in formal contradiction to the principle of individualism with its emphasis on ... universalism" (1973: 447). Moreover, "one of the historical gains of equality was the establishment of a principle of universalism so that a rule—as in the rule of law—applied equally to all, and thus avoided the administrative determination between persons" (1973:447). The counterpoint between the rule of law and "the administrative determination between persons" is, of course, the major theme of my own argument.

The conclusion Bell draws is that a terrific fragmentation of society is implied, a fragmentation that will surely impede the effectiveness of modern society as a social organization. He believes that society should be able to advance the citizen's rightful claim "to a basic set of services and income which. . . . Are matters of security and dignity which must necessarily be the prior concerns of a civilized society" without, nevertheless, the imposition of "a rigid, ideological equalitarianism in all matters" especially when it becomes "self-defeating" (1973:452).

In sum, therefore, a strong thread running through the above five criticisms of the welfare state leads back through the centuries to the individualistic values and the rule of law that gained political ascendancy at the time of the democratic revolutions. The principles of liberal rule imply an image of society as an order made possible by the voluntary rational contract. Free and equal individuals assume responsibility for their own behavior. Through enlightened self-interest, they enter into contracts that ultimately create order. This order is self-imposed and, therefore, "free." It is also affluent, providing a rich source of productive labor that relates individuals to one another as well as to their physical environment in a manner that allows them to reap the rewards of their own industry. The criticisms voiced above provide a contrasting image of society as an amalgamation of unfree individuals relinquishing responsibility for their fate to an omnipotent state. Such abandonment of individual freedom and responsibility to the pervasive state, it is argued, may result in any or all of these outcomes: state coercion of citizens, economic inefficiency within the productive sector of society, destruction of individual integrity, fragmentation of the citizenry in order to be first in line for government favor, and, worst of all, the disappearance of the rule of law.

The dilemma of the Western welfare state, thus, is clear: citizens do expect their government to protect them from falling below a certain standard of living. Yet, Western populaces have inherited political values that make them skeptical (and justifiably so, as will be seen) of the government's assumption of responsibility to assist them as dependents in complex political economies (Hacker, 1972; Wilensky, 1975). For these reasons the welfare state both succeeds and grows, while simultaneously undergoing exacting criticism. Accordingly, my argument will be that Western regimes gain legitimacy when they make redistributions in the form of social rights, that is, within the framework of national citizenship, itself protected by the rule of law. By contrast, contemporary Western regimes do not gain legitimacy, and, indeed, suffer "backlashes" as well as other criticisms, when they devolve largesse onto the citizenry in any manner that approximates patrimonial or premodern gratuitousness.

Although actions in this latter category have often been undertaken in the name of the welfare state, I will argue that this is a misnomer in terms of the definition of the welfare state which I will be advancing throughout this work. Here the Western "welfare state" as an analytic construct refers to a regime that guarantees the citizen social rights on a par with civil and political rights. Such social rights are the product either (1) of statutes that rest upon a substantive rationale legitimizing the content of the rights, or, alternatively, (2) of adjudication of claims between citizen and sovereign (in the roles of client and government agency) according to a format that guarantees that the decision will be unbiased. In either case, Weber's third type of legitimate authority, the rule of law (legal authority), provides the framework within which the tangible benefit is guaranteed by the state and enjoyed by the citizen. In turn, as bounty is dispensed successively outside the rights of citizenship, the welfare state fades gradually into the authoritarian protection of persons by persons. This was the hallmark of Weber's *traditional* type of (legitimate) authority, the type spurned with gusto at the time of the revolutions in the West. I now address the series of incongruities and paradoxes that, like the sword of Damocles, hang over the legitimacy of the Western welfare state as it redistributes societal wealth.

Chapter 2

BROTHERHOOD WITHOUT

PATERNALISM: IMPERSONALIZED RULE

AND THE WELFARE STATE

THAT SOCIETY is a moral order is sociologically axiomatic (Durkheim, 1947; Parsons, 1937; Kelsen, 1946).[1] But criteria of morality vary, both from culture to culture and throughout time within a cultural tradition. The very existence of the welfare state is evidence of the contemporary Western belief that society is a moral order. By way of social welfare transfers, we are our brothers' keepers. Hence, an important question arises: in what social structural way is the moral order implied by the welfare state distinguishable from the moral order of medieval society with its pronounced sense of Christian duty to protect the weak? It is a fact that "every society, preliterate no less than literate, makes some provision for those of its members who find themselves in distress" (Girvetz, 1968:512). Does this imply that the "welfare state" has existed since time immemorial?

In this chapter I will show why the Western welfare state is an analytically unique social phenomenon. During the centuries, indeed millennia, preceding the welfare state, protection of society's least well-off members was institutionalized through paternalism. Furthermore, under the paternalism of traditional authority, protection of the weaker by the stronger is essentially personal(ized) (Weber, 1968:1006–31). That is, persons protect persons. By contrast, under modern (Weber's "legal") authority, the protection of citizens is impersonal(ized). What are protected are rights, and they are protected by way of impersonalized law (Weber, 1968:217–19, 868ff.).

Administration and Adjudication:
Polar Types of Protection

Weber delineates two ideal typical constructs to account for the protection of persons by persons and the protection of rights by law: these are administration and adjudication. Administration and adjudication are alternative social structural modes through which political authority is enforced. The difference between them, according to Weber, is that administration is an arrangement in which only the political authority has rights; the ruled do not. Adjudication, however, is an arrangement in which the right of the political authority is limited, however rudimentarily, by the rights of subjects. The following excerpts from *Economy and Society* are as close as Weber comes to defining "administration" and "adjudication":

> The primeval form of "administration" is represented by patriarchal power, i.e., the rule of the household. In its primitive form, the authority of the master of the household is unlimited. Those subordinated to his power have no rights as against him, and the norms regulating his behavior toward them exist only as indirect effects of heteronomous religious checks on his conduct. [1968:645; see also pp. 1008–9]

> Originally, we are confronted with the coexistence of the theoretically unrestrained administrative power of the master and arbitration proceedings which originate in arrangements made between kinship groups and related to the proof and composition of the alleged injury. Only in the latter are "claims," i.e., rights, at issue and are verdicts rendered; and only in relations between kinship groups do we find established formalities, limitations as to time, rules of evidence, etc., that is, the beginnings of "judicial" procedure. None of these exist within the sphere of patriarchal power, which represented the primitive form of "government." [Weber, 1968:645]

Rather, through amassing historical illustration, Weber demonstrates the utility of his dichotomization of the modes of enforcing political authority.

I shall add to Weber's demonstration of the usefulness of this distinction. First, I shall sharpen Weber's constructs by relating them to Talcott Parsons's pattern variables as articulated in *The Social System*

(1951). Then I shall show how the historical movement from traditional to legal authority can be viewed as a continuum ranging from personalized protection by the political sovereign of subjects with no rights to impersonalized protection by law with the full development of citizenship rights. At one end of the continuum lies Weber's patriarchal household administration. At the other extreme lies the ideal typically drawn welfare state in which the status of citizen carries civil, political, and social rights guaranteed by an impersonal law. The law, in turn, is the sine qua non of adjudication, the institutionalized process of rendering a decision with legal consequences through the application of a norm (Weber, 1968:644–47, 653–54).[2] Such a norm, or rule, implies the right of an appellant to have the norm categorically (that is, impersonally) applied to his case (Weber, 1968:654).

In Chapter 3 the legitimacy of the redistributions of the welfare state will be analytically linked to the possibility that the law may be impartial; in this chapter the link is to the possibility that the law may be impersonal. If we recall that one criticism of the Western welfare state involves the potential for citizen subjection to loss of dignity through acceptance of "handouts," then it is easy to see that welfare state redistributions must, among other things, be impersonal. It is in this light that the Weberian distinction between administration and adjudication as alternative (ideal typically drawn) modes of enforcing the law will be viewed here: administration epitomizes personalized law enforcement with no subject rights, and adjudication, impersonalized law enforcement with full citizenship rights.

If we consider the political sovereign and the subject (or citizen) as "actors" in a relationship oriented around the well-being of the latter, we may derive insight into the relationship from an examination of Parsons's pattern variables. Parsons (1951:58–67) articulated five dichotomies as characterizing universal dilemmas of orientation among actors. These, he posited, need resolution before any determinate orientation can be achieved (Devereux, 1961:38–44).

The five dichotomies are as follows: (1) Affectivity/affective neutrality: Is affectivity (allowing oneself to be swayed by positive or negative feelings) present or absent? (2) Diffuseness/specificity: How inclusively defined is the scope of the relationship between the two actors? Does it range indeterminately over all areas or is the relationship confined by norms to specific circumstances and conditions? (3) Particularism/universalism: Do the actors judge one another in terms of a general referent or in terms of particular, idiosyncratic characteristics of one, the other, or both? (4) Performance/quality: Is the relationship defined in terms of what the actors can do or what/ who they are? Namely, are achievement or ascriptive criteria salient in the respective orientations of the actors? (5) Self-orientation/collectivity orientation: Does the actor orient himself toward the relationship in terms of what he can derive from it, irrespective of consequences for the other actor? Or does the actor orient himself toward the other actor in terms of a norm that directly or indirectly puts the latter's well-being foremost?

"Pure" administration, as Weber has defined the term, involves the enforcement of political authority at the household level by the patriarch. This enforcement of authority takes place in the complete absence of rights of members of the patriarchal household. In fact, a close reading of Weber's description of domination by patriarchalism in its pure form (1968:1006–10) reveals the predominance of the following five polar traits in terms of Parsons's pattern variables: (1) affectivity: the patriarch's "favor" is of importance to the subject in the domination relationship; (2) diffuseness: there is little or no delimitation as to the personal affairs of subjects upon which the patriarch may intrude; (3) particularism: the patriarch relates to each individual individually, as opposed to relating to household members in terms of a general norm; (4) performance: the domination relation from the viewpoint of the subject involves his performance of service to the patriarch, as well as his acting in terms of obedience and loyalty; (5) self-orientation: the patriarch relates to those within his charge primarily in terms of how his own personal desires and needs may be served—his rule is oriented toward himself. This is not to say that the patriarch fails to protect those for whom he is responsible; self-orientation is not equivalent to irresponsibility.

We may here observe that patriarchal domination, exercising itself through pure administration, has three polar variables in common with those posited as characterizing families: affectivity, diffuseness, and particularism (see Devereux, 1961:44). The domination is in this sense "paternalistic." But, because patriarchal administration is a system of domination, both performance (what one can do for the patriarch) and self-orientation on the part of the patriarch obtain, as distinct from the quality (who one is, that is, one's status as a family member) and collectivity orientations, which Devereux notes characterize families. These differences are important, for they imply that administration combines paternalism with demands for obedience and service on the part of a self-centered sovereign. The protection the subject obtains is unceasingly contingent upon his service to the whim of the political authority. An element of conditionality underlies paternalistic protection granted administratively.

Peter M. Blau's description of the character of "social exchange" would apply to the nature of the relationship between political authority and subject when administration is the mode through which the subject's protection is implemented:

> Social exchange . . . involves favors that create diffuse future obligations, not precisely specified ones, and the nature of the return cannot be bargained about but must be left to the discretion of the one who makes it. . . . Social exchange tends to engender feelings of personal obligation, gratitude, and trust; purely economic exchange as such does not. . . . In contrast to economic commodities, the benefits involved in social exchange do not have an exact price in terms of a single quantitative medium of exchange, which is another reason why social obligations are unspecified. [1967:93, 94, and passim]

By contrast, "pure" adjudication is treated by Weber as involving the application of rules or law that have been completely rationalized. Though the rationalization of the rules applied in the adjudication process will be treated in detail in Chapter 4, we may here note that the following (opposite) five polar traits in terms of Parsons's pattern variables characterize pure adjudication (see Weber, 1968:217–26, 654–58, 753–900 passim): (1) Affective neutrality: the political authority, in enforcing itself through adjudication, is neutral toward citizens; its favor cannot be curried; it is impartial. (2) Specificity: the areas of the citizen's personal life upon which the political authority can impose legal consequences are specified; specified, as well, are the respective degrees within each area (personal movement, speech, freedom to compete, and so forth) to which the sovereign can attach legal consequences to the citizen's behavior. (3) Universalism: the political sovereign invokes the general criterion of "citizen" in relating to individuals under its domination; hence, the enforcement of political authority through adjudication implies detachment (impersonality) on the part of the sovereign. (4) Quality: who or what the individual is, namely, a "citizen" (not what the person can do for the sovereign), determines the sovereign's orientation toward the individual. The ascriptive trait of citizenship of the individual in society, not his achievements in terms of obedience and service to the desires of the sovereign, conditions the sovereign's orientation toward the individual. (5) Collectivity orientation: by enforcing its authority through adjudication, the political sovereign shows its collectivity orientation in the recognition of citizenship rights. This is the exact opposite of the case in which the political authority recognizes only his own interest through administration, and only the political authority has a right, the subjects having none.

In turn, legal domination exercising itself through pure adjudication, that is, through the application of a rationalized system of rules, has three polar variables in common with those posited (see Devereux, 1961:44) as characterizing contractual relationships: affective neutrality, specificity, and universalism. Domination is, therefore, impartial, limited in scope, and impersonal. The two other polar traits that characterize domination through adjudication, but not the contractual relationship, are quality and collectivity orientation. The differences are important, for they imply that adjudication combines sovereign detachment toward the citizen without sovereign callousness. The performance and self-orientation of the contractual relationship by comparison implies an "each person for himself" frame of reference. At the same time, domination enforcing itself through adjudication escapes the paternalism inherent in the three other polar traits (affectivity, diffuseness, particularism) from which it is distinguished. In the ideal typically drawn case, then, adjudication enforcing legal domination through the upholding of citizenship rights combines the best of both worlds: the *Gemeinschaft* and the *Gesellschaft*.

From Patriarchal Administration to Adjudicated Citizen Rights

Viewed against the pattern variables, the gradual transition from paternalistic protection of subjects to detached concern for citizenship rights, including social rights, reflects a movement along five continua: (1) Affectivity/affective neutrality: political authority has become more impartial as protection has been carried out more and more in terms of adjudication than within the analytic confines of administration. (2) Diffuseness/specificity: political authority has become increasingly subject to limits upon the areas of citizen life to which it may attach the coercion of the law. (3) Particularism/universalism: political authority has become increasingly impersonal (detached). (4) Performance/quality: it is, increasingly, the status of the citizen, as distinguished from the performance of the subject, to which the political sovereign orients itself in enforcing its rule. (5) Self-orientation collectivity orientation: the right of the citizen has come to predominate over the right of the political sovereign. Rather than subjects serving sovereigns, sovereigns serve citizens through creating, enhancing, and upholding their rights.

An examination of *Economy and Society* shows that the transition from administration to adjudication in terms of these five continua was gradual. For example, pure patriarchalism did not reign for long: rather, as patriarchalism turned into patrimonialism, particularistic rights were subjectively granted by political authority to subjects (Weber, 1968:1031, 1040). Patrimonialism refers to that type of political rule in which offices originate in the ruler's household. Political authority is enforced through administration: the ruler directs his officials as to how conflicts will be settled according to his personally established regulations. Originally, officials are members of the family or personal dependents of the ruler and are fed at his table. As the territory governed by the ruler grows, decentralization becomes a necessity and officials are granted fiefs (see Bendix, 1962:344–48). This presents the prospect of the gradual attenuation of the purely discretionary administrative power of the ruler.

Eventually, "law communities" become established. Law communities represent groups of persons who share a common trait: mode of life or occupation, religious denomination, or membership in a fraternity may be the basis that unites the members. They bargain with the ruler to have "special law" applied in their favor. At this point in history, adjudication (the application of law recognizing "rights" of subjects) is particularistic (see Weber, 695–98, 880). The idea of generally applicable norms does not arise until the democratic revolutions, which mark the transition from traditional to legal authority. Rights cease to be personally granted from sovereign to subject, particularistic in their subjection to special law, and unspecified in their content. Rather, with the democratic revolutions, rights become the impersonally and impartially held territory of the citizen, the object of generalized law, and characterized by a specified and uniform content. Legal equality consists in uniformly held civil rights (see Sabine, 1952).

It is at this point in Western history that the impersonal market is regarded as an "authoritative" ordering device for social relations: let the market arbitrate social order through the impersonal and impartial law of supply and demand. This law, it is presumed, will operate efficiently (rationally) if restrictions upon the flow of money, materials, and men are removed. Paternalism (in terms of affectivity, diffuseness, and particularity) on the part of political authority is swept away. A new authority, symbolized in the apotheosis of freedom of contract, is instituted. This authority is affectively neutral, specific, universalistic, performance oriented, and self-oriented. If left to operate freely, all will "balance out" in the end, each self-orientation offsetting the others. The creation and recognition of individual rights are here identified with market processes, the market being the ultimate, impersonal judge of that to which the individual is entitled.

During the late nineteenth and early twentieth centuries, the market is exposed as a somewhat impervious and callous authority by virtue of the depressions and cycles of unemployment to which it subjects citizens. A rethinking of the "legitimacy" of such an authority ensues. The first acts of social legislation attempt to retain the detachment of the market while jettisoning its brutality. The adjudication of citizenship rights becomes a task for which the political authority begins to assume conscious responsibility. Affective neutrality, specificity, and universalism (the attractive qualities of the "authority" of the market) are held over from the eighteenth and nineteenth centuries. In turn, the status of the individual as a citizen (quality orientation) and the social responsibility of the sovereign toward the citizen and his rights (collectivity orientation) become an added double feature. The welfare state begins a lengthy engagement in the once purely libertarian West.

That society is, above all, a moral enterprise becomes explicit with the assumption of social responsibility toward the citizen by the political sovereign at the start of the twentieth century in Western regimes. Not, of course, that the underlying morality of social life was ever denied by contract theory. On the contrary, it was axiomatic that

> an obligation, to be really binding, must be freely assumed by the parties bound. . . . In the final analysis obligation cannot be imposed by force but is always self-imposed. It was this conviction which made all obligation appear under the guise of a promise; what a man promises he may reasonably be held to, since he has himself created the obligation by his own act. . . . As a conse-

quence a political theory based on natural law contained two necessary elements: the contract by which a society or a government (or both) came into being and the state of nature which existed apart from the contract. [Sabine, 1937:429–30]

Thomas Hobbes implied the morality of social life under the social contract most clearly when he described, by contrast, a life in the state of nature as a "war of every man against every man" and as "solitary, poor, nasty, brutish, and short" (see Sabine, 1937:464).

Thus, the morality of social order guaranteed by a political authority has never been in doubt in Western political philosophy. Its legitimate expression or manifestation has varied, however, according to differential emphasis of the various elements in the natural law tradition (see next chapter).[3] Under "administration," ideal typically considered, the patriarch protected his charges as extensions of himself. Self-orientation and collectivity orientation are analytically indistinguishable under paternalism. The natural law image of society as a brotherhood is somewhat distorted, but manifest nevertheless, under the oppressiveness of paternalism. Paternalism is, in its distinctive way, morally responsible. Charges against the prospect of the welfare state that suggest the identification of the individual's right with the right of the state as the "highest good" are rooted in a distaste for paternalism as expressed through pure administration. Fears that a welfare state presumes "totalitarian" control are, conceptually speaking, misgivings directed at the diffuseness of paternalistic protections. Finally, criticisms of the welfare state as coercive and restrictive of individual freedoms are rooted in that aspect of paternalism in which all protections are granted by the authority contingent upon the subject's obedience and service because, in any case, the subject has no formal "right" to these protections. Criticisms of the welfare state, thus, are frequently grounded in awareness of the dangers of paternalistic benevolence. Reluctance to make explicit that society is a moral order rests on the vivid and threatening image of the administration of protection under a paternalistic moral order.

The application of general norms, that is, the adjudicative process, in the enforcement of political authority makes possible the provision of protection without paternalism. When the adjudication of the citizen's right is self-consciously articulated and expressed by the political authority,[4] rather than implied by the operation of the impersonal market, the morality of society is announced rather than assumed (as under contract theory). To express this morality as "brotherhood without paternalism," the nature of the law upon which adjudication rests becomes of paramount concern. This concern will form the basis for discussions in Chapters 3 and 4. In Chapter 3, I show how law in Western regimes may acquire an aura of legitimacy by having the characteristic of impartiality. In Chapter 4, I discuss the relationship between rationalized (that is, impersonalized and impartial) law and the legitimacy of the state's making a transfer on behalf of citizen well-being.

Chapter 3

IMPARTIAL RULE, NATURAL LAW

LEGITIMACY, AND THE WELFARE

STATE: A WEBERIAN VIEW

AMONG THE generic characteristics attributed by scholars to natural law, the most important, for purposes of this discussion, is that natural law tenets contain the ideal that the political authority must impartially respect the dignity of all persons. "Right rule" is an implied amalgam of impartiality, fairness, and, therefore, legitimacy of authority. Though any number of scholars have treated natural law, I shall emphasize Weber's discussion here, for his treatment of the natural law legitimacy of positive law can offer much insight into the redistributional objectives of the Western welfare state. Weber did not, of course, treat the welfare state explicitly, but his elaboration of the rational grounds for the exercise of modern authority can be applied to contemporary Western regimes. Weber did not emphasize the quality of natural law that implies impartiality of rule, concentrating, rather, on the relationship between "Reason" and natural law. Therefore, I have called upon other writers to assimilate into the larger discussion the diverse notions of the reasonableness of natural law, its impartiality, and its capacity to imbue positive law with legitimacy. I will show that the precepts of natural law are compatible with both the individual rights tradition of the liberal state and the redistributional objectives of the welfare state.

As indicated in Chapter 1, one of the continuing debates regarding the welfare state involves its alleged threat to liberal principles. Through analyzing the elements of natural law as a legitimating ideal for the positive law promulgated by today's Western regimes, this tension can be shown to be more apparent than real. In fact, the implied antagonism in Weber's division of natural law into "formal" and "substantive" categories can also be reconciled by a careful examination of the generic qualities of natural law. In an attempt to unravel these timeworn but not very well-resolved issues, I will divide the discussion into the following sections: (1) the presuppositions of political liberalism and their relationship to those of welfare statism, (2) Weber's discussion of the rational grounds that legitimize legal authority, (3) Weber's articulation of the role of natural law in imbuing the rational grounds with "Reason," and (4) natural law and the objectives of the welfare state.

The Relationship of Liberal to Welfare State Tenets

Nineteenth-century economic liberalism held that, without the intervention of political authority, an "invisible hand" would automatically allocate a society's goods and services among a specific aggregate of individual actors. This was the view put forth by Adam Smith in *The Wealth of Nations* (1776). If men and money were entirely mobile (free of restriction or regulation), supply and demand within the scope occupied by the actors would be efficient. Such efficiency was valued as "good" by the political economists of the day. The relationship between government and the societal allocative process (referring to factors of production) "should" be one of nonintervention (laissez-faire). "That government which governs least governs best" expressed the value premise inherent in economic liberalism.

Economic liberalism engendered political liberalism. Political liberalism rested upon an analogous value premise that governments should not intervene in society's distributive system (referring to goods).[1] Until the twentieth century, the prevailing myth of liberalism was that this analytic parallel or isomorphism constituted a type of logical connection between the allocative and distributive realms of society (see Alfred Müller-Armack, 1947, as summarized by Rimlinger, 1971: 141–42). It was assumed that liberal governments would seriously compromise the legitimacy they enjoyed as respecters of individual freedoms if they altered the outcome (distribution) of the allocative process. This reasoning undergirded government reluctance to pass laws that would have mitigated the harsh contingencies of nineteenth-century working-class life. Laws that would have changed the terms involving labor, contracts, wages, or the ravages of unemployment were unthinkable at this point (Marshall, 1963; Bendix, 1977). If such laws were passed, what would become of individual freedoms and societal efficiency?

Yet intervention to change the outcome of the cards dealt society's players by the "invisible hand" is the sine qua non of the welfare state. The welfare state does exactly what the liberal state refused to do.[2] The philosophy of the welfare state does not deny the value of individual freedoms or societal efficiency.[3] Rather, the welfare state is fairly explicit in invoking the values of equality of opportunity and of human worth for persons at the foot of the stratification system. Humanitarianism (that ideal in which the concern of each is the concern of all) is emphasized as a necessary complement to libertarianism (that ideal in which each has social rights and freedoms to assume responsibility for himself).[4] But "the values of equality and humanitarianism that sustain the welfare state are in conflict with the free mobility ideology" that also characterizes Western regimes in the liberal tradition (Wilensky, 1975:29). Does this incongruity imply that the welfare state must, perforce, be a phenomenon of questionable legitimacy in the regimes in which it flourishes? Or, because it is a subtype of Weber's category of "legal authority," can an analytic justification for the welfare state be derived?

The "Rational Grounds" That Underlie Legitimacy

A connection between the objectives of the welfare state and the legitimacy of legal authority in Western regimes can be found in Weber's linkage of rational grounds (for legal authority) and natural law. This connection will be elucidated in this and the following sections.

Weber elaborates three types of legitimate authority that, analytically, comprise the whole of human political organization. Charismatic, traditional, and legal authority are his "pure types," though mixtures of them are to be found in virtually every empirical case (Weber, 1968:954). The validity of the claim to legitimacy of charismatic authority rests upon devotion to the exemplary character of an individual person as well as the normative order revealed by that person (Weber, 1968:215). The validity of the claim to legitimacy of traditional authority rests upon an established belief in the sanctity of immemorial traditions and the correlative legitimacy of the individual(s) exercising authority under those traditions (Weber, 1968: 215). In turn, the claim to legitimacy of legal authority rests upon rational grounds, themselves contingent upon the propensity of a people to believe in the validity of enacted rules and the right of those elevated to authority under such rules to issue commands (Weber: 1968: 215).

It is important to mention here that Weber fails to make explicit any logical connection between the pure type of authority he depicts and the "grounds" upon which the authority rests. Rather, he simply labels three sets of contingencies. For example, when an individual exercises authority in a manner compatible with immemorial traditions, we may say his legitimation rests upon traditional grounds. Similarly, we may say authority is "legal" and rests upon rational grounds when those exercising it do so by right of rules in which we believe. This merely raises the question as to why the rules should inspire belief in their validity among a populace in the first place. Weber never directly addresses this question in his ensuing description of the attributes of legal authority (1968:217–19).[5]

Weber's notion of legal authority refers to that type of political organization characterized by roles and relationships oriented to impersonal rules. Though Weber does not state this idea straightforwardly, it is implicit that the claim to legitimacy of a political organization so characterized rests upon a rationale that applies to those rules. Just such a "rationale" constitutes the "rational grounds" Weber portrays as underlying the validity of the claim to legality. Simply that the rules are impersonal or that they are established, for the most part, by intention (Weber, 1968:217–19) cannot be sufficient "grounds" for the validity of a claim that an order is "legal." Indeed, Weber makes clear that acceptance of the legal order implies that the rules will have the traits of impersonality and establishment by intention. Therefore, these traits cannot also be used to explain the initial legitimacy of the rules. Rather, this "explanation" must come from elsewhere. It is not until Weber discusses natural law as the ultimate source of legitimation for legal authority that the connection between rational grounds and legal authority is clarified.

Natural Law as the Rational Basis of Legal Authority

Philip Selznick makes an observation on the character of legality that supports the argument I shall present in this section. He writes, "The essential element in the rule of law is the restraint of official power by rational principles. . . . Legality imposes an environment of constraint, of tests to be met, standards to be observed, ideals to be fulfilled" (1969:11).

Natural law is the rational principle, or implied set of rational principles, that has provided an environment of constraint upon political power in varying degrees throughout the history of the West (Sabine, 1937; Brecht, 1959). The direction of Weber's argument, therefore, is consistent with what other scholars have inferred regarding the importance of natural law as an ideal informing the rightness of political authority. Weber writes that natural law is "the specific and only consistent type of legitimacy of a legal order which can remain once religious revelation and the authoritarian sacredness of tradition and its bearers have lost their force" (1968:867). Weber has here explicitly linked natural law (rather than "rational grounds") to the legitimacy of legal authority.[6]

It is as the very embodiment of "Reason" that natural law provides the "rational grounds" for the legitimacy of legal authority, however, and therefore, the positive law promulgated under such authority:

> "Nature" and "Reason" are the substantive criteria of what is
> legitimate from the standpoint of natural law. Both are regarded
> as the same, and so are the rules that are derived from them, so
> that general propositions about regularities of factual occurrences
> and general norms of conduct are held to coincide. The knowl-
> edge gained by human "reason" is regarded as identical with the
> "nature of things" or, as one would say nowadays, the "logic
> of things." The "ought" is identical with the "is," i.e., that
> which exists in the universal average. Those norms, which are ar-
> rived at by the logical analysis of the concepts of the law and
> ethics belong, just as the "laws of nature," to those generally
> binding rules which "not even God Himself could change,"
> and with which a legal order must not come into conflict.
> [Weber, 1968:869]

In short, natural law is "the sum total of all those norms which are valid independently of, and superior to, any positive law." Natural law, therefore, "provides the very legitimation for the binding force of positive law" (Weber, 1968:867).

Natural law rests upon the premise that men are equal in the eyes of God, who has revealed to each of them (by virtue of their capacity to reason) natural law's immanently valid "norms" (Weber, 1968:867). These norms provide the conception of the "rightness of the law." Weber notes that such an image is "sociologically relevant . . . when

practical legal life is materially affected by the conviction of the particular 'legitimacy' of certain legal maxims" (1968:866). What were
these "maxims" or "axioms," as Weber called them?

Weber emphasized that natural law axioms "fall into very different
groups," a distinction that is "not clear-cut" but "has great significance" (1968:868). The significance appears to be that the maxims
Weber collectively labels "formal natural law" imply an image of
society as a voluntary social contract. Therefore, the objectives of the
positive law of regimes legitimated by "formal natural law" center
upon the protection of individual rights and freedoms. More specifically, the protection of individual rights and freedoms from the de-
vouring attentions of political authority is a paramount condition if
the positive law of the regime is to be legitimate. Weber writes:

> The voluntary rational contract becomes one of the universal
> formal principles of natural law construction. . . . All legitimate
> law rests upon enactment, and all enactment, in turn, rests upon
> rational agreement. . . . The essential elements in such a natural
> law are the "freedoms," and above all, "freedom of contract." . . .
> Like every formal natural law, this type is conceived as a system
> of rights legitimately acquired by purposive contract, and, as far
> as economic goods are concerned, it rests upon the basis of a com-
> munity of economic agreement . . . created by the full devel-
> opment of property. . . . No enactment *can* validly limit the
> free disposition of the individual over his property and his
> working power. [1968:868–69]

According to Weber, therefore, "formal natural law axioms" served as
the value standard in terms of which the legitimacy of the law of Western regimes was judged until well into the twentieth century (1968:
870). Moreover, it is clear that the legal objectives of formal natural
law-legitimated regimes were the civil rights of which Marshall spoke
when he described the specific attributes of citizenship that were institutionalized in the eighteenth century in the West. Those included
"liberty of the person, freedom of speech, thought and faith, the right
to own property and to conclude valid contracts, and the right to
justice. . . . The right to defend and assert all one's rights on terms of
equality with others and by due process of law" (Marshall, 1963:74).

When, in turn, Weber elaborates the maxims he labels "substantive
natural law," the reader begins to appreciate the "great significance"
of the "difference" Weber has created between his two subtypes. It

appears that the objectives toward which the law of substantive natural law-legitimated regimes would be directed are diametrically opposed to the objectives guaranteed by the law of liberal regimes:

> For this view [substantive natural law] rejects not only all unearned income acquired through the channels of inheritance or by means of a guaranteed monopoly, but also the formal principle of freedom of contract and general recognition of the legitimacy of all rights acquired through the instrumentality of contracting. According to these theories, all appropriations of goods must be tested substantively by the extent to which they rest on labor as their ground of acquisition. [1968:871]

Having articulated that to which substantive natural law doctrines would be opposed, Weber then clarifies those objectives such a natural law would legitimize. Though Weber notes that the maxims of substantive natural law are somewhat ambiguous, he derives three related objectives a regime legitimated by substantive natural law would be likely to implement through its positive law. Substantive natural law can imply "in the *first* place the right to a share in the land to the extent of one's own labor power . . . or, *secondly*, a right to the ownership of land to the extent of the traditional standard of living. . . . In the conventional terminology the postulate thus means either the 'right to work' or the 'right to a minimum standard of living'; *thirdly*, however, the two may be combined with the demand for the 'right to the full product of one's labor'" (1968:871–72). Little strain on the imagination is required to recognize that the objectives Weber would impute to substantive natural law fall within the purview of the "social rights" articulated by Marshall (1963) and referred to in Chapter 1. The overriding characteristic of substantive natural law maxims, as Weber has depicted them, is that they imply legitimation of positive law that emphasizes the legal guarantee of humanitarian (as contrasted to libertarian) ideals. That is, substantive natural law implies an image of society as an order fairly explicitly connected by an overarching norm of social responsibility of each toward all. By comparison, formal natural law implies an image of society as an order automatically integrated by an overarching norm of individual responsibility (of each toward himself, with it all "balancing out" in the end).

Thus, each of Weber's subtypes of natural law contains a "rationale" that could render the "rational grounds" upon which legal rule is based "reasonable." That is, each type is capable of imbuing the positive law with the "meanings" or "reasons" that would make the law legitimate. The content of each is unique: the one containing civil liberties, the other, the right to a minimum standard of living.

I have argued that the presuppositions of liberalism and welfare statism are apparently contradictory. In fact, though, social welfare legislation is now enacted routinely in Western regimes that formerly eschewed such a use of political authority. Weber, too, took account of this change, though it had only recently been initiated (Weber cites court cases decided in the United States from 1898 to 1917 [1968:879 n. 17]). To provide a theoretical explanation for this seeming reversal of the legitimate uses of political authority, Weber spoke of "the transformation of formal into substantive natural law."

To account for such a "transformation," Weber's analytic task was to find an abstract feature of natural law that characterized both of his (formerly opposed) subtypes. He seized upon the notion of the law's "reasonableness":

> Natural law "reason" easily slipped into utilitarian thinking, and this shift expresses itself in the change of meaning of the concept of "reasonableness." In purely formal natural law, the reasonable is that which is derivable from the eternal order of natural and logic, both being readily blended with one another. But from the very beginning, the English concept of "reasonable" contained by implication the meaning of "rational" in the sense of "practically appropriate." From this it could be concluded that what would lead in practice to absurd consequences cannot constitute the law desired by nature and reason. This signified the express introduction of substantive presuppositions into the concept of reason which had in fact always been implicit in it. [1968:870]

Weber's explanation of the reconciliation of formal and substantive natural law leaves something to be desired. Did "formal natural law," as such, have as explicit a grip upon the consciousness of those exercising political authority as Weber implies in the above as well as in the following comment?

> [The] formalism of natural law . . . was softened in several ways. . . . In order to establish relations with the existing order, natural law had to accept legitimate grounds for the acquisition of rights [the social rights of citizenship] which could not be derived from freedom of contract. . . . [With a shift in meaning of

the term "reasonable" to allow for "substantive" considerations]
the Supreme Court of the United States was able to free itself
from formal natural law so as to be able to recognize the validity
of certain acts of social legislation. [1968:870]

Indeed, the first acts of social legislation (which will be treated in the
following chapters) may well have created a vague sense of inconsistency in the objectives of the law from the standpoint of those authorizing it. I would like to offer an explanation that is complementary to
Weber's regarding the relationship of natural law ideals to the legitimacy of social legislation in the Western welfare state.

Natural Law and the Objectives of the Welfare State

We may put aside questions regarding the degree of Weber's success in
resolving the implied incompatibility of the legal objectives associated
with his two subtypes of natural law. The fundamental question at this
point is whether the natural law tradition implies a standard for the
legitimacy of Western welfare legislation today. I have used Weber's
treatment of natural law to argue the plausibility of the case that the
welfare state is not as much at variance with the Western political
tradition as it may initially seem to be. In this section I shall reinforce
that argument.

I doubt, however, that any explicit notion of natural law per se
immediately affects the initiation or legitimacy of today's welfare legislation. Other variables (political expediency, the size of the GNP,
party politics)[7] are far more directly responsible for the format and
timing of specific acts of legislation. Nor is the presence of a natural
law tradition within the larger culture a necessary or sufficient condition for the emergence of a "welfare state" or for such a state's legitimacy if it does emerge. The establishment of such connections is not
my objective. Rather, given that (1) today's Western regimes enact
social welfare legislation, (2) the legitimacy of such legislation is often
problematic, and (3) part (though not all) of what is problematic
about the legitimacy of such legislation is that the political tradition in
Western nations enacting it is heavily steeped in the individualistic,
freedom-venerating side of the natural law tradition, then (4) are there
aspects of the natural law tradition that would be equally supportive
of the legitimacy of humanitarian (as they were of libertarian) legal
objectives?

Though natural law is a notion ostensibly remote from the machinations that underlie contemporary welfare deliberations, in fact, it can be argued that certain ideas within the tradition serve as standards against which Western government responsibility for citizen well-being is undoubtedly judged today. Collective responsibility for individual welfare is not as distant from the mainstream of Western ethics as the narrowly considered notion of "individual rights" would lead one to believe. Despite its numerous "eclipses," as discussed by Arnold Brecht (1959:138–41), the natural law tradition has stamped indelibly upon the Western cultural heritage certain predispositions toward conceptions of the "rightness of the law." By shifting Weber's emphasis and by relying upon the treatment of natural law put forth by other scholars, a position more relevant to today's world can be derived.

The following natural law notions were first articulated by the Greek Stoics and later incorporated into Christianity (Sabine, 1937:142–43). I shall be arguing that Western regimes have acquired legitimacy through the legal recognition (in varying degrees and at different times throughout Western history) of these related ideas:

1. Human consciousness and human nature are more or less identical everywhere. This commonality makes individual persons part of a universal brotherhood.

2. Not only are humans alike in nature but, by virtue that each possesses (unlike other animals) the faculty of reason, they are alike of mind. Accordingly, they are capable of concord or harmony in their relationships. This likeness of mind is a second basis of universal brotherhood.

3. Each individual has a private life, purely personal, and deserving of both dignity and the respect of others, including the state. Thus, the individual is important and significant in his own right, and he can "set up the claim of an inherent right, the right to have his personality respected" (Sabine, 1937:143).

4. That humans are alike in kind and in mind, and deserving of respect as individuals, implies their equality in an ethical sense. To recognize this equality of persons, the state should be impartial.

5. Because an individual has dignity in his own right, his interactions with political authority should be structured so that his dignity will be reinforced, not lost.

6. Ergo, power must justify itself: it is subject to rational criticism and inquiry.

7. "Mere" enacted law is to be judged in terms of the degree to

which it embodies the tenets of this "higher law," that is, the presuppositions of natural law.[8]

8. Enacted law is a localized phenomenon, whereas the "higher law" is universal in its application. Man has an individual nature that, nevertheless, partakes of the universal, and, as such, he has a place in the universe as well as in a particular locale.

At different times in the history of the West, legitimate political authority recognized or emphasized certain of the above natural law tenets over others. Traditional authority, though hardly impartial toward , and cognizant of, the reasoning power of each and every subject, nevertheless found it important to justify itself (Weber, 1968:227). Barbara Tuchman's *A Distant Mirror: The Calamitous Fourteenth Century* (1978) is overflowing with accounts of the abuses perpetrated by kings and popes alike against those below them on the medieval social ladder. Nevertheless, she emphasizes throughout that those assuming or holding power were constantly striving to legitimize themselves. Many of these legitimation stratagems involved implicit recognition of valued natural law tenets, particularly the one referring to the importance of man's place in the universal order. Bastardizations of this natural law view are manifested in papal pressure upon the underclasses to pay their tithe and their taxes upon penalty of forfeiting their place in heaven (Tuchman, 1978:173). In turn, the natural law tenet that man has an individual dignity was sufficiently part of medieval man's consciousness that he was able to feel a claim of "right" when he (albeit infrequently) confronted political authority with the prospect of reform (Tuchman, 1978:161–63). In addition, a harmony of interests among the classes was a cultural assumption held for centuries prior to the democratic revolutions (Sabine, 1937:318–22; see also Bendix, 1978:226; and Wolfe, 1977:42–79).

The democratic revolutions were themselves augured by the critical spirit inspired by natural law (Roth, 1975:152–54; Weber, 1968:866–68ff.; Sabine, 1937:546).[9] The democratic revolutions brought to the fore the more individualistic side of the natural law tradition, as well as that aspect of it calling for impartiality of the sovereign toward societal members. The establishment of the role of citizen with equal legal rights embodied several natural law implications. The citizen was presumed "reasonable," deserving of respect, and above all, legally entitled to impartiality of treatment from the political authority. It is the institutionalization of the right to impartiality upon which I predicate the remainder of my argument that the natural law legacy is of

continuing relevance to the contemporary Western welfare state and
to the legitimacy of its use of political authority to raise the standard
of living for citizens.

The interpretation of the ideal norm of impartiality implicit in the
natural law tradition has changed subtly from the time of the democratic revolutions to the present. Under the newly instituted democratic
liberal state, impartiality first meant government nonintervention into
the personal circumstances of citizens. We may call this "impartiality-
as-laissez-faire." In order to appreciate laissez-faire as, among other
things, a manifestation of the impartiality of the state, it is necessary to
understand just how partial political authority was before the democratic revolutions. Prior to the revolutions, government "intervention"
into the social realm was invariably particularistic: special law and
law communities are examples (Weber, 1968:694–704; Sabine, 1952:
461). Thus, Reinhard Bendix writes that spokesmen for the laissez-
faire position during the nineteenth century "insisted that to remain
legitimate the government must abide by the rule of law" (1977:94).
He notes the outcome as follows: "Legal equality advances at the
expense of legal protection of inherited privileges" (1977:92). It also
advances at the expense of the protection of those suffering social and
economic inequality in that the freedom of the wage contract destroys
the legal basis for such protections (Bendix, 1977:93: "For a time at
least, no new protections are instituted in place of the old").

If initial failure on the part of the newly instituted liberal governments to act on behalf of a certain category of individuals in society
seems brutal, it appears much less so when a longer historical perspective is taken. The larger perspective sharply highlights the partiality of
law and the restrictiveness of individual freedoms under laws promulgated by traditional authorities. "Outlawry," as indicated in the passage below, was a status into which an individual could easily be
driven under the laws of fourteenth-century England:

> Outlawry among free peasants had increased because their
> command of higher wages, as a result of depopulation [due to
> the Black Plague] brought them in constant conflict with the law.
> The Statute of Laborers, in a world that believed in fixed condi-
> tions, still held grimly to pre-plague wage levels, blind to the
> realities of supply and demand. Because the provisions against
> leaving one employment for a better were impossible to enforce,
> penalties were constantly augmented. Violators who could not be

caught were declared outlaws—and made lawless by the verdict. Free peasants took to the nomadic life, leaving a fixed abode so that the statute could not be executed against them, roaming from place to place, seeking day work for good wages where they could get it, resorting to thievery or beggary where they could not, breaking the social bond, living in the classic enmity to authority of Robin Hood for the Sheriff of Nottingham. [Tuchman, 1978:286]

This example makes eminently more understandable an interpretation of laissez-faire as simply a point on a continuum of impartiality of the political authority's orientation toward the citizen. This continuum is implicit in the natural law tradition, and nonintervention into the social choices of citizens was simply an early, if not altogether satisfactory, manifestation of this ideal.

Emphasis upon the central place of impartiality as a component of legitimate law in the West breaks the grip of the "individual rights– laissez-faire" frame of reference for judging the legislation of the welfare state. It becomes possible to see, in an analytic sense, that social legislation embodies the older notion of political authority as the impartial respecter of the dignity of every individual. By this logic, we may interpret social welfare legislation as embodying the ideal of impartiality through a new operational indicator: equity. Equity is giving each person his due. The welfare state increasingly uses the status of the citizen *qua* individual-deserving-of-dignity as the criterion of what is "due" him as a member of the larger collectivity. Finally, even the principle of equity has been elaborated in the welfare state. At least in the United States, "affirmative action" has become a reigning principle (see n. 26, Chapter 1, and n. 3 Chapter 11). That is, the state has undertaken the enforcement of conditions under which an individual can integrate himself into the social order in such a way as to be deserving of his "due" as a member of the collectivity.

The social critic can, from the above perspective, begin to appreciate both the advance of the welfare state in the face of laissez-faire and the skepticism of certain nineteenth-century social critics toward the notion of nonintervention. Even at its height laissez-faire was labeled an "upstart" idea in the history of Western ideas on moral, and therefore, legitimate rule. Richard Oastler, a severe critic of Britain's 1834 Poor Law (see Chapter 5), asserted that the "social state" was the "true state" of history: it was, rather, the laissez-faire political economists who were the "revolutionaries" (cited in Briggs, 1961:235). Briggs notes that "the idea of the 'historic rights of the poor' . . . provided a link between 'traditionalism' and modern working-class politics" (1961:235). Even Nassau Senior, an outspoken laissez-faire political economist who was also the architect of the 1834 Poor Law, was not the least dogmatic regarding the sanctity of nonintervention: "It is the duty of a government to do whatever is conducive to the welfare of the governed" (cited in Briggs, 1961:234).

In short, it is the duty of the government to exert social responsibility, opportunities and rights institutionalizing individual responsibility notwithstanding. Libertarianism (see above) as the lone ideal typical norm against which to measure the quality (legitimacy) of the citizen-sovereign relationship, was salient for only a brief period within the whole of Western history. According to the argument I have made here, the chance to assert individual responsibility was but the first institutionalization of the natural law principle that governments should be impartial toward their subjects. The establishment of this principle through law in the West transformed subjects into citizens. As the principle of impartiality continues to be elaborated through the notion of "social rights," the Western welfare state advances along a path potentially alight with its own legitimacy.

Finally, it should be recognized that the extreme point on a continuum of impartiality of the state implies the essential brotherhood of people. Welfare state embodiments of this notion would include any scheme in which "sharing the risk" is central. The welfare state is, in the last analysis, the risk-sharing state. Citizens "pay in" through discharging the normal duties of citizenship. They are thus "covered" and "eligible." The political authority, as the impersonal and impartial arbiter of the societal social insurance scheme, "pays up" through guaranteeing minimum standards of living in the degree that they can be economically justified by the size of the GNP and their relationship of the costs of other societal priorities. The welfare state, ideally, implies brotherhood without paternalism. The rule of law, which will be treated in Chapter 4, makes this possible.

Chapter 4

ENFORCING THE WELFARE STATE

THROUGH RATIONALIZED LAW

THE IDEALS OF individual dignity, a universal brotherhood, and collective social responsibility are integral to the natural law tradition. I have argued that such ideals indirectly legitimize the redistributional objectives of the Western welfare state, for redistribution is compatible with these natural law values. If each citizen is of equal worth as an individual, then governments achieve a corresponding degree of legitimacy whenever they impartially respect the dignity of all persons. Thus, the governmentally undertaken redistributions that distinguish the welfare state from the liberal state are a direct expression of the notion that citizens are equally worthy.

Redistribution is one species of the genus "social protection." By redistributing social wealth, governments act to the ultimate purpose of protecting individuals and families directly or providing people with the wherewithal with which to protect themselves. In Chapter 2, I pointed out that social protection can be offered through two fundamental channels: personalized and impersonalized. Under paternalism, as exemplified by patriarchal household administration, the protection of those within the purview of the political authority is a direct and personalized event, with those protected expected to offer service, loyalty, obedience, and gratitude to the patriarch. By contrast, under a system of legal authority with fully developed citizenship rights, as exemplified by the welfare state (in the ideal typically drawn case), the protection of those within the purview of the political authority is an indirect and impersonalized event. Those protected need only discharge the normal duties of citizenship. These duties, of course, ultimately involve obeying the law of the land and serving one's government (which represents the nation, the collectivity) in times of emergency such as war. Yet, the exchange of obedience for social protection is mediated through impersonalized institutions so that individual freedoms and dignity do not suffer. In this chapter, I will explicate the basis for the impersonalization of the citizen-sovereign relationship such that the welfare state may enhance the standard of living for citizens without simultaneously subjugating them.

Law as the Basis of Impersonalization

Law is the crux of the establishment of an impartial and impersonal relationship between citizen and sovereign in the modern state. The articulation of law is the articulation of a general norm. The generality of the norm, indeed, implies a "class" of events or persons, each of which is alike from a legal standpoint. Hence, a general norm implies impartiality on the part of political authority as it legally regards a member of this class.[1] Next, the general norm articulates a single legally relevant characteristic possessed by an individual which he shares in common with other individuals. The norm thus "detaches" the legally relevant part of the individual, separating that trait from his "personal" traits. Therefore, the articulation of law as general norms implies impersonality (detachment) in the citizen-sovereign relationship.[2]

Law is indispensable to the existence of rights. For Weber writes that the existence of a right is equal to "no more than an increase of the probability that a certain expectation of the one to whom the law grants the right will not be disappointed" (1968:666). Rights, in turn, are "claim-norms" and are amenable to guarantee through adjudication. Law as the articulation of a general norm is, therefore, the sine qua non of both rights and the institution of adjudication:

> Today we understand by lawmaking the establishment of general
> norms which . . . assume the character of rational rules of law.
> Lawfinding . . . is the "application" of such established norms
> and the legal propositions deduced therefrom by legal thinking,
> to concrete "facts" which are "subsumed" under these norms. . . .
> The distinction between lawmaking as creation of general norms
> and lawfinding as application of these norms to particular cases
> does not exist where adjudication is "administration" in the sense
> of free decision from case to case. In such a situation, it is not
> only the legal norm that is lacking, but also the idea of a party's
> right to have it applied to his case. [1968:653–54]

By contrast, "administration" involves the issuance by the political authority of "reglementations." These are norms that only embody instructions to state officials regarding their duties (Weber, 1968:642). If the citizen happens to derive a tangible benefit from the fact that an official has implemented a reglementation, the citizen does so only as a "reflex" of the reglementation (Weber, 1968:642). To benefit as a reflex or by-product of a reglementation is an altogether different case from benefiting by virtue of a "claim-norm," that is, a "right" (Weber, 1968:642ff.). Upon this difference turns a number of problems faced by the U.S. welfare state, in particular, as I shall show in Chapter 8.

For the moment, it remains to delineate the processes through which law, as the central feature of the impersonalization of the citizen-sovereign relationship, can effectively guarantee a citizen's right to a particular standard of living.

The Impersonalization of Law through Its Rationalization

In order to effectively guarantee a social (or any other) right, the law needs to have certain characteristics or qualities. Weber has treated these characteristics in terms of the process of rationalization. Rationalization is the process that systematizes, and therefore strengthens, a system of ideas, be that system law, philosophy, religion, or the like (see Swidler, 1973:36). Systematizing a set of ideas involves these steps (Gerth and Mills, 1958:267–301 passim):[3] (1) clarifying, defining, and distinguishing discrete elements within the idea set; (2) ordering elements according to an explicit criterion, which, in turn, provides internal consistency of relationships among discrete elements so systematized; (3) integrating discrete elements and synthesizing their relationships through using a criterion (or criteria) yet more abstract than the elements singly considered; and (4) extending the scope of comprehensiveness of the idea system through generalizing the criteria used to subsume concrete events to which the ideas refer. The rationalization of ideas contains its own dynamic for expansion and change—through raising the level of abstraction of ideas within a system, more and more concrete facts or fact situations can be subsumed within the purview of the law, philosophy, or thought-system being "rationalized." Through successive refinements in clarification, ordering, synthesizing, and generalizing ideas, comprehensiveness of the idea system is achieved (Weber, 1968:655–56). I shall be arguing that such systematization is the pivot upon which both the effective guarantee and the legitimacy of a social right turn. That is, if (1) law is the condition for the existence of a right, and if (2) systematization strengthens law, then (3) a systematized (rationalized) law strengthens rights.

In order to understand how rationalized law strengthens rights, it is necessary to be aware of Weber's definition of "rational law." Clearly, rationalized law, as Weber articulates it, is but a specification of the notion of the rationalization of ideas. The end-point of each (of rationalized law and the rationalization process in general) involves the comprehensivization of the idea system, as the following will show. Weber (1968:655–56) writes that rational(ized) law is (1) highly specified as to criteria of relevance for which aspects of an event will be taken into account; (2) general in that reasons relevant in the decision or concrete individual cases are reduced to one or more principles or "legal propositions"; (3) synthetically constructed in a way that (a) specifies which principles or propositions are in legally relevant relationships to one another, and (b) articulates legally relevant relationships so that, taken together, they are internally consistent; and (4) comprehensive in that it extends itself over all analytically derived legal propositions "in such a way that they constitute a logically clear, internally consistent, and at least in theory, gapless system of rules, under which, it is implied, all conceivable fact situations must be capable of being logically subsumed lest their order lack an effective guarantee" (Weber, 1968:655–56). With regard to this last point, Weber might better have used the term "determinate" rather than comprehensive, meaning that the permissible scope of the law's application is capable of being ascertained. In the degree that the principles guiding the law are abstract, then the scope would be very broad, that is, comprehensive.

To relate this abstract discussion of the rationalization (and hence impersonalization) of the law to the guarantee of social rights in the welfare state, I shall illustrate the relationship with a hypothetical case. Imagine that a Western welfare regime introduces and passes legislation that guarantees an annual minimum income supplement to all of the nation's "deserving poor." For the law to be "rational" (following Weber's outline above), the criteria of relevance for which aspects of the event to be taken into account must be specified. In this case, the law must specify criteria for determining (1) who is "poor" and then, within that category, (2) who is "deserving." To specify such criteria, principles (Weber's second step) will have to be invoked in order to ascertain the reasons relevant to each particular case to be decided. In other words, by what principle does the government deem a "poor" individual or family "deserving"? That is, why is this a "deserving" case?

In articulating the principles according to which certain "poor" members of the body politic can be certified as "deserving," Weber's third step, synthetic construction, will come into play. Namely, these criteria will have to be logically compatible with other criteria applicable to the citizen-sovereign relationship. This is what Weber means when he says that legally relevant relationships must be internally consistent for the system of law to be rational. In the United States, for example, the Bill of Rights articulates a number of "legally relevant" relationships between the citizen and the sovereign, among them freedom of speech, movement, and religion for citizens. Therefore, in selecting criteria of "deservingness," the government could not deem any of the poor "undeserving" on the basis of their religion, whether they have changed their residence in the last year, or their expression of political views. Again using the case of the United States, another legally relevant relationship between citizen and sovereign involves that implied by minimum wage legislation. The government could not deem a poor individual "undeserving" if he has refused to work for less than that to which he is entitled by minimum wage laws.

Finally, for the law guaranteeing an income supplement to all the "deserving poor" to be rational, it must be both determinate and, ultimately, comprehensive. That is, for every case considered, we must be able to decide if the criteria of "deservingness" and "poorness" apply. If we find cases for which we can make no determinate recommendation, then the system is not "gapless." Indeed, comprehensiveness relies, in the last analysis, upon the first step in the chain: clarity of definitions.

If, in fact, a body of law is rational, then it will have two very important characteristics:

1. Its guarantee will be effective. That is, none of the "deserving poor" will fall outside the law, thereby being deprived of their "rightful" due under the law.

2. The law will be legitimate. That is, the underlying principles according to which "deservingness" and "poorness" are articulated will be so well integrated with other legally relevant aspects of the

citizen-sovereign relationship that it will not seem incongruous (lacking in justification) from the viewpoint of the body politic that certain people (the deserving poor) should receive an income supplement.

Finally, again stemming from its rational character, the law will have one other notable characteristic: it will be capable of bestowing largesse upon the deserving poor impersonally. For the definition of the law's terms will state or imply eligibility criteria that, if met by the applicant, will automatically guarantee him, without further ado, the income supplement for a specified interval of time (until eligibility must again be demonstrated if the applicant continues to be "poor").[4] For example, in the United States, social security payments to the aged, the disabled, or the unemployed are "automatic" once eligibility has been demonstrated (see Bowler, 1974:9 and this work, Chapter 5).

Effectiveness and Legitimacy of Law as Outcomes of Rationalization

Weber dichotomizes the overall notion of the rationalization of the law into two subtypes of rationalization: formal and substantive (1968: 656–58 and 882–89). The analytic possibility that the law may be formally rationalized stems from the fact that the law has a formal (logical) structure. The possibility that the law may undergo substantive rationalization emerges from the fact that the law also has a substantive content.

Formal rationalization of law refers to the successive tightening (or rigidifying) of the law's logical structure as a system of ideas. It involves the processes aforementioned: (1) increasing clarification and specification of the law's concepts; (2) increasing generalization of the principles around which the law is oriented; (3) continued logical integration of the legally relevant relationships; and (4) successive extensions in scope of the determinateness of the law, such that social contingencies may be ordered "gaplessly" according to the law's principles.

Substantive rationalization of the law refers to the successive elaboration of the law's objectives. The objectives or purposes of the law are what give it its "meaning." The purposes toward which the law is oriented as a formally logical system may be ethical, religious, ideological, economic, expediential, and so forth (see Weber, 1968:809–64 passim). The purpose(s) toward which the law is oriented give the law its legitimacy, over and above the fact that it is the law. Thus, the substance, content, or concrete objectives of the law help us answer the question, "What good is this law?" or "What is it about this law that inspires our respect (and obedience) for it, other than that it is backed by the force of the state?" For Weber writes: "One specific characteristic of government . . . resides in the fact that it aims not only at acknowledging and enforcing the law simply because the law exists and constitutes the basis of vested rights, but also in that it pursues other concrete objectives of a political, ethical, utilitarian, or some other kind" (1968:644–45). Thus, as Selznick (1969:5) notes, it is not "orders backed by threats" that is central to the idea of law.

From a slightly different perspective, when it is said that "any law is better than no law," what is meant is simply that "order (any order) is preferable to disorder," for what "law" guarantees is an order (Weber, 1968:33–34). The substance of the law refers to the rationale that underlies the socially constructed relationships that are the order. It is the formal character of the law's rationalization that attaches legal consequences—and therefore the coercion of the state—to certain of these relationships. But the decision as to which of all possible social relationships to "legalize" requires a guiding substantive rationale (such as the paramount importance of freedom of contract, individual rights, social justice, or the like). Therefore, the law's legitimacy ultimately derives from its substance. Weber treats the continuing quest for the law's "spirit," "kernel," "real intent," or ultimate "meaning" in terms of the notion of the law's "logical sublimation" (1968:884ff.). Logical sublimation, as Weber uses the term, is essentially equivalent to the law's substantive rationalization. Both refer to the elaboration of the law's ultimate objectives.[5]

It is clear that if the law's guarantee is to be effective—to reach those whom it is intended to reach—the law needs to be formally rationalized. That is, the logical structure of the law should ultimately be gapless. This will come about if the concepts behind the law are both precisely specified and abstract so that the widest possible range of concrete events and fact situations may be subsumed within the law's purview. Correlatively, if the law is to be legitimate—in line with the values of the body politic—elaboration of the reasons behind the law (substantive rationalization) is necessary. In sum, formal and substantive rationalization are complementary and parallel processes. Unless they are synchronized so that they occur parallel to one another, their complementarity will be lost.

An illustration will make this relationship more apparent. If, for example, a regime extends the right to vote, in order to make this extension in a formally rational manner it will have to extend the right to general categories of persons. The categories must be named (specified), and they must be specified in abstract (general) terms. The vote, therefore, may be extended to such named and general categories of persons as "women," "minorities," and "those age eighteen and over." At this point substantive rationalization becomes necessary if this extension of the right to vote is to be made in a rational way. Reasons must now be elaborated as to why the right to vote is being extended in scope to this (or these) new category (or categories) of persons. Principle formation and logical synthesis permit the elaboration of such reasons. That is, a more general principle that unites both the old category(ies) of voters and the new categories to be added allows a consistent rationale to be articulated. Whereas the right to vote previously may have been held only by male propertyholders, presumed, therefore, to be interested in the political affairs of the government, the right to vote may now be predicated upon "all nondependent members of the society" (everyone over eighteen and not confined to an institution) on the strength of the rationale that they, too, have a direct interest in how the affairs of government are run. By articulating what both the old and new rightholders have in common, abstraction and synthesis make the law rational. Elaboration provides the "substantive rationale," while abstraction and synthesis constitute "formal processes" through which rationalization comes about.

When these two processes, formal and substantive rationalization, do not occur in parallel fashion, a disjuncture opens in their complementarity. Incongruity and the consequent image of "unfairness" arise. Incongruity can act as a spur to bring formal and substantive rationalization of the law into parallel alignment and thus make possible a complementary relationship. For example, in the United States, eighteen-year-olds were extended the right to vote by the Twenty-sixth Amendment to the Constitution proposed and passed in 1971. This was precipitated by the incongruity of a war being fought for which eighteen-year-old males were compelled to fight, risking their lives. Substantively, it seemed "unfair" that they had no say in electing the individual who would have the authority to make a decision with legal consequences that would be of vital importance to the well-being of their life, limb, and future social relationships. Why was the extension of the vote not confined to eighteen-year-old males (excluding females)? To do so would have introduced logical inconsistency into already existing legally relevant relationships between U.S. citizens and sovereign. Namely, the Nineteenth Amendment to the U.S. Constitution had already granted females the right to vote on grounds articulated in 1919 when the amendment was proposed (it was adopted in 1920). Too, the rationale under which eighteen-year-olds were extended the right to vote was articulated at a level more abstract than that males eighteen and over were vulnerable to loss of life through war (see Lowi, 1976:150–57, 245–47).

The complementary relationship between the law's formal and substantive rationalization is summarized in Figure 4–1.

Figure 4–2, by contrast, highlights those institutions within the structure of legitimate political authority that are most closely associated with various aspects of the rationalization of the law. When the legislative or adjudicative institutions of political authority fail to carry out their respective tasks of formal or substantive rationalization of the law, the welfare state (as a right-creating form of rule) is stopped in its tracks. Rather, discretion and patronization begin to characterize welfare transfers. This happens within the framework of "administration" (as distinct from "legislation" or "adjudication") and will be treated in detail in Chapters 7 and 8.

Finally, Figure 4–3 summarizes points made throughout Chapters 2, 3, and 4, indicating the historical transition from partial and personal to impartial and impersonal rule.

Paternalism unites the social order in that each member, regardless of how humble or insignificant, implicitly feels a relationship between himself and the individual at the "top" who is his protector. Rimlinger's (1971) discussion of czarism in prerevolutionary Russia articulates clearly the elements of paternalistic unification of a social order. The underplaying of linkages intermediate to the lowest and most exalted members of the political order marks paternalism as a threat to individual freedoms and integrity, for the individual stands alone against the sovereign, appealing to his benevolence. DeJouvenel (1963:169–304 passim) specifies in thoughtful detail the elements that constitute such a threat.

The social contract integrates the social order in that each member, regardless of personal characteristics, has a formal basis upon which he is free to relate to any other member of the society. This formal basis is his freedom to enter into contracts. Again, regardless of disparity in socially valuable traits (age, sex, wealth, prestige, and so forth), "A" is free to relate to "B" in the degree that each is willing to

FIGURE 4-1

*Outcome of the Degree of Rationalization of the Law**

		Degree of Rationalization of the Law	
		High Level of Rationalization	Low Level of Rationalization
Aspect of the Law Undergoing Rationalization	The Law's Form	(1) Formally rationalized law Makes effective the guarantee of the law, as well as the rights created by the law. Extends scope of law through abstraction (generalization) and closes scope of law through precise specification of categories.	(2) Formally irrationalized law Undermines the effectiveness of the guarantee of the law, as well as the rights created by the law. Undermines effectiveness of guarantee through leaving "loose ends," narrowness, or indeterminateness of scope through low-level abstraction or imprecise specification of categories.
	The Law's Content	(3) Substantively rationalized law Justifies the law. Justifies the content of rights granted by the law by elaboration of the ultimate purposes of the law.	(4) Substantively irrationalized law Undermines the legitimacy of the law or the content of the right granted by the law by bestowing or allowing through insufficient elaboration a sense of inappropriateness regarding the law's intent or the right's content.

*This figure is derived from Weber's discussion of the ways the law may be formally or substantively rational or irrational (1968:656–57). Max Rheinstein's (1967:xxxix–lv) introduction to *Max Weber on Law in Economy and Society* clarifies these issues and relationships, particularly on pp. xlii–xliii.

FIGURE 4-2

Type of Rationalization of the Law according to
Associated Institution and Aspect of the Law's Guarantee

		Institution (or Institutional Process) Most Closely Associated with Aspect of the Law's Guarantee	
		The Legislature (Legislation)	The Courts (Adjudication)
Aspect of the Law's Guarantee	The Law's Effectiveness	(1) Formal rationalization of the law: the passage of law whose categories are precisely specified, general, logically consistent with other legally relevant categories, and determinate in scope.	(2) X*
	The Law's Legitimacy	(3) X†	(4) Substantive rationalization of the law: the elaboration or articulation of the law's "real intent" such that the overall body of the law is interpretable as having a coherent purpose or mutually compatible set of ultimate objectives.

*The courts are but indirectly connected to the law's effectiveness. First, the legislature must pass a clear law. Second, the executive branch is entrusted to enforce the law, that is, make its guarantee effective. Only if one or the other of these two branches fails do the courts contribute to the law's effectiveness by either clarifying the intent of the law or deeming the law's enforcement consistent with the Constitution (or the law's lack of enforcement in violation thereof).

†The legislature is indeed associated with the law's legitimacy in that the legislature often enunciates a rational at the time of passage of the law. But because the courts are the ultimate arbiters of the "real intent" of the law, and because they may deem the intent of the law unconstitutional, I have listed the courts as the more closely associated institution with regard to the legitimacy of the law's guarantee.

FIGURE 4-3

Summary of Characteristics of the Transition from
Traditional to Modern Authority in the West

Traditional Authority	Legal Authority	
Authoritarian rule: Patriarch assumes responsibility for subject well-being.	Libertarian rule: Individuals assume responsibility for own well-being.	Humanitarian rule: Collectivity assumes responsibility for citizen well-being.
Paternalism unites	Social contract integrates	Brotherhood connects
Law is irrational: Formally—low level of generality of concepts, therefore law is particularistic and is not gapless. Substantively—ultimate purposes of the law as a coherent body are not well elaborated.	Law is rational: Formally—high level of generality of concepts; law is universalistic and gapless. Substantively—ultimate purposes of the law as a coherent system of ideas are well elaborated.	
Formal and substantive inequality before law	Formal equality before the law is paramount	Substantive equality before the law is added to formal equality

enter into a contractual relationship. Thus, social order under the auspices of the right to freedom of contract has a potential for a high level of integration: social relationships are not proscribed on the basis of age, sex, occupation, or the like.

The notion of brotherhood connects the social order in that each member, regardless of personal circumstances, has a substantive basis upon which he may feel an identity with any other member of the social order. This substantive basis consists in the recognition by each individual in the body politic that we are all alike as members of a universal order. A cultural ideal of the essential brotherhood of people implies a relinquishing of local, provincial, narrow definitions of the self and an embracing of cosmopolitan, universal, and even timeless criteria in terms of which to view the self. The broader the criteria invoked, the more alike we all seem to one another. The unification of the social order implied by a norm of brotherhood differs from the unification implied by paternalism. Paternalism implies a personalized guiding force to which each of us relates or may relate. Brotherhood implies an impersonalized universal standard in terms of which, comparing ourselves, we find ourselves to be in an equal relationship. This realization is what unites us.

I should mention, finally, that by offering these interpretations of the unification of society through paternalism, the social contract, or brotherhood, I am dealing essentially with relationships among abstract principles that may typify an era. In daily social life it is doubtful that anyone articulates these thoughts in relating to others in the social order. If, however, reigning principles may be said to characterize notions of "right" in various places at various times (see Chapter 3), then individuals cannot help but absorb some portion of that which is in their cultural ambient.

In Chapters 5 and 6, I will illustrate with historical material how the analytic processes outlined in Chapters 2, 3, and 4 unfolded throughout Western history. Special attention will be given to how the formal and substantive rationalization of the new laws embodying social rights passed by Western regimes managed both to effectuate their guarantee and to legitimize their content. These were the first steps toward legitimization of social rights in the emerging Western welfare state.

Chapter 5

APPROXIMATING THE WELFARE STATE:

A CENTURY OF ELABORATION

THE WESTERN WELFARE STATE, as such, emerged in Great Britain in the mid-1940s (see Chapter 6). For well over a century preceding its emergence, however, Western nations were faced with the dilemma of how a political sovereign might protect those most in need in society. The protection of the needy, as noted in Chapter 2, has been a timeless responsibility of those exercising legitimate political authority. Nevertheless, for reasons outlined in Chapter 3, liberal Western regimes found the discharge of this responsibility problematic. They were proscribed by the rule of law from interfering in the social circumstances of individuals as citizens. But the formal legal equality of citizenship by no means precluded the need of individuals in society for social protection under certain circumstances (see Bendix, 1977: 66–126 passim). But the paternalistic mode of and justification for helping had been halted by the democratic revolutions, and the liberal political sovereign was not legally free to provide assistance (see Chapter 3), creating an institutional gap into which the hapless fell. The promise of the democratic revolutions, "life, liberty, and the pursuit of happiness," "liberty, equality, fraternity," rang hollow in thousands upon thousands of ears throughout the industrializing West.

It is the task of any regime, welfare or other, to discharge certain responsibilities toward those who obey its commands. What those responsibilities are and the mode through which they are discharged has been the topic of this analysis, following Weber's treatment of the historical change from traditional to legal rule. Accordingly, the enlargement and legitimization of the scope of responsibility toward citizens that marked the transition from liberal to welfare regimes in the West will be the issue treated in this chapter.

The Point of Departure

To grasp the nature of the institutional transition from the liberal to the welfare state, it is necessary to have a clear image of the point of departure. To that end, I shall complete the picture of liberal regimes that was foreshadowed in Chapters 2 and 3. The transition will be discussed in terms presented in Chapter 4, namely, the formal and substantive rationalization of the law. The law of liberal regimes had both a formal structure and a content. Both will be described here. Then I shall show how the form and content of liberal regime law were successively rationalized throughout the late nineteenth and early twentieth centuries. The outcome of rationalization was to guarantee and legitimize a wider scope of government responsibility for citizen well-being prior to the definitive emergence of the Western welfare state.

Rationalized Law under Liberalism. The democratic revolutions, which "by common consent mark the beginnings of modern European politics" (Sabine, 1952:453), established formal rationality of the law as a new phenomenon in Western Europe.[1] The substantive content of the law whose rationalization was consolidated by the democratic revolutions consisted in individually held civil rights. Weber describes the specific character of these rights as follows: "Freedom of conscience may be the oldest Right of Man. . . . The other Rights of Man or civil rights were joined to this basic right, especially the right to pursue one's own economic interests, which includes the inviolability of individual property, the freedom of contract, and vocational choice" (Weber, 1968:1209)[2] The substantive rationale that underlay the civil rights was articulated in terms of the value of "Reason." The "Reason" inherent in natural law provided the charismatic grounds for legitimation of these rights:

> All of these rights find their ultimate justification in the belief of the Enlightenment in the workings of reason which, if unimpeded, would result in the at least relatively best of all worlds, by virtue of Divine providence and because the individual is best qualified to know his own interests. This charismatic glorification of "Reason," which found a characteristic expression in its apotheosis by Robespierre, is the last form that charisma has

adopted in its fateful historical course. [Weber, 1968:1209; see also Roth, 1975:152–54]

Such rights were unequivocally guarded by the law's formal rationality, for Weber writes, "[These rights exist] within the limits of a system of guaranteed abstract rules that apply to everybody alike.... It is clear that these postulates of formal legal equality and economic mobility paved the way for the destruction of all patrimonial and feudal law in favor of abstract norms" (1968:1209).

Under liberal rule, therefore, the legally relevant relationships between the political authority and the individual in society were articulated through a specific, abstract notion: citizenship. The content of the notion—individually held civil rights—was itself specified in abstract terms. Furthermore, the content was elaborated (justified) by a substantive rationale comprising the "charisma of Reason." Finally, the scope of the government's responsibility toward the citizen was eminently clear: "The law only defines his [the citizen's] legal capacity, but is silent on his ability to use it" (Bendix, 1977:92). The political authority, to remain legitimate, need uphold only a narrowly conceived notion of "equal rights under the law," which included that "the individual is free to conclude valid contracts, to acquire, and dispose of property" (Bendix, 1977:92). Thus, formal and substantive rationalization of the law under nineteenth-century liberal regimes initially provided a straightforward stance for governments to orient themselves toward the poor. That stance was manifest in the logic behind the Poor Law.

The Poor Law as Rationalized Liberal Legislation. Though various Western European nations passed poor laws throughout the nineteenth century (see Heclo, 1974), I shall illustrate the point to be made here with Britain's Poor Law Reform Act Amendment (1834).[3] If it were to remain faithful to the "rule of law," the liberal regime could not offer social protection to citizens: "It is consistent with this position that in most European countries the first Factory Acts seek to protect women and children, who at the time are not considered citizens in the sense of legal equality. By the same criterion all adult males are citizens because they have the power to engage in the economic struggle and take care of themselves. Accordingly, they are excluded from any legitimate claim to protection" (Bendix, 1977:94).[4] Therefore, social protection, when offered, had to be divorced from the status of citizenship. By this logic, the Poor Law Reform Act Amendment

> offered relief only to those who, through age or sickness, were incapable of continuing the battle, and to those other weaklings who gave up the struggle, admitted defeat, and cried for mercy. . . . Social·rights . . . were detached from the status of citizenship. The poor law treated the claims of the poor, not as an integral part of the rights of the citizen, but as an alternative to them—as claims which could be met only if the claimants ceased to be citizens in any true sense of the word. [Marshall, 1963:83][5]

Through this legislation the government of nineteenth-century Britain was able to discharge a modicum of moral responsibility to the poor without violating the dictates of formal rationality of the law.

A very well-elaborated substantive rationale reinforced the government's adherence to the letter of the law. The substantive rationale rested upon a market conception of society, the market, in turn, being subject to the "laws of political economy." The "laws of political economy" logically precluded the notion of social legislation. These "laws" comprised three arguments. The first was that relieving distress would aggravate poverty, for charity would destroy incentive. The second assumed that hunger would compel laborers to work to avoid starvation. (In turn, the wages that would result from availability of a large pool of laborers working to avoid starvation would be the "best" wage, over the long run, for the economy, if not for the laborer.) The third, a Malthusian argument, stated that populations tend to increase faster than the wherewithal of their subsistence. Poverty is therefore inescapable, as well as a stimulus to labor. Indeed, neither the upper classes nor the government could or should assume responsibility for a situation that could not, in any case, be changed (Bendix, 1977:69–71). The substantive rationale provided by the presumption that the market was the authoritative arbiter of the distribution of social wealth (see Chapter 3) handily complemented the formality of the law: "Civil rights were indispensable to a competitive market economy. They gave to each man, as part of his individual status, the power to engage as an independent unit in the economic struggle and made it possible to deny him social protection on the ground that he was equipped to protect himself" (Marshall, 1963:90). Given this superb synthesis of the formal and substantive rationality of the law, the nineteenth-century liberal regime as exemplified by the British government was easily able to close the scope of its responsibility toward the socially dependent while retaining its legitimacy. The Poor Law Reform Act Amendment stood as an example of thoroughly rationalized law.

The Transition: Britain

As indicated in the previous chapters, the revolutionary legitimating ideal of natural law greatly facilitated the transition from the paternalistic to the individualistic moral order. The democratic revolutions, bolstered by the natural law notion of the social contract, transformed authoritarian (traditional) society into libertarian (modern) society. But the transition from libertarian to humanitarian society, emphasizing collective social responsibility within the context of individual rights, has been far less definitive—it is still taking place. It began with a redefinition of the citizen-sovereign relationship in the late nineteenth century. This redefinition, in turn, was generated by a realization, in high political circles, of some shocking facts concerning the quality of citizen life in the most advanced industrialized nation of the day: Great Britain.

During the 1880s, a depression spread throughout the industrialized West. In England, the slump "gave Victorian courage and optimism the severest shock that it had yet received" (Marshall, 1970:25). Furthermore, during the 1880s and 1890s, dockers and match girls went on strike. Though they were working for a living, their standard of living was scandalously low (Marshall, 1970:25–26). Two British scholars, B. S. Rowntree and Charles Booth, studied and publicized the shabby life circumstances endured by working citizens.[6]

In addition to these revelations, another of equal embarrassment to Britain's liberal democracy came to light. In recruiting for the South African Boer War (1899–1902), the British government discovered that its young men were in such poor health that many potential recruits were rejected on medical and physical grounds. This finding led to a study resulting in the Report of the Interdepartmental Committee on Physical Deterioration (1904) (Marshall, 1970:26).

The cumulative effect of depressions, strikes, unemployment, and exposés during the late nineteenth and early twentieth centuries led the British government in 1905 to form the Royal Commission on the Poor Laws and Relief of Distress. Its task was to examine comprehensively the British poor laws (Girvetz, 1968:515). Thus, liberal governments established in the name of legal equality with its implications of social justice no longer were to take their cue solely from the market as they oriented themselves toward their citizens. In short, "men everywhere were beginning to envisage a turning point in national development" (Marshall, 1970:25).[7]

Articulating a New Substantive Rationale. As mentioned in Chapter 4, the rationalization of ideas involves their definition, clarification, and generalization and the establishment of mutually consistent logical connections among them. In turn, the substantive rationalization of an idea system involves the establishment of mutually compatible logical connections among ideas toward some ultimate objective, purpose, or meaning. In order to free itself from the letter, that is, the formality of the law, the turn-of-the-century British government needed desperately to reexamine the law's "real intent." For legal formality had surely ossified into legalism (see Chapter 7, n. 6). Even classical theoreticians of laissez-faire foresaw this danger. J. R. McCulloch wrote in 1848, "The principle of *laissez faire* may be safely trusted to in some things, but in many more it is wholly inapplicable; and to appeal to it on all occasions savours more of the policy of a parrot than that of a statesman or philosopher" (cited in Briggs, 1961:233–34). Escaping the policy of parrots, the British government made every attempt to redefine the situation so that its active efforts to aid the helpless would somehow be consistent with liberal principles, that is, could be "rationalized." To this end, subtle distinctions were drawn to make such a course possible.

Rowntree's work provided a logical underpinning that guided liberal governments in beginning to reorient themselves toward citizens. Rowntree distinguished between "primary" and "secondary" poverty, the former being "beyond the control of the wage-earner" (Briggs, 1961:253).[8] By viewing some types of poverty in this light, early attempts at social legislation could remain logically consistent with valued principles of individual rights and freedoms. The Pension Acts in both Britain (1908) and Sweden (1913) became the first attempts at acceptable social legislation. Heclo (1974) singles out these acts as landmark departures from the mentality of the Poor Law, which assumed that the fault for poverty lay with the poor. On this latter assumption, the rights of citizenship were forfeited. By recognizing a category of poverty as "faultless" and therefore certain of the poor as "deserving" of government help, however, the government was vindicated in assuming responsibility for their plight without simultaneously depriving them of citizenship rights. Heclo writes that prior to the Pension Acts, "the citizen's claim to state support rested upon either the performance of specific services as in the military or civil service,[9] or the submission to disqualifying restrictions in return for general public aid. Old age pensioners were the first significant portion of the population able to gain entitlement to state support by virtue of being citizens requiring such aid and without any effect upon their status as members of the community" (1974:156). The rationale of faultlessness enabled regimes under liberal rule to make this slight expansion of the citizen's right without compromising government legitimacy in terms of liberal values: "Conservatives could support it as an aid to social stability; socialists generally assented to the new approach as a first step toward greater government responsibility for citizens' welfare" (Heidenheimer, Heclo, and Adams, 1975:194).[10]

Finally, the logic of blameless or faultless dependency temporarily provided a convenient criterion to allow the scope of government responsibility to be closed. This is an important point, for in Chapters 9–11 of this work it will be seen that Western welfare regimes are having considerable difficulty in delineating and justifying a bounded scope of social responsibility (see especially Chapter 10, n. 1). In the discussion that immediately follows, the reader will note the relative ease with which other early social legislation closed the scope of government responsibility within the context of a justifying rationale.

Continued Articulation of a New Substantive Rationale. In 1909, the Royal Commission formed in 1905 made its two-part report. Both the Majority Report and the famous Minority Report led by Beatrice Webb agreed in recommending such government initiatives as "the adoption of preventive and curative measures in addition to palliatives (or mere relief), the extension of the public medical services, and the introduction of old-age pensions and some kind of facilities for insurance against unemployment" (Marshall, 1970:39). The Minority Report was adamant in recommending the application of scientific principles to social administration. It called for the "break-up" of the Poor Law, which "had the functions, but not the spirit, of a welfare service" (Marshall, 1970:44).

Indeed, it has been central to my argument that the Poor Law was never meant to have the "spirit" of a welfare service (in the sense probably meant by Beatrice Webb). As a rationalized act of liberal regime law, an embodiment of the "laws of political economy" as well as of the letter of legal equality, it could hardly have the "spirit" of collective social responsibility for individual hardship.

The economic logic of the Poor Law was heavily strained by the distasteful facts of British working-class life. The situation was ripe for a redefinition. Thus, the effect of the Report of the Royal Commission "was to give an entirely fresh impetus to the general adoption of the policy of security to every individual, as the very basis of his life and work, a prescribed natural minimum of the requisites for efficient parenthood and citizenship" (Webb, 1926, cited in Briggs, 1961:239). Though it would be many decades before these concrete objectives would be cemented by the formality of the law, only two years passed between the issuance of the report and Britain's institutionalization of the world's first national program of unemployment insurance.

The National Insurance Act: A Synthesis of Formal and Substantive Rationalization of the Law. The National Insurance Act (1911) was the legal embodiment of the world's first national unemployment insurance scheme (Heidenheimer, Heclo, and Adams, 1975: 195). As an attempt to surmount the limitations of the 1908 Pension Act, it had the following characteristics: (1) it expanded the scope of government responsibility for citizen welfare; (2) it articulated a principle of justification of the expanded scope of sovereign responsibility assumed; (3) through the clear articulation of categories of dependents in combination with a justifying rationale for government assumption of responsibility toward these categories of dependents, the act closed the scope of the government's responsibility. As such, the National Insurance Act was a synthesis of formally and substantively rationalized law.

Standing at the center of the act's rationalized quality were its justificatory principles. These rested upon two institutions—insurance and the labor exchange—that could be reconciled with liberal precepts. These two devices were articulated with the formal structure of the National Insurance Act. That is, legal consequences were attached to them in such a way as to be compatible with the liberal principles of the social contract—individual freedoms and "earned" rights. Heclo (1974) states that Sir William Beveridge's grasp of the relationship between insurance and the labor exchange was what made politically possible the legal guarantee of unemployment insurance in Britain. Beveridge noted that unions paid unemployment benefits using a system of insurance. They could do so because they had their own informal labor exchange service, through which they were able to detect whether one of their members was, in fact, able to find work. He observed, "The state is forced into the costly and degrading harshness of the Poor Law simply because it has no control or supervision of the labor market. . . . It must rely always on the assumption that the applicant for help could find work if he looked for it because it is never in the position to satisfy itself that there is no work for him" (quoted in Heclo, 1974:80–81). Beveridge worked out a scheme whereby workers had only to register at the employment exchange to demonstrate the integrity of their search for work. (Under the Poor Law, by contrast, such integrity could be demonstrated only by acquiescence to the status of pauperism and to the conditions of the workhouse.) By this device, Beveridge "believed he had circumvented an essential dilemma of the old poor law, and he was correct" (Heclo, 1974:81).

In turn, entitlement to insurance benefits stemmed from worker contributions. "Degrading means tests and the stigma of accepting charity were unnecessary since applicants had an earned right to benefits by virtue of past contributions" (Heidenheimer, Heclo, and Adams, 1975:193). Therefore, "with exchanges as the device for validating true unemployment and insurance as the device for establishing entitlement to benefit, Beveridge had the outlines of . . . the world's first national unemployment insurance. Conceptually, the grip of the poor law had been broken" (Heclo, 1974:81). According to the argument I have advanced throughout the preceding chapters, substantive rationalization (or logical sublimation) of the intent of the law had been elaborated so as to rise above the narrow conception of "individual rights" previously guaranteed by the formal structure of the law. Substantive rationalization of the ultimate purpose of the law created the conditions for the law's legitimacy. Because the law extended the coercion of the state into areas of citizen life hitherto untouched, the law's legitimacy would certainly have been precluded without a convincing (substantive) rationale.

Upon closer inspection it can be seen that the notion of social insurance was reinforced by joining it to the notions of "self-help" and the social contract. Expansion in scope of government responsibility for citizen well-being inevitably means expansion in scope of government authority, that is, legitimate coercion. The National Insurance Act heralded the "direct entry of British social policy into the life of the ordinary able-bodied workman" (Heclo, 1974:89). This meant that worker contributions to the unemployment insurance scheme were compulsory.[11] The articulating of such coercion with individual rights was artfully done by placing emphasis upon "self-help." Government facilitation of "self-help" was something of a "social contract" between sovereign and worker. In exchange for membership in a governmentally arbitrated scheme of protection for workers as citizens, the worker makes his contribution. This contribution is a form of helping oneself. Such a well-argued rationale made the act's passage unproblematic despite its unprecedented extension of the coercion of the (liberal) state into the life of the citizen (Heclo, 1974:80ff.).

Finally, both the formal and substantive rationality of the National Insurance Act was manifest in the way it defined, closed, reopened, and extended the scope of government responsibility while maintaining government legitimacy and economic feasibility. Thus, the act did not precipitate overextensions of the government's authority or budget in the years immediately following its passage. The act delimited specific categories of dependency (unemployment) and the conditions for granting the citizen's right to insurance benefits. Extension of the benefits of social legislation was always made categorically: "The categories of persons who were gradually extracted from the heterogeneous company of paupers were the children, the old, the sick, and the unemployed" (Marshall, 1970:36). In addition, there was always a justifying rationale deeming the government legitimate in extending its protection to the categorically dependent.

Thus, in early years of social legislation, extensions of scope were not too problematic. Heclo (1974:111) writes that in anticipation of unemployment unrest in Britain in the aftermath of World War I, insurance concessions were once again made. The substantive rationale of the law guaranteeing social protection was, however, still at the point where such extensions were seen as merely temporary. Behind these extensions stood "established principles of classical economics: government retrenchment and economy" (Heclo, 1974:113). This is not to say that the extensions were interpreted as either illegitimate or extravagant by those in charge of government policy or those eligible for coverage. Rather, the thinking of the day presumed that the states of dependency would be temporary. In fact, they were not (see Heclo, 1974:113ff.).[12]

In conclusion, Britain's National Insurance Act legally embodied the concrete realization in the industrializing West that "the unchecked insecurities produced by the market were a debilitating not constructive force, a social not individual failing, a public not private responsibility" (Heclo, 1974:88).

Clearly, the formal and substantive rationality of the act made social insurance the pivotal technique in the transition from the purely liberal to the emerging welfare state: "The advantages of the new technique [social insurance] were immense. Decisions on eligibility were automatic, since they were based on uniform insurance rules rather than on the discretion of poor-law officers. . . . After centuries of reliance on the medieval poor law, the advent of social insurance was one of the great watersheds in income support policy" (Heidenheimer, Heclo, and Adams, 1975:193). These advantages were not lost on the mid-depression United States, to whose case we now turn.

The Transition: The United States

As in Britain, an economic depression and resultant unemployment precipitated a redefinition of the citizen-sovereign relationship in the United States. Lowi (1969) adds the observation that fear of insurrection by those struck by the depression inspired the 1930s U.S. government to carefully reassess the relationship of liberal principles to social responsibility. Political authorities "were now prepared to see poverty as a social rather than a personal condition" (Lowi, 1969:218). As in Britain, so, too, in the United States the widespread effects of the depression dissipated the "old puritanical concept of poverty as the wages of sin, sloth, and stupidity" (Lowi, 1969:218). Nor were the U.S. poor during the 1930s a confined population sector: rather, they were a broad spectrum whose jobs were affected by the collapse of the market (Lowi, 1969:218).

Articulating a New Substantive Rationale. The U.S. government acknowledged the liberal principle that responsibility rested with the individual to succeed by his own efforts, working and saving according to his own defined needs (Rimlinger, 1961:106). Social insurance was then justified as an efficient mechanism by which the government could help the individual to do just that. Social insurance in the United States was elaborated in terms of "self-help," citizen "independence," and the "contributory-contractual principle."

Formalization of the New Substantive Rationale. The Social Security
Act (1935) virtually ushered in the welfare state in the United States
(Lowi, 1969:219). Specifically, Titles II and III (Old Age and Survivors Insurance and Unemployment Insurance, respectively) formalized social insurance. This was a contributory insurance system in
which compulsory contributions were to come from a tax on both
employers and employees. Unlike the British system, in which the
Exchequer also contributed from general taxation funds, this system
was entirely funded by the employer-employee payroll tax. In short,
the U.S. social insurance system was an actuarial one, with benefits
paid out equaling benefits paid in. The actuarial nature of the system
was a central justificatory element.

Benefits were a matter of "right" because none of their financing
came from general revenue. The official literature accompanying the
institutionalization of the new system emphasized that benefits were
not a matter of state benevolence that would subject citizens to state
whims. Rather, much was made of the "contributory-contractual"
nature of social security. In exchange for contributing a portion of
earnings to a compulsory system, the government would help the
individual achieve independence—would help him "help himself."
"According to this view, the American approach to social security is a
conservative force which strengthens rather than weakens economic
self-help and other individualistic values" (Rimlinger, 1961, 108).

Specification and Closure of Scope of Sovereign Intervention. Rimlinger points out the "restrictiveness of the approach to social security
embodied by Titles II and III of the Social Security Act. In terms
of the argument I am developing, "restrictiveness" allows closure of
scope of sovereign responsibility, as well as curtailment of sovereign
intervention into the social realm. The act "restricts benefits to those
by or for whom contributions have been paid" (Rimlinger, 1961:109),
that is, government discretion in the collection of contributions and
distribution of benefits was limited (Rimlinger, 1961:108–9).

The combined formal and substantive rationalization of the social
insurance titles of the act were, of course, what made possible the
delineation and legitimacy of the scope of government authority assumed. Namely, a relevant criterion (employability) was joined to
a justifying rationale (self-help through the contributory-contractual
principle). Together these made possible the specification of general-

ized categories of individuals eligible for participation in the program. The government formalized the program through law, thus lending the force of the state to the rights articulated through the rationale. In this way, the discharge of sovereign responsibility toward citizens under specific circumstances was easily achieved.

It was also easy to "rationalize" extensions of sovereign responsibility and citizen "rights." The pristine logic of the initial act facilitated successive logical deductions. In 1939, public complaints were voiced regarding the inadequacy of the benefits granted in relationship to the contributions paid in. The logic of the official response can only be admired for its smooth ingenuity: "Social security officials surmounted the problem by introducing the concept of family protection—an idea more collective than the one behind the previous individualized benefits. . . . Now widows, children, parents, or aged wives of contributors could collect benefits, while the breadwinners' own benefits became less closely related to their own contributions" (Heidenheimer, Heclo, and Adams, 1975:203). The notion of family protection logically sublimates the "intent" of the law. The intent of the law is to protect the employed against a certain range of contingencies. Gilbert Y. Steiner writes that "all social insurance is predicated upon sometime employment of an identifiable head of a household" (1966:28). Employment, therefore, is the definitive criterion of eligibility for protection through social insurance. The definitiveness of the criterion delimits the sovereign's scope of responsibility (in terms of arbitrating a social insurance scheme). The abstractness of the criterion allows a range of concrete outcomes to be justified, among them the notion of "family protection." Thus, the formal and substantive rationalization of the social insurance titles of the act both legitimized and made effective the government's guarantee of a social right. The formal and substantive rationality of the social insurance programs is the sine qua non of the impersonalization of the government's guarantee of the citizen's right to a benefit: "The administration of these programs and delivery of benefits is highly formalized, simplified, and automated, requiring a limited amount of contact between recipients and administrators" (Bowler, 1974:9).

The transition from the liberal to the welfare state in Western regimes was accomplished through a careful synthesis of the formal and substantive rationalization of the law. Law, which by its very nature is amenable to increasing generalization, is also amenable to successive impersonalization. The rationalization process (both formal and substantive) facilitates impersonalization of law. In turn, impersonalization of the law by which rights are created, enhanced in content, and guaranteed is the hallmark of modern, as contrasted to medieval, social protection schemes. Impersonalization of the law is the central feature of the notion of "collective" (versus "paternalistic") responsibility. Collective responsibility involves "spreading the risk." What is once "spread" or "dispersed" must oftentimes be brought together again. The government, therefore, as the impersonal arbiter of the societal social insurance scheme, serves as the organizational nexus —the juncture of integration—through which risks that have been spread can be compensated through a definable channel (social insurance benefit payments guaranteed by law). The discharge of social responsibility through impersonalization is not, thus, responsibility's evaporation through unruly diffuseness. Rather, it is responsibility's generalization through abstraction. The generalization of responsibility for individual hardship implies, in turn, the unification of the collectivity around the realization that we are all, in some ways, alike. We are all vulnerable.[13]

The following chapter treats the effect of World War II on the dawning of this realization upon Western leaders and their respective populaces.

Chapter 6

POSTWAR BRITAIN'S

INSTITUTIONALIZATION OF

THE WELFARE STATE

A SWORD that cut several ways, rationalized legislation in early twentieth-century liberal regimes added to the content of citizenship rights while both justifying and closing the scope of sovereign responsibility assumed for the guarantee of such rights. Changes in the larger social order, however, of which the legal order is only a part, virtually guaranteed that closures in the scope of liberal authority would prove temporary. This chapter addresses the next round (1946–48) of rationalization of the law in Western regimes, when the welfare state, as such, came into being. Its defining characteristic was its guarantee of the broadest notion of the rights of citizenship that had ever been proposed in Western history. Citizenship took the form of "social rights." These were the outcome of further elaborations upon the "real intent" of formal law guaranteeing legal equality.

Postwar Britain is generally acknowledged to have served as the model of the welfare state for other Western regimes (Briggs, 1961; Rimlinger, 1971). "In Great Britain," observes Morris Janowitz, "the elaborate welfare state as a societal definition came into existence in one dramatic step with the election of the Labour government in 1945" (1976:39). The emergence and institutionalization of the welfare state as a distinctive sociopolitical phenomenon, therefore, will be dealt with in this chapter as applied to the case of Great Britain. In succeeding chapters, the experiences of the U.S. welfare regime will be assimilated into the argument. Before describing the actual legislative embodiments of the British welfare state, however, the continued process of the elaboration of citizenship rights should be treated. The effect of World War II on this process was compelling.

Postwar Principles Reinforcing Extension of Citizenship Rights

Two postwar themes dissolved the strictures that had previously closed the scope of government responsibility toward citizen well-being. These themes were "universalism" and "unity" (Briggs, 1961; Rimlinger, 1971; Janowitz, 1976). "Universalism" is here defined as the idea of wider distribution of those things that society, acting through the government, has to offer the individual.[1] The unifying experience of the war implied that governments should act according to a norm of impartiality toward everyone, whether at home or on the front, who underwent the hardships of war. The stress, threat, and losses imposed by World War II underscored the essential equality of citizens, particularly equality of sacrifice (Janowitz, 1976:37). "The idea of 'citizens' standing by each other' had acquired a special meaning during the war and was now a dominant theme" (Rimlinger, 1971: 152). Together, therefore, the themes of universalism and unity reinforced one another as well as the liberal commitment to the equality of citizens.

The International Labor Office (ILO) noted in 1950 a trend toward universalism in the wake of the war. Operationally, universalism meant an expansion in both the content of citizen rights and the categories to whom the rights should be granted, in these words of the ILO: "There is a movement everywhere toward including additional classes of the population, covering a wider range of contingencies [i.e., right content], providing benefits more nearly adequate to needs and removing anomalies among them [i.e., introducing logical consistency], loosening the tie between benefit right and contribution payment and, in general, unifying the finance and administration of branches hitherto separate"[2] (cited in Briggs, 1961:224).

Janowitz delineates the specific social processes through which the increased solidarity of the populace resulted in a more refined notion of equality. In the passage below, Janowitz's usage of "universalism" refers to the breaking down of distinctions. This dissolution promoted unity and implied equality:

> In Europe, under total war, the distinction between civilians and the military narrowed—a new basis of universalism. In the United States and Great Britain, industrialization and the mobilization of women and minority-group members increased the

participation of these individuals in mass society. It took total war to create both the social and political demands for the welfare state and the social definition of the legitimacy of massive government intervention on behalf of the individual. [1976:39]

In sum, therefore, the welfare state both implies and is implied by a societal norm that calls for a generalized and impartial (that is, "universalistic") orientation of the political sovereign toward individuals in society: "The welfare state is a political arrangement that emphasizes universalism; mobilization for total war also emphasizes universalism and thus helps to create the societal and normative dimensions conducive to the welfare state" (Janowitz, 1976:36–37).

Acceptance of the Substantive Rationale. The themes of unity and universalism provided the raw material for a new product which the liberal state would henceforth offer in the line of citizenship rights: social rights. The creator of this new product was Sir William Beveridge, whose *Social Insurance and Allied Services* (1942) came to be known as "the Beveridge Report." It was "a comprehensive statement of the citizen's social right to freedom from want and of the means to implement this right" (Rimlinger, 1971:149). Of the acceptance of this new type of right, there was no doubt: "Although offering a blueprint of 'cradle to grave' protection, Beveridge did not find it necessary to also develop ideological arguments in order to justify its adoption. Nothing could be more indicative of the nearly unanimous acceptance in Britain of the basic concept of social rights" (Rimlinger, 1971:149). Indeed, the political "market" for social rights had been conditioned by over a half-century of formal and substantive rationalization of the law guaranteeing legal equality (as described in Chapter 5). "There is never any question about the desirability or legitimacy of the kind of social plan offered [by the Beveridge Report] only about its feasibility and about the best ways to achieve it" (Rimlinger, 1971:149).

Mode of Implementation of Social Rights. In subsequent chapters it will be seen that "only" the welfare state's feasibility and the best ways to achieve it have proved to be problematic for its legitimacy. As adumbrated in Chapter 2, the mode of implementation of social protection has important implications for individual freedoms. These implications will be treated in Part II. For now, it remains to note that in the early stages of welfare-state planning, an isomorphism was assumed to inhere between comprehensivization of coverage and comprehensivization of administration:

> For Beveridge, national solidarity logically led to a national pooling of social insurance risks and rewards, which meant one central fund and uniform benefits as opposed to the pattern of many separate funds, with diverse rules and benefits. . . . He considered the "unification of administrative responsibilities" as one of his basic social insurance risks, paid into one central fund, and one income maintenance payment. [Rimlinger, 1971:151–52]

Janowitz refers to this type of approach on the part of "cadres of administrators" after the war as "in essence a kind of societal 'breakthrough'" in both Britain and the United States. He writes, "The shift was from limited monetary expenditures for categorical groups to an emphasis on creating new arrangements and new institutions, which were presumed to have the capacity to alter the social structure and assist individuals and their families" (1976:38). The specific legislation that established the welfare state in Great Britain and therefore created the "new arrangements and new institutions" will now be described. In these arrangements it will be seen that the substantive rationalization of citizenship rights was joined to a formally rationalized law. In Chapter 7, I will treat the problems that have arisen in connection with the administrative side of the new institutions of the welfare state.

The Structure of the British Welfare State

Broadly speaking, the British welfare state comprises three analytic types of formalized guarantee of the social rights of citizenship. The three categories are (1) national insurance, (2) national assistance, and (3) the social services (health, education, the welfare services,[3] and housing). The formalization of each of these was accomplished, respectively, by the National Insurance Act (1946), the National Assistance Act (1948), and, collectively, the Education Act (1944), the National Health Services Act (1946), the Family Allowances Act

(1946), and the Industrial Injuries Act (1946) (see Marshall, 1970:86 and Rimlinger, 1971:153).

Though the British social services are usually seen from the vantage point of the United States as epitomizing "the welfare state," only passing reference will be made to them below. In fact, as I shall show, a good grasp of the political controversies surrounding the guarantee of social rights in the welfare state can be gained by analyzing the dilemmas presented by social insurance and social assistance.[4]

National Insurance. The National Insurance Act embodies the notion of the socialization of risk. The act's aim was to cover virtually the entire population with one comprehensive system of contributory social insurance, providing a minimum income for all insured persons who were unable to earn for themselves and their dependents (Sleeman, 1973:50). The relationship between contributions and benefits under the act was to be actuarial: though contributions came from the employed person, his employer, and the Exchequer, benefits paid out were to equal contributions paid in (Sleeman, 1973:51). National insurance in Britain, therefore, differed from the social insurance titles of the Social Security Act in the United States. In Britain part of the contribution from which benefits were drawn by citizens came from general revenue. Because the relationship between contributions and benefits was, nevertheless, to be actuarial, increases in benefits could come only from increases in contributions.

Within a decade, complaints arose regarding this seemingly impartial system of social insurance. Though impartial, it was inequitable. Its "universalistic" approach could not accommodate equitably a diversely situated population of legal equals. Because this was a flat-rate system that attempted comprehensiveness of coverage, the contributions had to be kept low enough so that lower income persons could afford them. But this seemed inequitable to the upper income groups: upon their retirement their pensions would be quite low because their contributions had been kept to a minimum by the flat-rate system which the lower income groups could afford. Their retirement pensions would represent a substantial drop in income for them and a correlative drop in their standard of living (Sleeman, 1973:51). Of the "subsistence principle" represented by comprehensive coverage under the flat-rate system, Rimlinger wrote, "Although it promoted equality, and perhaps a sense of solidarity, among benefit recipients, it generated economic inequality between them and those who still were actively employed. . . . There was a widening economic gap between those still at work and those living on social security" (1971:153). The response to this dilemma of "misplaced universalism" was the National Insurance Act of 1959 that "introduced a second layer of wage-related pensions to supplement the national minimum" (Rimlinger, 1971:153). Rimlinger refers to this superimposition of benefit differentiation upon an egalitarian base as a compromise solution combining several ideological positions (1971:153). In any case, the link between contributions and benefits was retained. Collection of benefits was clearly the citizen's right for he had earned the benefits through his contributions.

But a comprehensive system aimed at achieving subsistence for all must, in the light of costs (particularly rising costs over time), either compromise its "comprehensiveness" or lower its definition of "subsistence." These are the two choices available to meet rising costs as long as the principle of benefits-related-to contributions is maintained. Abandoning or supplementing the earned-right-to-benefits framework opened up a third alternative. This alternative was embodied by Britain's National Assistance Act (1946).

National Assistance. Though the National Assistance Act is considered one of the pillars of the British welfare state (Marshall, 1970:86), in fact, it legalizes the principle of selectivity. This approach to citizen welfare presents a dilemma for the legitimacy of the welfare state, as will be shown below.

National assistance is a tribute to the inescapable fact that "it is a truism that a given volume of resources can be more effectively used in combating need and increasing opportunities, if they can be concentrated on those who can be identified as being the most in need or most disadvantaged, rather than being dispersed over a much wider number, many of whom could afford to provide for themselves" (Sleeman, 1973:98). Accordingly, assistance is given under a test of means to ascertain need. But, because the benefits are not "earned" through contributions from beneficiaries, they retain, for Britons, some of the stigma of the old poor laws.

At the time of the act's passage it was assumed that the need for national assistance would decline as pensions rose in connection with national insurance. Thus, national assistance was never intended to be a central feature of the welfare state. But national assistance came to play a larger and larger role in the British scheme of social security

(Sleeman, 1973:56). In the first place, the comprehensive flat-rate benefits introduced under the National Insurance and Family Allowance acts were not, indeed, up to the subsistence level envisioned by Beveridge. This precipitated reliance upon means-tested assistance to bring citizens up to a minimum acceptable standard of living (Sleeman, 1973:97). Thus, the majority of national assistance payments are made to supplement inadequate national insurance benefits, particularly old age pensions, although widows and the chronically sick are also assisted in large numbers (Sleeman, 1973:56).

In the second place, the role of national assistance was, perhaps, bound to expand once the feasibility of universalism began to be questioned: "The continuance of considerable poverty and lack of opportunity in the generally prosperous Britain of the 1960's and 1970's has led many people to question the principles on which the Welfare State was based in the early post-war years. . . . Would it be more effective now to follow a more selective ideal, of providing services more generously to those in real need and less generously to those who are not?" (Sleeman, 1973:97). To doubt universalism is to doubt the sine qua non of the welfare state: formally guaranteed social rights, equal in content, impartially and impersonally adjudicated, and distributed according to the most general (abstract) criterion of all— the legal equality of citizens. To doubt universalism is, implicitly, to endorse selectivity. Selectivity, regardless of how noble the cause to which it is harnessed, involves the use of the means test. Herein lies a genuine dilemma, namely, that "means tests are anathema to the welfare state" (Girvetz, 1968:515).

Means tests are intended to discriminate among those most in need in order to help them. Though this may seem to be a reasonable solution to the exorbitant costs of universalism, a clamorous voice has arisen in Britain against this approach. This voice articulates the fear that a selectivist solution will patronize the needy and draw a sharp distinction between needs and rights, stifling the development of the latter: "That discretion can obtain more for a specific individual is difficult to dispute. The critical question is: What does discretionary administration do for the poor as a whole? Does it reduce poor people to grateful suppliants? Although discretion may provide for the exercise of humanity in an especially difficult case, it also acts as a rubbery defense against the possibility that a need could be generalized into a right" (Eimicke, 1973:87). In fact, this is exactly what happened in the United States during the Progressive Era (see Chapter 8).

William B. Eimicke (1973:85–87) argues that universalism implies that people have a right to benefits: social unity is emphasized and discrimination is minimized. To prefer a universalistic approach is, in the terms I have been using here, to keep rights as rights. Administrative case-by-case consideration of individual circumstances is seen as backsliding toward an era when assistance was not rightful, but stigmatized, personalized, and discretionary. Therefore, some parts of the British political spectrum have supported a state-backed earnings-related insurance scheme which J. F. Sleeman notes "cuts across the selectivist-universalist division" (1973:166–67). A basic flat-rate social security benefit has also been advocated (Sleeman, 1973:167). Finally, interest in the "reverse" (the British term—see Clark, 1977) or negative income tax has found its source in this and related welfare state financing dilemmas (Chapter 9, n. 5 amplifies these concerns). In Chapter 8, I will expand upon these issues through a discussion of events in the United States, where social insurance and public assistance parallel the British categories of national insurance ("rightful") and national assistance (problematic). As in Britain, the controversies associated with the welfare state have been most virulent when aimed at the contingencies surrounding public assistance. This association with the "welfare state" is ironic, however, because the values that have given rise to public assistance and the institutional context of its administration long predate the welfare state and are anything but "modern," as I shall show in Part II.

The Social Services. The social services in Britain, called "services in kind," are distinct from the cash benefits treated above. The social services include the national health service, education, the welfare services, and, to a lesser degree, housing. (Housing cannot be fit into the usual social policy analysis of the British welfare state because it is "in a kind of half-way position between the social services and the ordinary commercial market" [Sleeman, 1973:153]. The fair rent principle of the 1965 Rent Act is representative of a trend in welfare government policy on housing [Sleeman, 1973:154].) The social services are state supported and all citizens may use them as a "right." Those who favor the continuance of the social services in Britain see "participation in the social services by everyone on more or less equal terms irrespective of income . . . as one of the rights and duties of citizenship" (Sleeman, 1973:166).

Because the emphasis in this analysis is on the evolution of citizenship rights, as such, a protracted discussion of the British social services would be inappropriate here. (Richard M. Titmuss's *Essays on the Welfare State* [1969] would be the definitive starting point for addressing issues surrounding the British social services.) Suffice to say that the use of the social services in the British welfare state is considered a "right." As will be emphasized in the following chapters, the exercise of a social right involves the use of a government-provided commodity or service without the recipient being stigmatized.

This chapter has shown how the notion of legal equality was logically sublimated to the point where a distinctive sociopolitical phenomenon emerged to guarantee it formally. This new phenomenon is the welfare state. Though the welfare state is, analytically speaking, a straightforward set of legally relevant relationships joining citizen and sovereign, the administration of the welfare state raises other issues. Making the welfare state "happen" after it has been substantively rationalized and formally guaranteed through law is an entirely separate matter. In the present chapter, I have called attention to the proverbial tip of the iceberg in referring to Britain's universalism-selectivity debate. This debate goes to the very heart of the process of legitimizing social rights. The issue at hand is the problematic movement away from the protection of persons by persons and toward the modern notion of the protection of citizens by law (part of the content of which is the right to a minimum standard of living).

In Part II, I will show that it is not only the costs of universalism that have raised the issue of what the welfare state stands for. Another issue associated with the universalism-selectivity debate has even more complex implications, and that issue is administrative discretion. Accordingly, Eimicke has written that "the real center of the debate over selectivity revolves around the question of discretion" (1973:87). Just how crucial is the control of discretion for the ultimate legitimacy of the welfare state and the social rights it creates will now be explained in detail, for, as Lawrence M. Friedman has noted in *The Legal System*, "a right is, by definition, not a matter of discretion" (1975:229). Therefore, Chapters 7–10 are oriented around the irony that, at the very heart of the welfare state with its delicately rationalized notion of social rights, stands the sturdy, historically indefatigable organizational unit that affixes itself to every effective rulership: the administrative staff, the "bureau."

Part II

Chapter 7

ADMINISTRATION AS THE ACHILLES HEEL

OF THE WELFARE STATE

The Gratuities-Rights Continuum

"Wherever there is official conduct, the possibility of arbitrary decisions arises" (Selznick, 1969:14). The implications of this statement for one set of processes by which welfare state redistributions ultimately accrue legitimacy to themselves will be the topic of this chapter.

Following Weber, Chapter 2 depicted the essentially antithetical character of administration in relationship to adjudication. The latter involves the subjection of official conduct to general rules. Rules are the sine qua non of adjudication and therefore provide the prospect of appeal. Weber's ideal typically drawn "administration," by contrast, refers to authoritative decision making unencumbered by a framework of rules. Rather, decisions are made upon a case-to-case basis according to expediency or some other principle useful to the purposes of the ruler. The absence of rules allowing for appeals to be made precludes the possibility that a claimant might become an "appellant." Rather, the individual is confronted with the very real possibility of arbitrary official decision.

Weber, however, recognized that the transition is gradual from the case in which a right exists to one in which "the legally secured interest of a party is but the 'reflex' of a 'regulation' and where the party does not possess a 'right' in the strict sense" (1968:667). Weber here posits a correspondence between empirical reality and an analytic continuum for ranking the status of a benefit. At one end of the continuum is the right, created by legislation and amenable to adjudication in the regular courts of law. At the other end is the entirely gratuitous benefit enjoyed by dint of the discretion of the one granting it. The benefit is gratuitous from the viewpoint of the benefactor: he dispenses the benefit not from legal obligation, but from personal motive. The benefit, in turn, is but a contingency from the standpoint of the beneficiary, who, as mentioned, usually must "curry favor" or otherwise serve, please, or obey his patron. Because the benefit enjoyed stems purely from the discretion of the one bestowing it, there exists no right of appeal should the giver, for whatever reason, decide to discontinue providing the gratuity. Ideal typically, therefore, the "administrative principle" and the "adjudicative principle" form two poles of a continuum, here referring to the chances of an individual to enjoy benefits either by discretion of the benefactor (gratuitously) or by law that guarantees the right to them (rightfully).

History has filled this continuum with an endless variety of events that can be analyzed in different ways. In Part I, I showed how the continuing formal and substantive rationalization of the civil or statute law measured progress on this continuum from gratuities to social rights. I emphasized, essentially, how, through legislation, favors become guarantees. In Part II, I will emphasize how, through continually rationalizing administration, gratuities become entitlements and how, in turn, entitlements may become rightful.

There is an interval on this continuum that belongs to the analytic territory of administrative law, which, as I mentioned in the opening chapter, is the law promulgated by modern administrative agencies (see Shapiro, 1968:104–9). Administrative law is contrasted in the literature with the common law, constitutional law, the civil law, statute law.[1] Through legalization and judicialization administrative law can undergo rationalization. Figure 7–1 diagrams the relationships that will be explicated in this and the following chapters.

Rationalized Administration

I have mentioned that Weber treated "administration" in two different senses (see Chapter 1). Administration may be a form of domination in which the three functions of government are merged and rule is, in this narrow sense, "arbitrary" (Weber, 1968:641–58). Administration may refer, in turn, to a staff of individuals organized into role relationships for the purpose of task implementation. The more systematic the arrangement of these roles, that is, the more rationalized the administrative staff arrangements are, the more does it approximate "bureaucracy" or "bureaucratic administration" (Weber, 1968: 956–1005). It is clear that Weber's "bureaucracy" is an organizational tool for putting into effect objectives formulated elsewhere (whether

FIGURE 7-1
The Gratuities-Rights Continuum

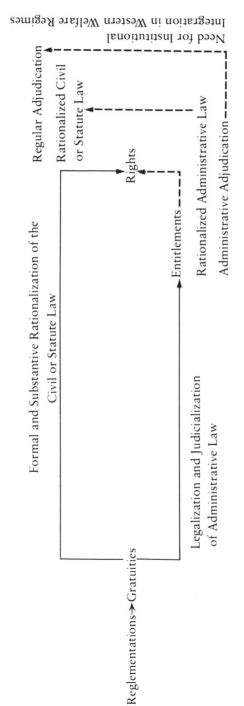

Legitimation of Social Rights "From Above"
(through Legislation and Adjudication in the Regular Courts of Law)

Need for Institutional
Integration in Western Welfare Regimes

Regular Adjudication
Rationalized Civil
or Statute Law

Formal and Substantive Rationalization of the
Civil or Statute Law

Rights

Entitlements

Rationalized Administrative Law
Administrative Adjudication

Legalization and Judicialization
of Administrative Law

Reglementations→Gratuities

Legitimation of Social Rights "From Below"
(through Rationalized Administration Leading to Claimant "Entitlization" from
which Vantage Point a "Right" May Ultimately Be Articulated by the Courts)

in political, religious, or private sectors of society). It is not itself a type of domination as is "administration" (see Chapter 2). Bureaucracy has authority, to be sure. But this authority is, like moonlight, only the reflection of some larger societal sun of which bureaucracy is the satellite. Similarly, the legitimacy of objectives or tasks toward which bureaucracy is oriented is but a reflection of their legitimacy as articulated elsewhere in the social order. This "light" cannot come from inside the bureaucracy itself.

Before the democratic revolutions in the West, when bureaucratic staffs carried out political objectives, they did so in terms of reglementations that benefited subjects gratuitously, if at all. Weber referred to these units in the context of patrimonial administration or administration by notables. This means that before the democratic revolutions and the establishment of the rule of law, "administration" did not simply mean role organization, but "domination." The revolutions did much to sweep away administration as domination. Administration as role organization for task implementation, however, survived.

Figure 7–2 shows that we may analyze the phenomenon of administration in the same terms used in Figure 4–1 to analyze law. That is, if we agree that administration, like law, has both a formal structure and a substantive set of objectives toward which it is oriented, each of which can undergo rationalization, two distinct types of administration emerge. Administration in which either dimension (formal structure or substantive objectives) has a low level of rationalization is always domination. Administration in which the two dimensions have undergone a substantially high level of rationalization becomes analytically divorced from domination and may be thought of as "organization." Weber's ideal typical "bureaucracy" is within this latter category. As I noted in the opening chapter, if, as organization, administration's impersonal purposes also happen to be public purposes defined by a political unit, administration then becomes associated with domination. Its authority is derivative authority, the legitimacy of its substantive objectives, derivative legitimacy.

In the modern state, administrative staffs (or agencies or units) derive their authority from the rule of law: either the legislature passes a statute creating the agency, specifying (in broad or narrow terms) the agency's objectives and scope of authority, or, alternatively, an agency is created by executive order. In either case, the rule of law provides a formal, legal basis for the existence, authority, and legitimacy of the agency. In theory, therefore, the agency's sublegislation (administra-

FIGURE 7-2

Outcome of the Degree of Rationalization of Administration

		Degree of Rationalization of Administration	
		High level of Rationalization	Low level of Rationalization
Aspect of Administration Undergoing Rationalization	The Administration's Form (the structure of roles oriented around task implementation)	(1) Formally rationalized administration Technical competence and efficiency (Weber's ideal typical bureaucracy) (Weber, 1968:217–26, 956–63)	(2) Formally irrationalized administration Technical incompetence and inefficiency (Weber's depiction of administration by notables) (Weber, 1968: 973–75)
	The Administration's Substantive Objectives (the goals the administration is established to carry out)	(3) Substantively rationalized administration The clear articulation of impersonal, public purposes (Weber, 1968: 959, 1006) (Weber's ideal typical bureaucracy)	(4) Substantively irrationalized administration The articulation of purely personal purposes ("Originally, patrimonial administration was adapted to the satisfaction of purely personal, primarily private needs of the master" [Weber, 1968:1013]). (Weber's ideal typical patriarchal or patrimonial administration)

tive law) should be congruous with the "spirit" of the objectives stated in the statute or executive order that initially gives the agency authority to sublegislate.

For any number of reasons, however,[2] administrative officials need or otherwise receive a range or a latitude within which they have discretion to make rules and regulations oriented toward the public. Mechanisms of discretion control, thus, are necessary so that the rule of law can be maintained; otherwise, administration would revert to domination. Whereas the rationalization of the civil or statute law involved imbuing it with an impersonal and impartial character, the rationalization of administrative law involves imbuing it with definiteness, uniformity, and the chance for appeal. Not, by any means, are these latter traits mutually exclusive of the law's impersonality and impartiality. Rather, for purposes of this discussion, it is a matter of emphasis whose implications will shortly become clear. Jeffrey L. Jowell defines "legalization" as "the process of subjecting official decision to the governance of predetermined rules" and "judicialization" as "the process of submitting official decision to adjudicative procedures" (1975:2–3). Together these two processes increase the rationality of administrative law. Figure 7–3 portrays premodern and rationalized administration in terms of the degree of legalization and judicialization of the directives promulgated by administrative officialdom.

Legalization. Legalization rationalizes administrative law by requiring officials to make determinations through the use of definite rules and standards.[3] Eligibility criteria should be uniform, written, and open to public view. The archetypal arbitrary decision, for example, is that based upon bribes or nepotism. Though legalization counters these obvious sources of official abuse, it does not eradicate more subtle administrative maneuvers that agencies have actually used to keep applicants at arm's legnth from a benefit the agency was dispensing.

Michael B. Rosen's "Tenants' Rights in Public Housing" (1967) gives a remarkably detailed account of how local housing authorities can surmount the niceties of legalization and still produce arbitrary decisions concerning eligibility claims. As required by federal law, the housing authorities may publicly post eligibility criteria based on, say, income limits of applicants, as well as of what constitutes the definition of "unsatisfactory" housing in which the potential beneficiary may now be living. More applications will be received than there will be public housing units available to accommodate them, however, and the agency must then establish a ranking of eligibles according to, perhaps, some third (or more) criterion. Here is where the dictates of legalization may be evaded by agency officials if they are so inclined. The agency can shield its selection criteria from public view by charac-

FIGURE 7-3

The Character of Administration in Terms of Discretion Control

		Mode of Discretion Control	
		Legalization	Judicialization
Degree of Discretion Control	High	(1) Norms that can be applied through (a) predetermined rules (b) definiteness of standards	(2) Institutionalized processes of appeal (therefore, the existence of entitlements)
		MODERN RATIONALIZED ADMINISTRATION	
	Low	(3) Few or no norms that can be applied because of (a) lack of predetermined rules (b) vagueness of standards	(4) No institutionalized processes of appeal (therefore, the absence of entitlements of any kind; only gratuities exist)
		PATRIARCHAL OR PATRIMONIAL ADMINISTRATION (Weber, 1968:1006–1110)	

terizing these criteria as "internal procedures"[4] (Rosen, 1967:166). There is evidence that these criteria can be arbitrary in the extreme and have resulted, upon occasion, in the rejection of applicants who, upon obtaining legal counsel, were reclassified as "eligible" or as higher up the eligibility list after all (Rosen, 1967; see also Baum, 1974).

Part of the explanation for why legalization does not more thoroughly eradicate arbitrary official decision lies in the slippage that occurs through the delegation of authority (Handler, 1979:8–18). In the United States, the federal government delegates its authority to the states, which, in turn, redelegate their authority to local agencies to implement social welfare programs. The local agencies may be subject to very little restriction in their decisions to operationalize the program (Handler, 1966, 1979; Rosen, 1967:157–64; Gronbjerg, 1977). This raises the question of the aforementioned congruity of agency sublegislation with the intent of the statute that establishes the legal basis for social welfare benefits in the first place. If such harmony is to be achieved, a mechanism of appeal is necessary. Accordingly, judicialization is a device for addressing slippages in legalization or any other questions that arise in connection with agency rule application.

Judicialization. Judicialization is the attempt to make agency decisions accountable by subjecting them to the process of elaboration. As I mentioned earlier, judicialization refers to the process of administrative adjudication, that is, adjudication within the agency: the agency itself conducts the hearing procedure. Citing Lon L. Fuller (1963), Jowell describes administrative adjudication as "a social process of decision which assures to the affected party a particular form of participation, that of presenting proofs and arguments for a decision in his favor" (1975:25). In this regard, judicialization is a device for establishing some approximation of due process as a major characteristic of the relationship between client and agency.

In the United States the Administrative Procedure Act (1946) embodied a step taken by the legislature to hasten the rationalization of administrative law through judicialization. Peter Woll (1963:22) writes that the act was the outcome of a concern by lawyers and others "to establish a meaningful concept of due process of law[5] with reference to administrative proceedings, thereby protecting the citizen under the jurisdiction of administrative agencies. . . . Generally speaking, due process of law in administration requires that fundamental procedures such as notice, hearing, adequate record, and appeal be maintained." The scope of the act is limited, however, to only those cases in which a statute provides that an agency's decisions may be subjected to a hearing process (Woll, 1963:20). Although the act does provide for the greater independence of hearing examiners from the prosecuting arm of the agency, such "independence of hearing examiners may not be strictly observed in all cases" (Woll, 1963:21). Daniel J. Baum observes that the fair hearing process is by no means a friendly affair "in which the interests of the federal government, the states, and the individual claimant meld." Rather, pressures can be exerted that can "cause distortion, leading even to the breakdown of the process itself" (Baum, 1974:58). These points lend credibility to the observation that "the effect of the APA is equivocal. Widely hailed as the most important enactment of the century in administrative law, the pre-ABA and post-ABA operations of administrative agencies do not differ from each other greatly" (Woll, 1963:20).

Nevertheless, Jowell's argument cannot be disregarded when he notes that one of the greatest merits of administrative adjudication involves its intrinsic function of elaborating the principles behind the rules, for rules "do not carry with them any explanation. . . . Nothing in the rule itself explains to a welfare recipient why she may be permitted, as a 'special need,' a washing machine, but not a television set or dishwasher" (1975:22–23). He specifies the connections among legalization, judicialization, and the ultimate objectives of agency decisions: "The adjudicator's obligation to reason will provide a check against the use of criteria that are improper, arbitrary, or legalistic,[6] or fail to achieve congruence between the effect of the decision and official objectives" (1975:27).

Judicialization, therefore, is clearly a step in the direction of due process in the application of administrative law. It brings more visibility to the relationship between sovereign (as represented by the agency) and citizen than would otherwise exist.[7] It also brings more formality as well as articulateness to a situation in which a conflict develops over a claim. Thus, while the regular courts of law decide whether citizens have rights in terms of the civil or statute law, administrative adjudication stipulates whether claimants have entitlements in terms of administrative law. Figure 7–4 summarizes the outcome for the individual of the degree of rationalization of either the civil or statute or the administrative law.

The "Administrative Imperative"

Figure 7–4 raises the question, "What is the relationship between entitlements and rights?" What implications does this distinction have for citizens' enjoyment of benefits and/or for the legitimacy of the act of redistribution assumed by the Western welfare state? What point is there in differentiating between the entitlement as the outcome of administrative adjudication and the right as the outcome of adjudication in the regular courts of law? Is this just hairsplitting? I will show in Chapter 9 that the distinction reaches paramount significance at the very juncture at which administrative adjudication pronounces a decision that does not favor the applicant.

This does not imply that agencies ought not to have the authority, through administrative adjudication, to declare applicants ineligible for benefits. Indeed, many applicants do not qualify for the benefits for which they are applying. Too, beneficiaries may become ineligible

FIGURE 7-4

Outcomes for Subjects or Citizens of Degree
of Rationalization of Law

		Type of Law	
		Administrative	Civil or Statute
Degree of Rationalization of the Law	Low	(1) No Entitlements (only gratuities exist)	(2) No Rights* or Primitive Rights Particularized Rights
	High	(3) Entitlements	(4) Generalized Rights (substantively rationalized and formally guaranteed)

*This represents only the extreme case. See Chapter 2 for the continuum of rights that preceded the establishment of the modern state.

for continued benefits at some point which administrative agencies need authority to declare. The redistributional state can hardly function without criteria of redistribution. Moreover, the administrative agency is unquestionably the appropriate institution to establish and implement such criteria. Frederick F. Blachly and Miriam E. Oatman (1934:43–53) treat this issue with a thoroughness that I need not reiterate here. Legislative bodies would not have the time or the expertise to attend to the myriad details, not to mention the major analyses of alternatives and consequences, connected with setting up and implementing social programs on a societal scale.

Criticisms of administrative adjudication (to be treated forthwith) are categorically unaccompanied by any suggestion that it be done away with. Indeed, as early as 1934, Blachly and Oatman noted that "the decisions of the various authorities which exercise administrative judicial power are several times as numerous as the recorded decisions of all the federal judicial courts. . . . Their published rules and regulations cover altogether about eight or ten times as many pages as the acts passed by Congress" (p. 11). A more recent statistic is no less staggering. In the United States, "the Social Security Administration (SSA) hearing system, administered by the Bureau of Hearings and Appeals (BHA), is probably the largest adjudicative agency in the western world. Its more than 625 administrative law judges disposed of 180,000 cases in the fiscal year of 1976. By comparison, the judicial system of the United States, including the District Courts, the Courts of Appeal, and the Supreme Court, has 505 judges and in the fiscal year 1976 terminated 129,683 civil and criminal cases with court action" (Mashaw et al., 1978:xi). It is evident that modern rulership could not be carried out without vast apparatuses of administration, including administrative adjudication. We might label this incontrovertible fact "the administrative imperative."

If administration, including administrative adjudication, is imperative, then a true dilemma exists from the standpoint of Western welfare regimes and their commitment to the tradition of individual rights. That dilemma lies squarely upon the fact that unless the applicant (who is also a "citizen" under the rule of law) has some independent authority to whom he can appeal in the event that his claim was turned down under administrative adjudication procedures, the agency has exercised all three functions of rule over him. Analytically, this is the trademark of premodern rulership, that is, administration as domination, and it undermines the legitimacy of the redistributions made in the name of the welfare state in two ways. The first is obvious: it compromises the notion of the supremacy of the law, the cornerstone of which is the individual's right of appeal to an independent judicial authority once an "enforcing" arm of the regime has restrained or otherwise exercised authority over him. The specters of "authoritarianism," "tyranny," "totalitarianism," "despotism," and the like are invariably raised.[8] The second way in which a purely administrative determination of the eligibility of a claimant undermines the legitimacy of welfare state redistributions is more subtle and applies especially to the United States. It will be treated in Chapters 8–10. Briefly, it has to do with the fact that once "cases" move from the purview of administration into the regular court system, issues become more visible to the public. The elaboration of the judges becomes part of the larger ambient of legitimation for the claim to a benefit. This will become especially apparent in the discussion in Chapter 9 of a famous U.S. Supreme Court case, *Goldberg* v. *Kelly* (1970). In cases such as these, the twilight zone between entitlements and rights (see Figure 7–

1) becomes illuminated by the society's changing values as reflected through new court decisions. These decisions articulate new rationales and thus legitimize new standards of living for the regime's citizens.

Returning to the first criticism of administrative adjudication from the standpoint of its effect upon the legitimacy of the use of government authority, the fear that the rule of law would be its first casualty was voiced loudly and early. It has not abated. In 1914, Roscoe Pound described administrative adjudication, which he called "executive justice," as the very antithesis of law, "one of those reversions to justice without law" (quoted in Woll, 1963:12). Arthur V. Dicey viewed administrative law as "an invasion of the rule of law by imposing judicial functions upon officials" (quoted in Woll, 1963:11). Lowi's contemporary statement draws the logical inference of Dicey's criticism: Lowi states that "broad discretion makes a politician out of a bureaucrat" (1969:300–301). Jowell (1975) notes that judicialization in and of itself does not mean that the agency rule that was applied was a good or a fair rule. Judicialization cannot change such a rule; it can only try to explain it. If, in fact, the rule is at variance with the intent of the social legislation the agency was meant to implement, judicialization can help to reveal this fact, but it cannot "right a wrong." Harvey Wheeler points out that "a vast world of substantive injustice has grown up in the name of fair administrative procedures" (1965:12). This has happened because an administrative agency "may do things that are wrong, but if it does them in the right way, administrative law must be satisfied because it cannot cope with the substance of the law itself" (Wheeler, 1965:12).

In this chilling revelation lies the reason why the categories "formal and substantive rationalization of the law" are not directly transferable to an analysis of administrative law. Administrative law is not oriented toward "substances," ergo it cannot undergo "substantive rationalization." Selznick says it best when he distinguishes between the objectives of the adjudicator and the administrator:

> In the determination of rights, "discretion" is compatible
> with the rule of law when it remains essentially judicial rather
> than administrative. Like any other discretion, judicial discretion
> involves a certain freedom of choice. The choice, however, is of
> a special kind. From among many possible ways of classifying
> the events at hand, the court selects that particular classification
> which will fix the rights and obligations of the parties. To this

end, judicial discretion may carpenter doctrines and otherwise rework the legal materials. But the objective remains: find a rule or a rule-set that will do justice in a special class of situations. . . . Administrative discretion is of another order. The administrator . . . is also interested in diagnosing and classifying the world. But he properly looks to an end-in-view, the refashioning of human or other resources so that a particular outcome will be achieved. [1969:159]

Not oriented toward substantive values per se, administrative law indeed "cannot cope with the substance of the law." Put slightly differently, the substantive rationalization of the civil or statute law (as discussed in Chapter 4) has no analytic counterpart in administrative law. By this very token, administrative adjudication cannot elaborate rationales that provide ultimate legitimation for the objectives toward which administrative law is oriented.[9] In Selznick's terms, the elaboration that occurs under administrative adjudication can only go as far as the "ends-in-view" toward which administrative law is oriented.

This immediately raises the question as to what exactly is the relationship between administrative "ends-in-view" and the "substantive" or "ultimate" values to which the civil or statute law gives crystalline form. If administrative agencies, whether regulatory, redistributive, or otherwise, are created by statute or executive order to give concrete form to an ideal, how can incongruities arise between administrative ends-in-view and the ideals that inspire the statutes? Various analysts have answered this question by noting that the objectives of legislatures are not always either clear or consistent (Blachly and Oatman, 1934; Leys, 1943; Landis, 1966; Handler, 1966, 1979; Shapiro, 1968; Lowi, 1969). Martin Shapiro notes that in many instances the statute will vest great powers of discretion in an agency,

allowing it to engage in wide-ranging policy making of its own. The statute may establish few if any outer limits to the agency's discretion. In such statutory schemes it is usually clear that the statute maker did not intend to leave the agency totally free. But it is typically not clear what limits were intended, and indeed it must frequently be admitted realistically that no exact limits have been stated precisely because the various participants in statute making could not agree or had not thought about what the limits should be. Such statutes are open invitations to all supplementary

lawmakers to make large amounts of law to fill in their meaning.
. . . Such statutes are in effect announcements by the statute
maker that the agency is being granted an exploratory commission to develop a new jurisdiction and new power that will only
become clearly defined as the agency explores what limits on
its power and what substantive policies ought to be written
into the statute. [1968:100–101]

Applying these observations directly to the case of the redistributive
agencies of the welfare state, we can see that there might very well
arise a gap between that to which an agency is willing to "entitle" an
"applicant" and that which a regular court of law is willing to declare
as the "social right" of the "citizen." In fact, one of Shapiro's points is
that, because the legislature has neither the time "nor the institutional
memory necessary to spot and turn back" agency decisions that may
be incompatible with its statutes, "it was therefore natural for the
statute maker to set its judicial subordinate [the courts] to watch its
administrative one [the agencies it creates]" (1968:100).

Returning to Figure 7–1, then, we see that even rationalized administrative law and its adjunct, administrative adjudication, can go
just so far toward the creation of a "right" for a citizen. The journey
of rationalized administrative law promulgated by the redistributive
agency of the welfare state stops at the "entitlement." Accordingly, the
major points to be treated in the following chapters, are foreshadowed
by what has been said in this one. Namely, what evidence is there that
the redistributions that stem from administrative rules and regulations
are occurring within a framework of increasingly rationalized administrative law? Why will "entitlements" always have a character different
from "rights" from the standpoint of rationales that attach legitimacy
to the redistributions of the Western welfare state? Stated in different
terms, why does a gap open up between (1) entitlements and rights,
(2) rationalized administrative law and rationalized civil or statute
law, and (3) administrative adjudication and adjudication in the regular courts of law (see broken lines in Figure 7–4)? What does this gap
mean for the legitimation of social rights? How can it be bridged? I
will treat these issues as they apply to the specific case history of the
U.S. welfare state, for under the U.S. federal system, they have surfaced
clearly. In addition, the position of the U.S. court system is unique
among Western regimes. It reviews much legislation and agency action
and in so doing it raises diverse issues associated with the ultimate

bases of legitimacy of welfare regimes. By treating the U.S. case in detail, I gain a vantage point for dealing with general issues of concern to regimes that undertake to redistribute their surpluses in the name of humanitarian values under the rule of law.

In this chapter, I have emphasized an ineluctable attribute of administration, namely, that it merges all three functions of traditional rulership: legislative, executive, and judicial. As we have seen (Chapter 2), the merging of all three governmental functions into a format of domination by administration is the oldest form of rule. James M. Landis, whose well-known work, *The Administrative Process*, initially appeared in 1938, nevertheless analyzed the outcry against modern incarnations of administration as lying, in part, in its comparative novelty within the Western political tradition: "There has been too little history to give the term 'administrative power' a content in any way comparable in impressiveness and historical significance to that conveyed by expressions 'legislative' or 'executive power.' The boundaries of any grant of administrative power are still a matter of interpretation of statutes" (1966:49). Discussions of administrative power by various contemporary analysts suggest that Landis's observation still holds (Handler, 1966, 1979; Reich, 1966; Shapiro, 1968; Wheeler, 1965; Lowi, 1969, 1979; Street, 1975). Certainly the excerpt given above from Shapiro's *The Supreme Court and Administrative Agencies* says as much. Lowi (1969:129–32) points this out, too, in noting that the era of modern administration did not begin in the United States until 1887 with the passage of the Interstate Commerce Act, creating the Interstate Commerce Commission.[10] Indeed, "delegation of power did not become a widespread practice or a constitutional problem until government began to take on regulatory functions. The first century was one of government dominated by Congress and virtually self-executing laws" (Lowi, 1969:128).

A systematic and professionalized approach to administration has characterized the British and Continental traditions for far longer than such an approach has inhered in the United States, as I shall discuss in Chapter 9.[11] Yet, administration, however rationalized, is still a sociopolitical phenomenon whose relationship to the legitimate uses of authority in the Western tradition needs to be resolved. Landis was certain of this when he wrote in the 1930s, and some would today agree with his assertion that "a consequence of an expanding interest of government in various phases of the . . . scene must be the creation of more adminstrative agencies if the demand for expertness is to be met" (1966:24). Wheeler's call (as noted in Chapter 1) for the provision of "appropriate controls" and the "fitting of the system of administrative law into the legal order" is a contemporary reiteration of Landis's implied warning: administration in the modern state is indispensable; therefore, reconcile it with the traditional functions of the state. Do not try to avoid the issue. I would add: avoiding the issue simply aggravates the Achilles heel of the Western welfare state.

Chapter 8

THE ADMINISTRATIVE HERITAGE

OF U.S. ASSISTANCE

ADMINISTRATION AS an Achilles heel on the body of the welfare state is much in evidence in the United States. In this and the following two chapters I will deal with only the U.S. welfare state, punctuated by references to events and issues in Britain that reinforce various themes. My overall argument, however, is applicable to Western welfare regimes as an analytic type. All face the fundamental problem of how to protect individual rights in an age when government and citizen may become adversaries on a scale and in ways unknown before the twentieth century. From the standpoint of the liberal tradition, that is, the guarding of individual rights, the overriding objective of the Western welfare state would be to reach that point at which social rights were protected with the same sense of urgency that has affixed itself to the protection of civil and political rights. For reasons to be presented in this chapter, that sense of urgency has been slow to materialize in the United States, a nation that Wilensky (1975) has labeled a "welfare laggard."

I have advanced the definition of the welfare state as that distinctive type of regime that formally guarantees and substantively rationalizes statutes of a certain type. These statutes are laws whose content is the social right to a minimum standard of living based on an agreed-upon range of commodities and services. With the sharp knife of analysis we may carve out a specific set of institutional processes in Western political history and call these, collectively, "the welfare state." In fact, however, despite quantum leaps in Britain and the other Western nations after World War II and in the United States during the 1960s, we must admit that the welfare state is also the outcome of an accretion of sundry policies and administrative practices that, as indicated in Part I, were expediently oriented toward crises and contingencies that arose throughout the twentieth century in the West.[1]

Nowhere among Western welfare regimes is this description of the desultory governmental recognition of sizable needs of citizens more true than it has been in the United States. The emergence of social rights—either legislatively or through articulation in the courts—was seriously shackled by the federal structure of the U.S. political system. The federal structure entails a division of sovereignty between the national government and the states. The hallowed institution of "states' rights" allowed administration to emerge as domination over those receiving assistance, subjecting them to the indignities of being pushed around by Achilles heel. As I argued in the previous chapter, one crucial task of the Western welfare state is to curb the inherent tendency of administration to become domination by (1) rationalizing its law, and (2) institutionally tethering administration to the other branches of rule. This would dissolve the gratuitous nature of the benefits so dispensed. By allowing the states the "right" to "administer" assistance to their residents, however, the doctrine of states' rights also allowed the institution of the gratuity to become entrenched in the grass roots of the U.S. assistance system. It was here, at the level of local responsibility for the needy, that the train of events by which assistance would ultimately become "rightful" in the United States made its inauspicious departure. Accordingly, this chapter deals with the condescending character of early U.S. assistance and how this initial orientation has continued to the present day to reinforce administration as domination, an influence that subtly pervaded the War on Poverty and foreshadowed the backlashes associated with it. At the conclusion of this chapter I discuss three legislative attempts to entitlize the U.S. poor to assistance during the 1970s. These attempts fundamentally differ from the approaches employed in the War on Poverty.

Early Impediments to Institutionalizing Social Rights in the United States

Certain assumptions born of the Progressive Era (roughly 1895–1917) as well as the tradition of states' rights with its cloying and arbitrary paternalism have served as obstacles to the emergence of the U.S. welfare state. The welfare state rests upon the possibility that adjudication procedures exist for the arbitration of claims. For one of society's institutional sectors to be capable of deciding the rightfulness of a claim, however, opportunity must be present for an adversarial relationship to arise. Adjudication cannot flourish in a setting that precludes adversarial relationships. This overall observation sets the tone for the discussion immediately to follow, as well as for treatment in Chapter 9 of the increasing role of adjudication in U.S. assistance cases.

Assumptions of the Progressive Era. Assumptions of administrative benevolence during the Progressive Era in the United States completely obviated the idea that state and citizen could be adversaries. Willard Gaylin et al. (1978) provide the historical background to this issue in their illuminating volume, *Doing Good: The Limits of Benevolence.* In "The State as Parent," one of the selections in *Doing Good,* David J. Rothman analyzes legislation of the Progressive Era. Such legislation presumed no antagonism between officialdom and beneficiary. For this reason the normal safeguards to civil liberties, enjoyed routinely by the rest of the citizenry and guarded jealously by the courts, were abrogated in the name of "helping" the client. The passage below indicates the conditions under which help was offered to widows during the Progressive Era:

> Enabling legislation and agency practice enhanced the prerogatives of state officials and reduced—and almost eliminated —legal protections and rights for those coming under their authority. To call the acts "widows pensions" was really a misnomer. The widows did not receive their allowance as a matter of right, the way a pensioner received his. Rather, the widow had to apply for her stipend, demonstrate her qualifications, her economic need, and her moral worth, and then trust to the decision of the welfare board. At their pleasure, and by their reckoning, she then obtained or did not obtain help. [Rothman, 1978:78]

Institutionalizing the process of claim settlement was unthinkable: "Since the state . . . was to help and not to punish . . . it was unnecessary—in fact it was counterproductive—to limit or to circumscribe officials' discretionary powers" (Rothman, 1978:77).

This assumption (that administrative discretion is "good" for the client) is alive today, manifest in the statute that established the Veterans Administration in 1934, requiring that all veterans' claims be handled within the VA: "It is provided by law that 'all decisions rendered by the Administrator of Veterans' Affairs . . . shall be final and conclusive on all questions of law and fact, and no other official or court of the United States shall have jurisdiction to review by mandamus or otherwise any such decision" (Woll, 1963:151). Woll describes the Veterans Administration as "the best example of the pure administrative process in the benefit field," but adds that the contact staff is highly oriented toward helping the applicant to secure benefits from the agency (1963:146, 148).

Thus, the assumptions of "doing good" that underlay administrative arrangements initiated during the Progressive Era had sunk foundations deeply into the soil upon which architects of the welfare state would much later wish to build. In the meantime, the public assistance titles of the U.S. Social Security Act (1935) were a natural outcome of these institutional foundations.

Assumptions Underlying Public Assistance. Called by some an "omnibus bill," the U.S. Social Security Act had a distinctly dual nature at its inception. The social insurance titles formally guaranteed substantively rationalized rights. They embodied the notion that "the benefits they provide for the worker and his family 'grow out of his own work,' or that they are a sort of an extension of the individual's own earnings. . . . The benefits are 'earned' . . . eligibility is a matter of 'right.' . . . If an individual can fit himself into the legal definition of a beneficiary, the official in charge has no discretion to withhold his benefits" (Bowler, 1974:9). By contrast, the public assistance titles of the act solidly formalized administration as domination. The administrative agencies set up by the act to dispense public assistance had, and have, executive, sublegislative, and adjudicative powers over the applicant to a far wider degree than was, and is, the case with the social insurance titles: "[A] . . . 'fundamental doctrine' of the original Social Security Act that contained both the social insurance programs and public assistance was that the types of programs were to be carefully distinguished in terms of administration, funding, program purpose, the nature of benefits, and the recipients" (Bowler, 1974:10). We can quickly see that there was to be no early institutionalization of the adversarial claim to benefits under the public assistance titles of the act, for, "as contrasted with Social Security or unemployment insurance, public assistance benefits are considered unearned, and not to be received by anyone as a matter of right but as public charity. Any stigma associated with the notion of charity or the 'public dole' is justified as a means of preventing idleness and discouraging individuals from applying for public assistance" (Bowler, 1974:10). This orientation toward those on public assistance was heavily reinforced by the three-tiered (federal/state/local) structure of U.S. rulership, as will be shown in the following sections.

Continuity between Progressive "Benevolence" and Public Assistance. The public assistance titles of the Social Security Act were the federal government's response to the separate states' inability to cope with the depression crisis. Steiner writes that those titles were "meant to shore up, not to replace, state old age and mothers' pension laws" (1966:80). Rothman points out that "between 1900 and 1920 practically every state passed widow-pension laws" (1978:76), which were the antecedents of the Aid to Dependent Children program begun under Title IV of the Social Security Act. Vince J. and Vee Burke write that when the act was passed, Title IV related to a particular category of the needy whom "everyone agreed should not work, even if jobs were available: dependent children and their mothers deprived by death or other causes of a male breadwinner" (1974:8). Since the 1930s, however, not only has this category of the needy grown larger, but, as Steiner (1966:33) wrote, by the 1960s had taken on a completely different set of sociological characteristics: the children were primarily the offspring of unwed black females (see also Baum, 1974:47).

Given the assumption of the Progressive Era that aid was gratuitous when given to mothers and their dependent children, we can readily see as the inevitable outcome the curtailments of civil liberties that would eventually be faced by mothers under the Aid to Families with Dependent Children program (AFDC).[2] In the early 1970s, Frances Fox Piven and Richard A. Cloward wrote:

> That recipients are denied commonly accepted rights was dramatically illustrated by a recent district court in Washington, D.C. in the matter of a group of AFDC mothers who took the rare step of suing the welfare department for declaratory and injunctive relief against unreasonable searches, harassing surveillance, eavesdropping, and interrogation concerning their sexual activities. The court not only ruled against the mothers, but rendered the opinion that welfare benefits are a gratuity: which of the eligibles are actually to receive benefits is, the court held, within the absolute discretion of administrative functionaries who may impose such requirements as they deem appropriate. [1972:166–67]

In short, during the Progressive Era the seeds of administration as domination were planted. Social rights to benefits were not likely to sprout from them. Rather, removing weeds from the United States' garden of civil liberties has been a never-ending process, as an episode during the early 1970s demonstrated: at one point a federal Senate-House conference committee considered (but ultimately rejected) a plan to attach to the continuing AFDC program the establishment of "a national apparatus for tracking down runaway fathers of welfare families and forcing them to support their families. This rejected plan envisioned the establishment of regional blood-testing laboratories to determine paternity of welfare children, as well as a 'parent locator center' in the Justice Department" (Burke and Burke, 1974:187n.). Individual states, however, did not necessarily relinquish such ideas. In 1979, the state of Washington's Office of Support Enforcement was attempting to establish the paternity of children of unwed mothers through questionnaires that asked far more intimate sexual questions than were necessary to achieve program objectives (Bryant, 1979).

When, therefore, the political sovereign (represented by an agency) enters the life of the citizen in a context that presumes gratuitousness, beneficiaries become what Ira Glasser calls "prisoners of benevolence." He points out that "the midnight knock at the door is always inherent in governmental power. In one century, it comes in the form of a British soldier; in another, a caseworker. The encroachment of power upon liberty has many disguises" (1978:168). Lionel Trilling, reading a paper in the late 1940s at the Conference on the Heritage of the English-Speaking Peoples and Their Responsibilities, stated the problem in yet another way: "Some paradox in our natures leads us, when once we have made our fellow men the objects of our enlightened interest, to go on to make them objects of our pity, then of our wisdom, ultimately of our coercion" (1950:215; also quoted by Rothman, 1978:72). In view of the argument I have presented throughout, when administration becomes domination, it brooks no adversaries. Its handmaiden is the gratuity, not an entitlement, and certainly not a "right" to which claim can be made within a well-institutionalized adversarial format.

States' Rights Reinforce Paternalism. Assumptions of benevolence were not the only hindrances to the eventual articulation of social rights in the United States. States' rights was, and is, an ideal that has complicated matters enormously, saddling the United States with a problem not faced by Britain, France, West Germany, and Scandinavia, for example. In this section, I will indicate how the principle of states' rights precipitated an initially low level of legalization of public assistance.

Before the passage of the Social Security Act, there was a strong tradition of local responsibility for the poor in the United States (Steiner, 1966; Feagin, 1975; Meenaghan and Washington, 1980). The act was not meant to interfere with the parochial, discretionary orientation of the separate state administrations to needy populations. Legalization (uniformity and definiteness of rules and standards) within state agencies was quite low. Steiner notes that "without a demonstration that relief of the poor was a problem that required uniformity of policy, efforts by economists and social workers to impose such uniformity were resisted" (1966:80).

The wording of the public assistance titles of the act allowed the low level of legalization to persist, leaving room for wide administrative discretion: "The conditions for approval of state plans are stated negatively, so that the states are able to impose any conditions they see fit, except that age, residence, and citizenship qualifications may not be more stringent than the maxima set forth in the Act. This leeway permits the imposition of income and property restrictions, lien laws, and other such qualification features as a creative state may invent" (Steiner, 1966:85). Such discretion, naturally, spawned glaring inequities: "In the early days of the new state-federal welfare program, it was customary in some areas to offer smaller payment, if any, to blacks than to whites. The rationalization was that blacks could get by with less" (Bowler, 1974:8).

Efforts to legalize administration of benefits under public assistance titles of the act met with early sabotage. These attempts were rapidly dissolved in the acid of racial rejection of the equitability that would have followed legalization: "Before enacting FDR's 1935 bill, Congress erased a welfare provision that would have required states to furnish sufficient aid to provide 'a reasonable subsistence compatible with health and decency' . . . because suspicious southern members feared that it might give Washington authority to compel states to give poor blacks as much as poor whites" (Burke and Burke, 1974:8). Therefore, states themselves have been permitted to decide whether to provide welfare, how much, and to whom (see Handler, 1966, 1979; Steiner, 1966; Gronbjerg, 1977). This arrangement ensures that it can only be a misnomer to call the U.S. approach to public assistance a "system": "Imagine a Social Security 'system' that paid five times more to a New York family than to a corresponding Mississippi family; that reduced benefits in almost half the states in a period of rising living costs; that penalized those whose behavior offended the community; that could be abolished overnight by the state legislature" (Burke and Burke, 1974:7).

How could a system emerge, complete with legalization and judicialization, when various ways were open to the states to elude the national intent of the act? First, states could "go it alone," for "unlike the unemployment insurance program, no special earmarked tax, with a forgiveness feature for complying states, is imposed to support public assistance" (Steiner, 1966:80). Second, states could articulate a plan and then negotiate with the federal government to approve it. Steiner calls this "an agreement to play a somewhat modified version of the original game" (1966:81). Third, states have engaged in outright noncompliance with the federal program stipulations (Feagin, 1975:75ff.). States may deliberately flout federal law, expecting either that the state case is sufficiently strong that the federal agency will ignore or justify the disobedience or that a change in the federal law may be brought about as a result of the state's noncompliance (Steiner, 1966:81).

A Comparison with Early British Approaches to Assistance

By contrast, the British approach to assistance has, from the beginning, been far more legalized. Beveridge had recommended a single, comprehensive system of social assistance, making payments on a test of need on a uniform basis. Under the National Assistance Act a National Assistance Board was set up with a network of local offices. Uniform scales and conditions of benefit were instituted. A minimum subsistence income for families of different sizes was fixed through standard income scales. The difference was paid between the means of the applicant and his direct dependents and the standard scale applicable, disregarding certain minimum means (Sleeman, 1973:55).

Britain's tradition of legalization in the matter of assistance long predates the National Assistance Act and the welfare state. Derek Fraser notes that certain aspects of the 1834 Poor Law were revolutionary in relationship to the Elizabethan Poor Laws. These innovative elements involved the standardization and centralization of relief. He writes: "In order to ensure equitable and efficient treatment of paupers in all areas a uniform administrative regime was attempted, under the guidance of a central Poor Law Commission. Less-eligibility, the workhouse test, uniformity and centralisation: such in outline were the main landmarks of the 1834 revolution" (Fraser, 1976:1). In theory, then, nineteenth-century British paupers were subject to less arbitrariness than twentieth-century U.S. black citizens in southern states.

Administration as Domination

I have been arguing that in order to achieve legitimacy redistributions made by Western welfare regimes need to be channeled through the institution of the social right. The social right is the outcome of the development to a high degree of rationality of a society's legal system. That is, the law that creates the right is clear, formal, and adjudicable, thus making the law's guarantee effective. In turn, the rationale underlying the law is well elaborated, its principles synthesized smoothly with principles that underlie other laws in the legal system. This strengthens the law's acceptability or legitimacy.

Tangible commodities and services form the content of social rights; therefore, administrative agencies or bureaus must be created to deal with the practical side of service delivery, including eligibility determination. An agency's rules must ultimately be brought into conformity with the intent of the laws that make up the broader, more abstractly (or idealistically) oriented legal system. I showed in the last chapter and in Figure 7–4 that legalization and judicialization together initiate the important processes by which this compatibility of principle and practice can be achieved. When Jowell (1975:17) writes that "a rule is formal notice of entitlement," he is referring to the fact that legalization ultimately results in "entitlization." Entitlization, in turn, provides applicants with a legal vantage point to make an adversarial claim against the agency. In parallel terms, individual rights (including social rights) provide citizens with a legal vantage point to make an adversarial claim against the sovereign. The task of the welfare state, thus, requires continued construction of institutional bridges between the entitlement and the social right.

Articulating entitlements with social rights widens the arena within which the adversarial process can take place. Entitlements are adjudicated administratively (see Chapter 7). Social rights, as a subcategory of individual rights associated with citizenship in Western regimes, theoretically open the entire court system to the citizen to have the law applied in his favor. Bridging entitlements and rights also opens the processes of entitlization to public view because the determinations are made in the open forum of the courts. The courts, in examining the issue of whether or not a right exists, figuratively speaking, shine a searchlight down the entire corridor that led to the legal location of citizen and sovereign when a case comes up for review.

In the above sections, I have shown that early applicants for assistance in the United States either were in no position or were in a remote position to make adversarial claims against service agencies. The low levels of legalization and judicialization precluded entitlization. In short, applicants had no "standing" (in legal terminology), that is, no legal catapult from which to launch their claim. In the following sections, I will show how the United States has continued to reap the dubious harvest of the paternalistic seeds planted during the Progressive Era. Part of this harvest included severe legitimation controversies and backlashes surrounding programs aimed at "helping people." Help was given gratuitously, outside the context of social rights. Administration continued to be domination. Legitimation could not attach itself to the format within which the help was given.

Perihelion and Aphelion in Pennsylvania. From 1967 to 1973, the Pennsylvania State Department of Public Welfare announced a series of policy changes toward AFDC applicants and others requesting assistance (Ritti and Hyman, 1977). In the late 1960s, a new governor issued an executive directive that would make it easier for applicants to receive help: "self-declaration" was institutionalized. "With self-declaration . . . the potential AFDC recipient was to be taken at her word," whereas under earlier policy, "questions [were] asked and doubts expressed" (Ritti and Hyman, 1977:166). Governor Branch Offices were opened throughout Pennsylvania to act as advocates for the poor. The state's official welfare directives reached their perihelion: they came as close to the glittering sun of "full rights" as ever they would during those tumultuous years.

Welfare administration policy now stressed these objectives: "Sound judgment, quick action, and respect for human dignity must prevail over procedural detail. A continuing and constantly renewed stress on courtesy, prompt service, and a scrupulous regard for the full rights and entitlements of citizens [will demonstrate our commitment to serve]" (Hyman, 1975:12, as cited in Ritti and Hyman, 1977:167; brackets are the authors'). Under this policy the welfare caseload increased 400 percent (Ritti and Hyman, 1977:168). Perihelion was expensive and a point too hot for policy makers.

By 1971, a massive reaction was well under way: the public assistance program was referred to as an "unbridled monster," and the state executive office explained the rise in the welfare caseload as resulting from "waste, inefficiency, and cheating" (Ritti and Hyman, 1977:169, 172). In the face of a worsening economy, policy was reversed and self-declaration was terminated "even over the objections of the Federal HEW" (Ritti and Hyman, 1977:168). The state government "reinstituted rigorous verification procedures before payment could be obtained" (Ritti and Hyman, 1977:172). Aphelion had now been reached: the state of Pennsylvania's assistance to the citizen in need attained its most distant orbital point from the scorching sun of social rights and its attendant capacity to sear the state's treasury.

In fact, the changes in Pennsylvania's welfare policy paralleled the rise and fall of the emotional temperature of its inner cities during those years (Ritti and Hyman, 1977). Cool authoritarian benevolence was poured upon the hot issues of the day. Legitimation of the financial outlays could not be, and was not, the outcome. No social rights were created. Applicants had no grounds for an adversarial claim against the policy changes surrounding "self-declaration," the benefits of which were entirely gratuitous. In the light of these events, an observation of Selznick's is revealing: "Administration may be controlled by law, but its special place in the division of labor is to get the work of society done, not to realize . . . ideals. . . . Adjudication also gets work done, in settling disputes, but this is secondary and not primary. The primary function of adjudication is to discover the legal coordinates of a particular situation. That is a far cry from manipulating the situation to achieve a desired outcome" (1969:16). The Pennsylvania State Department of Public Welfare used administration to manipulate and control a situation involving a political turmoil. The "job to be done" was to quell the unrest. The rightness or wrongness of the department's motives is not the point here. My point is, rather, that legitimacy did not attach to the benefits dispensed, as the violent backlash and stark policy reversals were quick to disclose.

The War on Poverty. The War on Poverty, launched by the Economic Opportunity Act (EOA) in 1964, has been referred to by Lowi (1969: 231) as one more attempt among a proliferation of uncoordinated government programs dedicated to "helping people." The act enlarged the purview of administration, not social rights. "It is a catchall of job-creating, job-training, and money-providing programs aimed largely at making lower-class life a bit more comfortable for the present lower classes" (Lowi, 1969:234).

Consider the difference between the notion of a "right" as something that attaches to the citizenship status and the notion of a program that local administrators have discretion to bestow upon their communities: "In the United States localities have had to be induced by federal grants to initiate many programs in the areas of housing, welfare, and education, because these programs remain voluntary. As Daniel Elazar points out: 'Though both national and state governments permit local governments to bend any given grant program in the direction desired locally . . . if local initiative is not present, the opportunities remain unrealized'" (Heidenheimer, Heclo, and Adams, 1975:266). Kenneth C. Davis, the administrative law specialist, refers to this approach as the discretion to do nothing (cited in Handler, 1966:175). We might call it "the optional welfare state," which, from the standpoint of social rights, is no welfare state at all. Thus, the War on Poverty essentially relied upon a format of devolving government benefices onto twentieth-century patrimonies:

> The Act is only concerned to establish the incidence of need,
> and kind of programmes which qualify a proposal for support,
> indifferent to the planning methodology by which it was devised.
> Any community with many poor is entitled to support, if it
> is genuinely prepared to undertake programmes of employment,
> training, health, housing, social welfare and remedial education
> likely to put people on their feet. It need not offer a sophis-
> ticated justification of these innovations. [Marris and Rein,
> 1973:213]

Far from articulating any rationale connecting the expensive benefits to justifiable citizenship rights, the act simply articulated what Lowi (1969:235) calls "open-ended sentiments": the arrangement of education and training programs to provide enrollees with "useful work experience," the combating of poverty, the provision of services and activities of sufficient scope and size to give promise of progress toward eliminating poverty, and the creation of maximum feasible participation of residents in the communities in question. Viewed under this uncomplimentary light, the act by no means made possible the creation of entitlements by administrative agencies, for how does an agency go about entitling a citizen to "maximum feasible participation," which, in any case, is neither a commodity nor a service? Thus, Lowi's point regarding the act's "sentimental" orientation is well taken and reinforces the argument I am making.

The dispensation of governmental largesse during the War on Poverty took place outside the context of a clear right to benefits. Unsurprisingly, legitimation controversies arose. Unremitting backlashes enveloped the War on Poverty. Even beneficiaries of various social programs experienced vast degrees of frustration and vented much bitterness (Lowi, 1969:239–40). By these observations I do not, however, mean to indicate that the War on Poverty achieved nothing of value. It did much good, as even some of its severest critics would attest. My point is simply that social rights were not created as this largesse was dispensed, nor could the programs gain legitimacy merely by putting new names on the ancient process of administration as domination.

Legislative Initiatives toward Entitlization during the 1970s

In this section I will treat three legislative packages[3] that either proposed or actually initiated entitlization programs. These three programs were attempts to legalize, judicialize, and, hence, entitle the U.S. poor to assistance. Their structural differences from the bulk of the War on Poverty programs will be quite evident, as these latter did not formally link assistance to the citizenship status or, more loosely, to the individual or family in need. Rather, the communities or even the programs themselves were the centerpieces of the War on Poverty's assistance effort. The three programs to be discussed here are Supplemental Security Income (SSI), the Family Assistance Plan (FAP), and the Program for Better Jobs and Income (PBJI). It will be seen that the journey toward entitlization has been characterized by much limping and halting.

SSI. SSI is the high point of the legalization of general assistance in the United States, general assistance being that financed from general revenues as distinct from payroll taxes. Since 1 January 1974, the U.S. government "has guaranteed to those over 65 years of age, and to the blind and disabled of any age, a minimum income" (Burke and Burke, 1974:189). SSI is one of three income-tested programs, along with the food stamp and AFDC programs, and enjoys by far the greatest degree of rationalized administration: "For an unfair and confusing maze of state rules to decide who among the aged, blind and disabled is poor enough to be helped, SSI substitutes objective and national standards of income and resources" (Burke and Burke, 1977:203–4).

The Burkes refer to SSI as having "transformed adult welfare in philosophy, procedures, and financing" (1974:204), and other authors would concur (see Bowler, 1974; Meenaghan and Washington, 1980; Stein, 1980). In philosophy, SSI breaks the link between work and governmentally guaranteed cash benefits. Furthermore, it grants these payments without stigmatization (Burke and Burke, 1974). In procedures, SSI represents a federal takeover and standardization of the various sublegislation that emanated from state governments as they carried out the tradition of local responsibility toward the poor. In financing, the bulk of the payments comes from the federal treasury with a smaller percentage coming from the state (see Stein, 1980). When Burke and Burke (1974:204) state that "the new law has begun a quiet revolution," they are referring to the logical endpoint of a trend implied and initiated by legalization: the categorical rejection of the gratuity in favor of the entitlement in the modern state.

FAP. FAP was part of the same congressional bill (H.R. 1) as was SSI, both before the floor of Congress in October of 1972. Proposed by the first Nixon administration, FAP was an attempt to convert a congeries of assistance programs (in differing stages of legalization) into entitlements for certain old and some new categories of the population. Public surprise ran high when, in 1969, Richard Nixon "proposed unprecedented federal intervention in welfare, advancing far ahead of the goals made explicit or those actually achieved by FDR's New Deal, Harry Truman's Fair Deal, or LBJ's Great Society" (Burke and Burke, 1974:130). But public commitment to old-style, grudging paternalism ran higher. FAP did not make it through the Congress. Rather, "the story of FAP confirmed the dangers inherent in trying to move American income support policy away from the consensus established in the 1930's" (Heidenheimer, Heclo, and Adams, 1975:219).

The consensus of the 1930s linked legitimacy of government help to the citizen to employability and earnings through social insurance (see Chapter 5). FAP, by contrast, would have shifted the eligibility criterion away from employability of the household head to the hard fact of income deficiency in families with children (Bowler, 1974). Administrative discretion over eligibility determinations would have been sharply reduced, for, in Daniel P. Moynihan's words, FAP would have been a guarantee "for every family, united or not, deserving or not, working or not" (quoted in Burke and Burke, 1974:178). Questions of who "can" work or who "won't" work, as well as associated issues of "deservingness" or "blame," would have been rendered obsolete (Bowler, 1974:28–29; see also Moynihan, 1973).

FAP, thus, would have introduced legalization into government assistance on two levels: first, the criterion of eligibility (income deficiency in families with children) would have lent itself to greater definiteness and standardization than the criterion of employability. Second, FAP entailed a federal takeover of the welfare system that, of course, would have imposed uniformity upon what was then, and continues to be, a veritable jungle of variously sized and shaped assistance programs. Because financing of FAP would have come overwhelmingly from the federal government, legalization, judicialization, and entitlization would have had a sure path upon which to advance.

The three categories of the poor toward which FAP addressed itself indicate where entitlization would have been institutionalized: (1) intact poor families whose fathers had low-paying jobs and which had hitherto fallen through the net of other cash assistance programs; FAP would have supplemented the earnings of these families, thus raising their children out of poverty (Burke and Burke, 1974:135); (2) the welfare poor in southern states where state-determined payments were lower than elsewhere in the nation and where eligibility rules were strict (Burke and Burke, 1974:135); (3) the welfare poor in industrial states in the North and West where benefits were highest. No increases would have accrued to the welfare poor where benefits were highest, but vastly higher payments would have gone to those recipients where the payments were lowest (Burke and Burke, 1974:135).

FAP failed to pass Congress for a number of reasons, including ironically, opposition from the National Welfare Rights Organization

(NWRO). NWRO originated in the late 1960s and became the successful organizational representative of several hundred welfare groups in about seventy cities and twenty-six states (Piven and Cloward), 1972: 322). The organization marched, demonstrated, and campaigned on numerous occasions to protest welfare restrictions and to stop cutbacks in welfare appropriations (Piven and Cloward, 1972:323). It served, therefore, as an effective agent to hasten the introduction of legalization and judicialization into the welfare system so that recipients could then claim entitlements, not just gratuities. When FAP was proposed, however, some years after NWRO's outstanding victories, the latter failed to recognize the enduring gains embodied by FAP, and the organization vigorously opposed the impending legislation.

NWRO, representing particularly AFDC mothers, opposed FAP on two grounds. First, AFDC mothers in the industrial states receiving the highest public assistance payments would gain no increases under FAP. But neither would they have suffered decreases. Under FAP the states were required to supplement the difference between the federal FAP payment and current public assistance benefits received by those under AFDC (Burke and Burke, 1974:136 and passim; Bowler, 1974). Second, and the analyst of the welfare state can only emit a sigh of despair, "it would be harder for NWRO to wrest from local welfare departments special grants—in excess of regular benefits—for school clothing, household items . . . or for whatever special purpose NWRO might campaign" (Burke and Burke, 1974:159–60). And yet, the initial FAP plan, which required the state supplement, was "a federal guarantee against a reduction in the above-FAP welfare benefits that their [AFDC recipients'] states had granted them and could withdraw from them" (Burke and Burke, 1974:136). No clearer example can be found of a case in which adaptability to the present system on the part of a sector of the population receiving public assistance curtailed further gains, not only for others, but for themselves. NWRO acted to help bring about rationalized administration and entitlization, up to a point. But the organization was unable to see beyond that point to a state of affairs allowing the scope of legalization to be advanced immeasurably and the advantages of entitlization generalized to far more of the needy than the membership of NWRO.

Finally, FAP failed because it became identified in the public mind, as well as in political circles, with a massive expansion in the "welfare rolls." Under FAP about ten million new recipients would have been guaranteed federal cash benefits, most of them the working poor who slip through many other income nets (Burke and Burke, 1974:35). Arnold J. Heidenheimer, Hugh Heclo, and Carolyn Teich Adams (1972:219) get to the core of FAP's problems in gaining public assent when they write that "the plan itself was formulated and perceived as a comprehensive reform of the public assistance system rather than as part of an integrated income support policy." I agree with them, but would rephrase their observation as follows: the legitimation of social rights "from the bottom" (starting from gratuities and moving toward entitlements) is a journey that takes place on a sharply inclined path. Nor is arrival at the destination inevitable.

PBJI. PBJI was announced by the Carter administration in 1977 as a plan that would "consolidate three major components of the current welfare system and provide, for the first time, a nationwide minimum federal cash payment for all the poor. . . . Earnings, welfare, manpower policy, and taxes would be interrelated through an expanded earned income tax credit and a new, nationally uniform system of basic income support payments" (Danziger and Plotnick, 1978:16). For purposes of the discussion at hand, the important aspects of the above brief description of PBJI are, first, that it called for rationalized and comprehensive administration of the three income-tested (SSI, AFDC, and food stamps) welfare programs.[4] Legalization would have been achieved through uniform national standards (this is already true of SSI—see above). Systematization would have been achieved by consolidating three separate programs, each in a different stage of entitlization, into one programmatic arrangement linking the citizen-in-need and his sovereign as represented by an administrative bureau. Second, the proposal of PBJI clearly indicated that the problems to which FAP addressed itself yet exist, although FAP failed as a proposed solution. The Program for Better Jobs and Income Act, introduced in late 1977, died in committee in 1978.

The experiences of two U.S. presidents suggest that there are, to date, grave obstacles to reforming "welfare" because alternative attempts to impose rationalized administration upon the congeries that passes for the public assistance "system" are consistently voted down. Rationalized administration leads inevitably to entitlization. Entitlization radically reduces the stigmatization and confusion surrounding the social transfer that takes place between state and citizen. Entitlization appears to be an idea whose time has come, an idea embodied in both FAP and PBJI, and, of course, SSI. Certainly the idea of a guaranteed income is a topic that has been kicked around bureaucratic corridors within the capital for well over a decade. Certainly a former poverty-program official under the Johnson administration noted enthusiastically that the ideas embodied by FAP were "very, very sound —the basis for the next important round in the development of social welfare administration" (quoted in Burke and Burke, 1974:137). Certainly "we are approaching the limits of our tolerance for the current transfer system" (Danziger and Plotnick, 1978:16). And yet, the transition from gratuities to entitlements by way of legislation has been beset by political obstacles. What apparently is needed, in the words of an old Beatles tune, is "a little help from our friends." Such friends are most sustaining if they are at the very top, far from Achilles heel. I turn now to judicial review and its effect upon the emergence of entitlements and the gradual conversion of some of them into social rights in the United States.

Chapter 9

FROM ADMINISTRATION TO

ADJUDICATION: LEGITIMATION OF

SOCIAL RIGHTS IN THE UNITED STATES

"THE WELFARE STATE has brought with it a series of fundamental transformations that have not yet acquired jurisprudential recognition" (Wheeler, 1965:14). But the process of according jurisprudential recognition to these transformations has well begun. The legitimation of social rights has been closely associated with such recognition in the United States. That will be the topic of this chapter.

The legitimation of social rights in the United States is taking place through a complement of social processes. I have labeled this complement "legitimation from above" and "legitimation from below," elaborating somewhat upon Piven and Cloward's (1972) usages of these terms, to be discussed shortly. On the one hand, social rights can be created directly by statute. Such statutes explicitly articulate that a right to a benefit legally exists and offer an accompanying rationale for the right. I illustrated this method of right-creation in Chapters 4–6 when I discussed the social insurance titles of the U.S. Social Security Act, as well as the specific legislative acts that created the British welfare state. Claims involving rights to benefits under such statutes have always been much more amenable to adjudication in the regular courts of law in the United States than have claims involving types of assistance to which rights have not been created. Each time courts defend rights created directly by statute, the right and its content gain reinforced legitimation beyond the justification initially accompanying the statute. When courts defend rights, therefore, legitimation comes "from above," that is, from the highest locus of legitimation in the legal system (see Figure 4–2, n. †).

By contrast, social rights in the United States have not always had to emerge through legislation. They have also emerged circuitously "from below" (see Figure 7–1) as I shall show in this chapter in my discussion of the significance of the 1960s and their culmination in cases such as *Goldberg* v. *Kelly*. Social rights can come into being "from below" once redistributive administrative agencies have become sufficiently rationalized (through the legalization and judicialization of their rules and regulations) that the claim becomes one of whether the individual has an entitlement. Once the issue becomes one of whether an entitlement exists, the groundwork has been laid for a further determination: whether the individual has a "right." This is a far cry from the Progressive Era in U.S. history when assistance was only a handout, when it was merely "charitable" (and the irony of that term was apparent in Chapter 8). Under such conditions, claims of an appellant against an agency rarely, if ever, reached the lofty levels of regular court review, for gratuities are merely "administered," whereas "adjudication" is reserved for rights. By this line of reasoning, it can be understood that the entitlement is indeed a crucial point on the gratuities-rights continuum, for entitlements are "adjudicated administratively" (I will reinforce this point in Chapter 11). Entitlization, accordingly, dissolves the worst excesses of administration: the complete dependence of the recipient upon a benefactor for discretionary assistance. At the same time, the entitlement provides, as mentioned earlier, the legal catapult from which an appellant may ultimately launch a claim that may (or may not) be deemed a right by a regular court of law. That the entitlement provides the possibility, however, is a central point in my argument.

We saw in the last chapter that entitlization through the legislative route has been variously successful: SSI is a program that entitles eligibles to benefits. No gratuitousness is involved in determination of eligibility or of amount of award. FAP and PBJI, however, did not make it through the Congress as programs entitling potential claimants to assistance. In this chapter, I shall treat the interplay between agencies and courts as a route that has strengthened both the principle of entitlization and the connection between entitlements and social rights. Thus, in the absence of explicit legislative creation of a benefit using the vocabulary of individual rights (as with retirement pensions), bounty that flows to the individual as a result of agency sublegislation remains analytically at the level of successive approximations of entitlements (as with general assistance). The degree of approximation is contingent upon the extent of legalization and judicialization that characterizes the agency's rules connected with the dispensation of the commodities or services at issue. In the United States today, court review is the primary vehicle for determining whether an entitlement (or an approximation thereof) has the prestige of being socially rightful. Legitimation of social rights "from below," therefore, refers to the outcome of a case in which an appellant has "exhausted his administrative remedies" (submitted to administrative adjudication at the agency level), has taken his case into the regular court system, and has won his claim by virtue of the court's having enunciated his social right to benefits of that type. Finally, the importance of the finely honed distinction between entitlements and rights reaches its height only at the time when an applicant is refused benefits by the agency and this denial is upheld by the agency's administrative adjudication procedures.[1]

"Ripeness" and the Decision to Review

The events of the 1960s in the United States ripened the times for court review of cases of the type having to do with subtle distinctions among gratuities, entitlements, and rights. Shapiro's (1968) discussion of the notion of "ripeness" is here instructive. Ripeness has to do with the court's idea of whether the time is right (ripe) for it to decide upon a certain type of case: "When a judge asks whether a matter is ripe for adjudication, he is asking, 'Is it the sort of question that the courts are competent to decide?'" (Shapiro, 1968:117).

Shapiro argues that the Court's stance on "ripeness" is largely concerned with the issue of timing, as well as with the political impact of court decisions: "Because the Supreme Court's power to declare statutes unconstitutional obviously carries with it the potential for major political clashes with other branches of government and major segments of the public, the Court has always sought doctrinal stances that would allow it to retreat from such clashes when it wanted to" (1968:117). On the other hand, the Court can about as easily "insist that it was especially competent, and was compelled by 'the law,' to decide those major political questions it wanted to decide rather than retreat from" (Shapiro, 1968:117). In that case,

> The problem is then essentially one of degree and timing, and when a matter is ripe for adjudication will vary on pragmatic grounds from area to area. . . . A court speaking of ripeness today is probably balancing the desirability of two sets of factors.

> Should it intervene only after the individual and the agency have come to final loggerheads, when the issues and facts are full, firm, and concrete, the injury certain not speculative, and thus when the problem is clearly and unavoidably judicial? Or should it step in to mitigate the very real damage to the interests of individuals and businesses that delay may cause in certain instances? Because of its constitutional concerns the Supreme Court has probably erred on the side of overripeness. [Shapiro, 1968:120, 121]

I would like to emphasize that by no means do I wish to imply here that courts usually differ with agency decisions. Usually they do not (Shapiro, 1968). For the sake of the argument at hand, I am elaborating what can happen in the ultimate case, when a client takes an agency to court. For one, the court can uphold agency regulations or the agency decision.[2] For another, the court may simply say that the agency has acted "illegally" regarding a straightforward point of law. Prototypically illustrating this latter issue is a report on a ruling against the state of Washington that noted: "The state overstepped legal bounds by ending a welfare program that helped tide over employable adults during hard times, a Thurston County Superior Court judge ruled. . . . Although the Department of Social and Health Services has power to cut welfare grants across the board, it doesn't have the authority to wipe out a whole program mandated by law" ("State Welfare Cut Illegal, Court Rules"). In such a case, the court is saying that an entitlement exists, independent of the generousness of its actual content. For a third, the court might go beyond strict statute construction and say that an agency's actions, in fact, an agency's regulations, are not in keeping with the "spirit of the law" by which the agency was given authority to act. From here the court may go on to declare that the type of benefit at issue is a right of every citizen. At this point the court has engaged in interpretation of the law, and the type of benefit at stake can gain legitimation as socially rightful. This happened in *Goldberg* v. *Kelly* in which it was ruled that an individual must have an evidentiary hearing before assistance may be terminated, for eligibles, the Court emphasized, have a right to such assistance (see below). But I am jumping ahead of the story: we shall first consider what happened during the 1960s to raise the probability that a case such as *Goldberg* would be accepted by the Supreme Court for review.

The Strengthening of Entitlization in the United States during the 1960s

Kirsten A. Gronbjerg (1977) has observed that the 1960s were a "water shed in the extension of citizenship" in the United States (see also Piven and Cloward, 1972; Baum, 1974; Wilensky, 1975; Janowitz, 1976). Writing of that era, she states that "rules concerning eligibility for public assistance under the Social Security Act had rarely before been subject to court interpretation" (1977:122). In turn, "there is some reason to think that court decisions . . . have succeeded in preventing arbitrary or illegal denials of aid to eligible recipients" (Gronbjerg, 1977:122). The events leading up to these decisions encompassed forces in the larger society that, in turn, precipitated a modicum of entitlization of recipients of public assistance. These processes, events, and redefinitions of the situation created an atmosphere that encouraged court review of such cases on an increasing scale.

Piven and Cloward (1972) are detailed in their portrayal of this atmosphere under the Johnson administration. One of the many programs generated by the EOA was the Community Action Program (CAP). As part of CAP, the Office of Economic Opportunity sponsored approximately one thousand Community Action Agencies (CAAs) during the 1960s. The CAAs, or "storefront service centers" as they were called, became nexes around which gathered social workers, lawyers, churchmen, students, and slum dwellers (Piven and Cloward, 1972:288). The lawyers in particular helped potential and actual claimants deal with public agencies. In so doing, "the attorneys challenged a great variety of welfare decisions" (Piven and Cloward, 1972:292).

In these challenges were the underpinnings of legalization: for example, lawyers undertook group action that implicitly forced the articulation of a rule or standard by the agency. Rather than bargaining with the welfare agencies for winter clothing allotments for each of fifty families, lawyers bargained just once on behalf of an aggregate of fifty (Piven and Cloward, 1972:293). Piven and Cloward speak of these assaults upon irrationalized administration as changes generated "from below," that is, from neighborhood action through the CAAs up through the actions of lawyers in relationship to the agencies. Correlatively, they speak of the effect of court decisions upon welfare administration as emanating "from above": "A series of judicial decisions in the 1960's had the effect of undermining some of the regulations by which relief rolls have been kept down. For decades, reformers had lobbied unsuccessfully for legislative repeal of residence laws, man-in-the-house rules, and employable-mother rules. But in the 1960's these ... were washed away by one court decision after another" (1972:306).

That court review forced welfare administration to become more rationalized is beyond a doubt, as evidenced by HEW rule changes in the wake of the "Fleming Ruling" (1961). The "Fleming Ruling" said "that states cannot deprive children of welfare because of the behavior of their parents" (Gronbjerg, 1977:46). After that HEW "ruled that in order for states to obtain federal matching funds for foster children, *all* AFDC children in the state had to receive maximum grants. . . . This was an attempt to prevent the states from shifting children to the foster care segment of the AFDC program by using the suitable home clause as a punitive measure" (Gronbjerg, 1977:46). Next, in *Golden Gate Welfare Rights Organization* v. *Born* (1972) the court ruled that "the welfare department must take your application and they cannot take longer than thirty days from the time you first ask for food stamps to decide whether or not you will get them" (Law, 1974:119–20).

Thus, cases such as *Golden Gate* revealed and halted the arbitrary, unsystematic, or otherwise "irrationalized" nature of administrative regulations. As I noted briefly in Chapter 7, rationalized regulations are ideally impartial and impersonal, as are rationalized laws. By forcing administrative regulations to become more rationalized, the *Golden Gate* case indirectly enhanced individual rights: such rulings helped establish the citizen's right to rationalized administration of the legally relevant relationships between himself and his sovereign, as represented by the agency. Viewed in this light, it is clear that rationalized administration helps make the law's guarantee more effective and is therefore an extension of the formal rationality of the law. Rationalized administration brings clarity, predictability, logic, and consistency to the citizen-sovereign relationship, the very traits that imbue law with formal rationality. The advance toward rationalized administration and the extension of the formal rationality of the law were thus major outcomes of the strengthening of entitlization during the 1960s.

The Increasingly Closer Articulation
of Entitlements and Rights

Weber's description of the relationship between administrative "reflexes" and full-fledged rights anticipated the subtle and elusive character of the transition that the United States has been experiencing from the 1960s to the present:

> We have previously defined the existence of a right as being
> no more than an increase of the probability that a certain
> expectation of the one to whom the law grants the right will not
> be disappointed. We shall continue to consider the creation of
> a right as the normal method of increasing such a probability, but
> we must recognize . . . that there is but a gradual transition from
> this normal case to the situation where transition from this normal case to the situation where the legally secured interest of a
> party is but the "reflex" of a "regulation" and where the party
> does not possess a "right" in the strict sense. [1968:667]

In *King* v. *Smith* (1968) we encounter yet a slightly more advanced point on the continuum that runs from gratuities to rights. *King* v. *Smith* required states to grant aid to a child regardless of the status of the substitute father, where the family income was insufficient. No longer could state administrative agencies assume that a substitute father's income was available to support a child (Gronbjerg, 1977:45). While manifestly forcing administration to become more rationalized with regard to the overseeing of availability of material support for children, this decision latently endorsed the "right" of children to a modicum of security. Such court decisions made the notion of the security of children a safe enough part of the political environment that Nixon felt encouraged to propose a program such as FAP though, as the demise of the proposed legislation became imminent, Nixon did not force the issue. It is no coincidence that Bowler (1974) and others referred to FAP as "a guaranteed income for the nation's children."

   Anderson v. *Burson* (N.D. Ga. 1968) and *Shapiro* v. *Thompson* (1969) made certain that administrative rules and regulations by which potential recipients would be entitled to assistance did not clash with long-established civil rights. The compatibility of entitlements with rights was reinforced when *Anderson* v. *Burson* struck down as illegal work rules that were unfair and unequal. Prior to this ruling the state of Georgia would terminate welfare payments to blacks during the cotton-chopping season. The state insisted that there was work available for everyone and that cotton chopping was suitable work for black mothers. A federal court declared this approach illegal for various reasons, among which, there might not be enough work for everyone, or a particular mother might not be suited to such field work and even if so, she might not make enough to support her family. Finally, the court ruled that "field work is no more 'suitable' for black people than it is for white" (Law, 1974:71). In turn, *Shapiro v. Thompson* declared unconstitutional the requirement that an applicant for general assistance must have lived in the state for one year prior to the claim. The grounds were that such a requirement interfered with interstate travel (Gronbjerg, 1977:43). Thus, although the court did not explicitly grant the right to general assistance, it guaranteed that the condition for receiving it would not be incompatible with the right to freedom of movement.

Civil rights were the first content of individual rights (Chapter 3); thus any rationale that links enjoyment of benefits to civil rights (either directly or by making certain that the enjoyment of benefits does not clash with civil rights) enhances the legitimacy of the benefits so enjoyed. This reasoning is consistent with the argument I presented in Chapter 4: namely, the guarantee and the legitimacy of a regime's law grows stronger the more the law's various legally relevant principles are synthesized with one another. *Goldberg* v. *Kelly* embodies such a synthesis.

Goldberg v. *Kelly*: A Turning Point

Goldberg v. *Kelly* was a genuine judicial turning point in the rationalization of assistance as not charitable, but rightful. The rationale behind *Goldberg* went far to associate assistance with the other rights of citizenship, thus imbuing certain types of benefits with the character of social rights. As touched upon earlier, "The Supreme Court was faced with the narrow but important question of whether the due process clause required that the recipient be afforded an evidentiary hearing before the termination of benefits. For thirty years that question, as a matter of administrative practice, had been answered in the negative by the Social Security Administration. In 1970 the Supreme Court held otherwise, in sharp, unequivocal language" (Baum, 1974:16). Indeed, assistance is here divorced from charity, from patronization, from any attitude of superiority on the part of the government vis-à-vis the citizen. Rather, assistance is associated with both the dignity of the individual and due process of law, becoming, under these particular circumstances, a social right. The Court stated:

> We agree with the District Court that when welfare is discontinued, only a pre-termination evidentiary hearing provides the recipient with procedural due process. . . . For qualified recipients, welfare provides the means to obtain essential food, clothing, housing, and medical care. . . . Thus the crucial factor in this context—a factor not present in the case of the blacklisted government contractor, the discharged government employee, the taxpayer denied a tax exemption, or virtually anyone else whose governmental entitlements are ended—is that termination of aid pending resolution of a controversy over eligibility may deprive an *eligible* recipient of the very means by which to live while he waits. Since he lacks independent resources, his situation becomes immediately desperate. His need to concentrate upon finding the means for daily subsistence, in turn, adversely affects his ability to seek redress from the welfare bureaucracy.
>
> Moreover, important governmental interests are promoted by affording recipients a pre-termination evidentiary hearing. From its founding the Nation's basic commitment has been to foster the dignity and well-being of all persons within its borders. We have come to recognize that forces not within the control of the poor contribute to their poverty. This perception, against the background of our traditions, has significantly influenced the development of the contemporary public assistance system. Welfare, by meeting the basic demands of subsistence, can help bring within the reach of the poor the same opportunities that are available to others to participate meaningfully in the life of the community. At the same time, welfare guards against the societal malaise that may flow from a widespread sense of unjustified frustration and insecurity. Public assistance, then, is not mere charity, but a means to "promote the general Welfare, and secure the Blessings of Liberty to ourselves and our Posterity." The same governmental interests that counsel the provision of welfare, counsel as well its uninterrupted provision to those eligible to receive it; pre-termination evidentiary hearings are indispensable to that end. [as cited in Baum, 1974:16–17]

Due Process as the Solvent for "Executive Justice"

With this mention of the core feature of the *Goldberg* decision and its emphasis on due process, we are now able to pick up important threads of the argument first treated in Chapter 7. Namely, how can the gap between administrative adjudication and regular court adjudication be bridged in the modern era when the former is indispensable to the operation of a complex welfare state? Due process is a central element in such a bridge. Of major importance in the *Goldberg* decision is that the Court related specific criteria for fair hearings to the ideal of due process of law. In so doing, it colored in a gray area that had long characterized the U.S. administrative picture. Writing in 1963, Woll stated:

> As presently defined, in order for due process to be operative
> in administrative proceedings, private parties must have oppor-
> tunity for recourse to the formal hearing stage within the agency,
> for only at that stage are procedures sufficiently formalized and
> opportunity present for further appeal to the judicial branch.
> Unfortunately, aside from these general observations, it is impos-
> sible to define with any degree of precision standards of due
> process in administrative law. The District of Columbia Court of
> Appeals noted in the 1942 case of *NBC v. FCC*: "Nor has it
> been made clear by judicial decision what constitutes a minimum
> compliance with the due process in the way of administrative
> hearing." . . . Although the Administrative Procedure Act was
> designed to remedy this situation, the indefiniteness of standards
> of due process remains today. [p. 22]

The Court replaced indefiniteness with specific standards in 1970. These standards concerned the conditions surrounding hearing and notice, the probability that the judgment would be impartially adjudicated within the agency, the right to counsel, the right to confront adverse witnesses, and the right to know the reasons for the agency's determination as well as the evidence that was used as the basis for the ruling (Baum, 1974:17–18; Law, 1974:72–79). Before the ruling, the welfare agency in New York City failed to allow the recipient to appear personally or to face and cross-examine adverse witnesses. The Court noted this and was quite specific about the unfairness of the expectation that welfare recipients reply to charges in writing or second-hand through a caseworker (Baum, 1974:17).

It is important to be aware of the historical background against which the *Goldberg* ruling stands out practically in neon letters. We saw that in the early days of U.S. assistance to citizens the question of how citizens might be protected from agencies did not arise. This is truly a modern query in the sense that the idea that benefits are rightful, not just charitable, is a modern idea. Nevertheless, lawyers and others especially oriented toward the protection of civil liberties have always been concerned with this question, as was evident in the proposal of the Walter-Logan Bill. This was an early attempt to proceed in the direction of the destination reached with the *Goldberg* case.

The Walter-Logan Bill. The Walter-Logan Bill, which was vetoed by FDR in 1940, was an early effort to introduce protections to citizens in their relationships with administrative agencies. But the bill was inflexible and unrealistic: "The effect of the bill would have been to make *any* administrative decision reviewable by the courts. The bill was a direct outgrowth of the common-law insistence upon the supremacy of law, and upon the right of the citizen to appeal to the 'ordinary' courts of the land government actions which purportedly violate constitutional or legal rights. . . . The bill attempted to safeguard the citizen by remaking the administrative process in the judicial image" (Woll, 1963:20). The flaws of this approach to guarding citizens' rights have been fully documented (Woll, 1963; Wheeler, 1965; Shapiro, 1968; Handler, 1966), and in general, they expand upon FDR's sentiments in his veto: "The conventional processes of the courts are not adapted to handling controversies in the mass. . . . All laymen and most lawyers recognize the inappropriateness of entrusting routine processes of government to the outcome of neverending lawsuits" (quoted in Woll, 1963:25). In short, administrative agencies and courts each simply have different tasks in the societal division of labor, and forcing agencies to become more like courts by no means resolves the dilemma.

Early U.S. Incognizance toward Professionalized Administration. Before dismissing the Walter-Logan Bill as a ludicrous solution to a very real problem, however, a point raised by Alan Wolfe in *The Limits of Legitimacy* (1977) may be mentioned here. Wolfe has called attention to the accident of U.S. history that inextricably entwined notions of rulership with notions of laissez-faire. Specifically, Wolfe argues that U.S. political philosophy was heavily steeped in conceptualizations that denied that anyone was controlling the state. Ergo, the question of professionalizing (in my terms, "rationalizing") administration never arose at the outset of U.S. history:

> Consequently the promotion of uniform standards of justice, criteria for government service, the rules for dispensing public largesse had been passed over in favor of a system that allowed the strong to take control of administration for their own private ends. . . . In America the absence of a public administration was ideological; since the state was not supposed to be used, even though it was being used, it made little sense to professionalize the task of administering it. . . . Laissez faire and vast corruption go well together; the periods of the greatest success of the one also saw the greatest amount of the other. [1977:66, 68]

By contrast, "England was different; there the rise of the Administrative Reform Association, plus the Benthamite concern with a constitutional code, underscored the preoccupation of a new class with matters of administration" (Wolfe, 1977:66). Though Samuel P. Huntington (1966) would not give the same reasons as those adduced by Wolfe for the United States's early lack of preoccupation with rationalized administration, he, too, notes that "the rationalization of authority and the differentiation of structure were slower and less complete in America than they were in Europe" (reprinted in Bendix, 1968:90). Huntington's discussion of the differentiation of structure roughly corresponds to Weber's distinction between authority by administration or through use of adjudication procedures, as well as to my discussion of the attributes of rationalized administration. In any case, compared to Britain, France, Germany, and Scandinavia, the pace in the United States has been lethargic. Perhaps, then, the drastic measures proposed in the Walter-Logan Bill were but a swing of the pendulum from the nineteenth to the twentieth century in the politicization of concern for better administration in the United States.

Early Attention to Due Process in Britain. In contemporary Britain there is continuing concern with improving the position of the citizen vis-à-vis the processes of administrative adjudication (Eimicke, 1973; Street, 1975). Nevertheless, British attention to ideals of due process and its institutionalization at the administrative level made an early showing by way of the National Health Insurance Act in 1911: "The 1911 Act set up special tribunals to handle contested claims for unemployment benefits. These tribunals worked exceptionally well, so much so that the sceptical became convinced that the judges were not the only ones who could do justice in disputes between the government and the public. These unemployment tribunals became the pattern for many others" (Street, 1975:2). The belief that only judges could do justice, so rigid in the United States, was less entrenched in Britain.

In turn, the belief that only formal court procedures could result in "just" decisions was also a less firmly fixed idea in the early twentieth-century British mind. In 1932, the notion of "natural justice" was elaborated in the Report of the Committee on Ministers' Powers: "It is beyond doubt that there are certain canons of judicial conduct to which all tribunals and persons who have to give judicial or quasi-judicial decisions ought to conform. The principles on which they rest are . . . implicit in the rule of law" (quoted in Woll, 1963:183). Natural justice involves (1) impartiality ("a man cannot be judge in his own cause"), (2) hearing and notice ("no party ought to be condemned unheard" and "he must know in good time"), (3) a person must know the reason for the decision made in his case, and (4) a person must know the nature of any material or recommendations made at an initial administrative level that is taken into account by officials authorized to render a final decision (Woll, 1963:183–84). The committee noted that no one procedure, either of notice or of hearing, need be regarded as fundamental: ministers or tribunals need not use procedures identical to those used by the courts to achieve natural justice. Therefore, an early foundation was established in Britain for the ideal that justice could be done without using a formal court procedure, as long as certain tenets consistent with the "rule of law" were incorporated into the decision-making procedure. Combined with the success of the tribunals set up after the 1911 act, the British had paved their own pathway for combining informality with due process within the context of an expanded tribunal system after World War II.

At least one other set of circumstances hastened the British toward an elaborated tribunal system in the late 1940s. The empirical experience from 1897 to 1946 of trying all workmen's compensation cases "by the ordinary courts in the usual way" was heavily disillusioning. The exclusive use of the courts "proved disastrous. For instance, thousands of cases were taken to appeal on one point alone. . . . The law became extremely complicated and detailed, and bitterness between workmen and employers resulted" (Street, 1975:11). With the emergence of the British welfare state in toto, however, an overarching tribunal system was institutionalized following the Beveridge Committee's review of the social services. Street writes: "What has emerged is a comprehensive parliamentary scheme of social security administered by the Department of Health and Social Security. There is a uniform machinery for handling claims to the various forms of benefit: sickness benefit, retirement pensions, death grants, family allowances, industrial injury benefits, maternity benefits, unemployment benefits, widow's benefits, guardians' allowances and child's special allowance" (1975:12). Thus, while the United States, through its 1946 Administrative Procedure Act, was making fledgling attempts to grapple with due process in administration, the British were already crystallizing that principle in a tribunal system that flexibly combined informality and rule of law within the context of "natural justice."

I need not reiterate here Street's (1975:12–17) detailed description of the procedures by which the tribunal system works. Suffice to note that "the tribunal does everything possible to make claimants feel at ease" (Street, 1975:16), whereas, by contrast,

> Unless a litigant engages a lawyer he is never at ease in court. The judge is aloof, the procedure is formal, there is an atmosphere of uncomfortable dignity. A man likes to be able to have his say in his own way, unrestrained by the niceties of the rule against hearsay evidence and the rest. He does not want to be reprimanded every time—and it will be often—that he fails to distinguish between cross-examining a witness and making a point in his own favour. Administrative tribunals are sufficiently informal to permit these liberties; courts never are. Many believe that a man ought not to be compelled to pay for legal representation in order to get a fair hearing of his case. [1975:9]

Goldberg: A Convergence with British Tradition. The *Goldberg* decision unmistakably coincides with tenets of natural justice as mentioned above and converges upon the types of assumptions that underlie the British tribunal system. That is, formality and rigidity are by no means synonymous with justice. The concept transcended the specific forms that had evolved in the United States to implement it. Justice underwent substantive rationalization, its "kernel" ferreted out by the judges. In *Goldberg* the Court ruled:

Written submissions are an unrealistic option for most recipients, who lack the educational attainment necessary to write effectively and who cannot obtain professional assistance. Moreover, written submissions do not afford the flexibility of oral presentations; they do not permit the recipient to mold his argument to the issues the decision maker appears to regard as important. Particularly where credibility and veracity are at issue, as they must be in many termination proceedings, written submissions are a wholly unsatisfactory basis for decision. The secondhand presentation to the decision maker by the caseworker has its own deficiencies; since the caseworker usually gathers the facts upon which the charge of ineligibility rests, the presentation of the recipient's side of the controversy cannot safely be left to him. Therefore, a recipient must be allowed to state his position orally. Informal procedures will suffice; in this context due process does not require a particular order of proof or mode of offering evidence. [Quoted in Baum, 1974:18–19]

The convergence of notions of due process and fair hearings in the United States with the assumptions underlying natural justice and the tribunal system in Britain is consistent with the fact that both nations share a common-law heritage. Woll has noted that due process was long ago identified with common-law procedures: "In the development of the common law the courts have decided that although due process does not necessarily mean judicial process, fundamental judicial procedures of *notice and hearing* should be preserved" (1963:23). In fact, "ideally, under the terms of traditional common-law theory, *judicial* review must be maintained over administrative adjudication. The possibility of such review should be open, even if rarely used, for a system to be in accordance with common-law doctrine" (Woll, 1963: 184). *Goldberg*, in effect, was a reaffirmation of the United States's common-law legacy, central to which is the ideal of "supremacy of the law," the very antithesis of "executive justice."

Due Process: A Panacea?

From the description I have given of due process as a pivotal notion facilitating "legitimation from below," it may appear that due process is a panacea for the various disjunctures noted in Chapter 7. Indeed, I have shown how it is possible, analytically speaking, for due process to bridge the gap between (1) entitlements and rights, (2) rationalized administrative law and rationalized civil and statute law, and (3) administrative adjudication and regular adjudication. Rejoicing, however, would be premature. Unfortunately, this bridge is literally stopgap (temporary). It cannot be a long-term solution to the larger dilemma.

For one, there are far more adversarial claims between agencies and clients over potential benefits than could possibly be adjudicated by the regular court system (see Chapter 7). The few cases that have been tried so far have been crucial to maintaining the rule of law at a point in U.S. history when other solutions have not yet been devised to address the gaps between the elements in the above series of relationships. Second, as I will discuss in the next chapter, the court-agency relationship is subtle and complex. This was true during the early days of regulation, and it is even more true in the era of the redistributional state, not to mention the era of "the New Regulation" (see Chapter 11). Due process does not address such complexities, foremost among which is that when courts make interpretations that imply the implementation of costly social programs in the name of guarding individual rights, they overstep a hazy line between their own purview and that of administrative agencies. Such missteps bode ill (as I shall show) for the legitimation of social rights. Legitimation is inextricably conditioned by how much redistribution the society can afford. This is not for the courts to decide. Yet, court decisions that are indistinguishable from orders to effectuate expensive programs seriously compromise the separation of powers in the U.S. welfare state. Such decisions also compromise the integrity of budgets, federal, state, or municipal. Can benefits that flow from the court's overstepping of its authority be "legitimate"? The question can only be rhetorical.

Toward Parity among Civil, Political, and Social Rights

As the title of the present chapter indicates, the legitimation of social rights in the United States has, indeed, been facilitated by the movement, broadly speaking, from administration to adjudication. But the very nature of the terrain guarantees that such movement cannot be in a straight line, nor can the path be expected to be smooth and well-traveled. Ergo, that destination cannot rapidly be reached at which social rights are protected with the identical commitment that attaches to the protection of civil or political rights. There are compelling reasons why this is the case, and I will elaborate upon a few of them at this point, foreshadowing some of what will be discussed in Chapter 10.

First, we should remember that centuries of human struggle and institutional flux preceded the firm establishment of civil and political rights. Using this yardstick, perhaps the materialization of social rights has not been so sluggish after all.

Second, as mentioned, the concretization of social rights requires the type of societal work done by administrative apparatuses. The institutionalization of civil and political rights did not necessitate the establishment of these problematic sociopolitical units. Sharing the scale with social rights are the weighty relationships between citizen and administrative agency, thus holding down the chance of the social right to rise to the level of protection held by civil and political rights in the larger balance by which Western legal systems are measured. The weight of the citizen-agency relationship must somehow be counterbalanced in order for social rights to achieve parity with civil and political rights as elements of Western citizenship.

Third, within the Anglo-American tradition, the protection of civil and political rights has rested largely upon the common law, which has been an ingenious device for reconciling the generality of the law with the uniqueness of the individual case to achieve an admirable approximation of substantive justice under the rule of law. But the common law is an inappropriate device for addressing the types of grievances that stem from the application of the administrative rules and regulations of the regulatory and redistributional states. In such cases, the common law method of dispute resolution "is cumbersome, lengthy, and overly complex. It is tentative and indecisive, to the detriment of individual rights, because of the very excellence of its appeals system which so carefully protects individual rights in criminal proceedings. Common law adjudication is also extremely expensive. . . . A citizen should not have to run the financial gauntlet of a long common law war of attrition merely in order to force the telephone company or the Veterans' Administration to provide him with the service to which he ought to be entitled by law" (Wheeler, 1965:13–14). Wheeler (1965) points out that novel forms of injustice arise in an era of administrative law.[3] He likens the application of the common law to their resolution to operating "a complex welfare state with legal machinery appropriate to a simple agrarian society" (1965:14).

In the degree that the protection of social rights involves, largely, protecting the individual from certain consequences of the application of administrative law, the common law format is inadequate.

Analysts express this view in various ways. Harry Street, writing of the British case, states that "what is needed above all else is a cheap and speedy settlement of disputes. For these cases we do not want a Rolls-Royce system of justice" (1975:3). In particular, the adversarial approach characteristic of the common law has been singled out for criticism: "Lawyers tend to focus on restraining officials, preventing them from doing wrong by attacking through the adversary system. . . . The costs might outweigh the gains" (Handler, 1966:186). Moreover, initiative lies with the aggrieved individual or the offended public-at-large (Landis, 1966: Shapiro, 1968; Wheeler, 1965). Thus, the common law, so useful for the protection of civil and political rights in Anglo-American nations, is not necessarily well suited to the protection of social rights. It is inappropriate in that the result of using common-law procedures to protect individuals from abuses stemming from the application of administrative law appears to take the urgency out of the whole issue of citizen protection. That initiative lies with the individual and that the expenses in time and money to both individual and society are large are factors that contribute to the impression that the game of protecting social rights is hardly worth the candle. For this reason, some nations have instituted counterbalances to protect the citizen or the public from officialdom: Britain's parliamentary commissioner (Street, 1975), Sweden's ombudsman, France's conseil d'etat all fall into this category (Rowat, 1965; Gregory and Hutchesson, 1975). But these are short steps toward a distant goal.

Finally, a fourth reason why social rights have not received the same urgency of gurantee as have civil and political rights is the fact that social rights cost a fortune. They cost the "fortune" that the collectivity in question has produced in terms of the societal surplus. These costs manifest in two ways. First, there are the costs of the actual goods and services which the government assumes responsibility to guarantee its citizens.[4] Second, there are the costs of establishing, maintaining, and constantly expanding the administrative staffs who formulate the programs and put them, as the current vernacular has it, "in place."[5] As Gerhard E. Lenski (1966) has shown definitively, questions of allocating the societal surplus, once a society has produced one, are inevitably surrounded by conflicting interests, purposes, values, and the like. To guarantee social rights is to set up and defend criteria aimed at containing the ever-explosive issue of "who gets what and why." Add to this the fact that both sources of the costs of social rights are expanding, and it becomes clearer why social rights are the hand grenades of our time: at what point do Western regimes let go the humanitarian ideal before it destroys the solvency of the state? By contrast, the costs associated with the guarantee of civil and political rights are approximately the same as those associated with establishing and maintaining a solid court system. Here we are talking about a far lower figure. For these several reasons, then, it is not surprising that social rights have emerged in a halo of diffidence compared to their confidently established older siblings, civil and political rights, within the Western tradition.

Chapter 10

COURT-AGENCY RELATIONSHIPS IN

THE U.S. WELFARE STATE

LEGITIMATION PROBLEMS in the U.S. welfare state do not rest per se upon the differential sociopolitical character of entitlements versus rights. Indeed, the differences between these two allow flexibility among choices open to the redistributional state. Making a benefit "rightful" is to legally commit a portion of the budget to it in a way that makes the commitment very difficult to reverse (see below). If all benefits were rights, the overall standard of living in the society could drop drastically if redistribution were made to the point of endangering the surplus or its production. This is where the legitimation of social rights reaches its upper limit. By contrast, the discretionary element that attaches to the level of benefit that is "only" an entitlement allows the regime to cut the costs of social spending if the economy or the taxpayers so demand.[1] Thus, it is not that rights, entitlements, administrative law and regular (civil, statute, the common, or constitutional) law, administrative adjudication and regular adjudication are distinct in character that is problematic. What is problematic, as Landis (1966) would have predicted, is that the relationships between and among them are not yet clearly articulated (see Wheeler, 1965; Handler, 1979; Lowi, 1979: Preface to the 2d edition and Chapter 10). In this chapter, therefore, I will treat some important features of the court-agency relationship in the United States and the effects of these features upon both the costs and the legitimation of social rights.

Specifying Ideals for the Court-Agency Relationship

What is the ideal, or optimum, relationship between the courts and administrative agencies? "Optimum," of course, means the "most favorable," raising the question, "most favorable for what?" Therefore, (1) what would be the most favorable court-agency relationship for balancing the citizen's rights and freedoms against the undeniable need for agencies to have authority to adjudicate hundreds of thousands of cases between themselves and their clients each year? (2) what court-agency relationship would ideally maintain their mutual integrity in the governmental division of labor?

A consideration of the effect of the *Goldberg* decision upon (the former) Department of Health, Education and Welfare's fair hearing regulations serves as a departure point for addressing these two issues:

> Just before the Court's enunciation of due process principles in *Goldberg v. Kelly*, a revised set of fair hearing rules was proposed by HEW. Indeed, the Court noted this fact in its opinion, but it nevertheless preferred to test and weigh the constitutional question against state practice.
>
> As finally promulgated, the regulations of HEW were comprehensive in their substantive terms. These were given definition in fair hearing guides published by the Assistance Payments Administration of the Social and Rehabilitation Service. . . . They were designed to cover all categorical aid programs, not merely AFDC. It can be safely stated that the regulations went beyond the constitutional minima of *Goldberg v. Kelly*. Key to the new regulations was the requirement that aid could not be discontinued until after the state fair hearing decision, if it involved an issue of fact or judgment. It was this key restriction, coupled with advance notice requirements, that placed real and new responsibilities on several states. [Baum, 1974:18]

On the surface, it would appear that *Goldberg* and its aftermath represented an ideal court-agency relationship, each doing its job and enhancing citizenship rights in the bargain. In the terms I have been using throughout this argument, we could describe what happened as follows: The Social Security Administration (a subdivision of HEW) used its properly delegated authority to issue regulations concerning distribution of certain benefits to claimants. By 1970, however, social forces in recent U.S. history had brought about a redefinition of the situation involving government assistance: citizens were applying for "entitlements," not "gratuities." Accordingly, when the question of termination of the entitlement arose, as it did in *Goldberg* v. *Kelly*, the recipient had sufficient legal standing to take his case into the regular court system and, indeed, as high as the Supreme Court. The Court, in turn, elaborated a rationale that logically connected the entitlement at issue to the larger tradition of individual rights, dignity, and the government's responsibility to promote the general welfare. Thus, the assistance was a social right of eligible recipients. Denial of the benefit to eligible recipients would violate the constitutional principle of due process of law. Strictly speaking, therefore, the Court did not tell HEW and its associated welfare administrative agencies what to do. It simply told them what they could not do: they could not violate the ideal of due process of law, that is, they could not discontinue benefits without pretermination evidentiary hearings. HEW, in its turn, promulgated two new sets of regulations: one set was issued prior to *Goldberg*, possibly in anticipation of the issues to be raised by court review, and another set was issued after *Goldberg*. The post-*Goldberg* regulations went beyond the constitutional minima set forth by *Goldberg* and reflected the Court's interpretation of assistance as socially rightful.

The foregoing interpretation of the effect of *Goldberg* upon agency regulations and the expansion of social rights is adequate as far as it goes. But it is incomplete. Indeed, the Court decision imposed greater rationalization upon the administration of assistance. Certainly the rationale underlying agency regulations was forced to conform more closely to the intent of the statute as interpreted by the Court, namely, to promote the general welfare. The tone of the above interpretation implies, however, that agencies are not themselves in the business of impartially and impersonally issuing sublegislation that captures the intent of the statute by whose authority the agencies make available tangible goods services to citizens. Second, this interpretation does not account for the fact that some would think of the Court as having legislated, not merely applied, the law. Some would say that the Court's decision in *Goldberg*, in effect, committed tax dollars, a commitment only the Congress may legally undertake. The Congress delegates its authority to redistributive agencies, so they, too, have the authority to commit tax dollars in certain ways by virtue of their eligibility regulations. Ergo, some would see the Court as having usurped the prerogative of the agencies in the court-agency division of favor. After all, the practical effect of the *Goldberg* decision was to "place real and new responsibilities on several states," responsibilities that cost them dollars they could not recoup (Baum, 1974:70). Did, therefore, the relationship between courts and agencies, as represented by *Goldberg*, actually embody an ideal? The answer is, "up to a point." In the immediately following section, Courts and Agencies as Interpreters of Statutes, I will show that in various ways, the *Goldberg* decision did embody certain desirable objectives in the court-agency relationship. In the subsequent section, Courts and Agencies as Uncertain Adversaries, I will show that the implications of court decisions for both the objectives and the costs of the modern state (whether regulatory or redistributional) can have a disorienting effect upon the other branches of rule that, after all, create agencies to carry out various objectives.

Courts and Agencies as Interpreters of Statutes

To treat this issue, I shall refer to some observations made by Shapiro in *The Supreme Court and Administrative Agencies* (1968). Shapiro has noted that debates over jurisdiction between courts and agencies are debates over which consequences a judge should concern himself with and which he should leave to others (pp. 84–85). Traditionally, courts have concerned themselves with issues of law, not fact. Agencies, with their specialized staffs, were presumed to have the facts well in hand. This was especially true during the era when agencies were predominantly regulatory: issues of fact involved, for example, complicated rate structures and had policy implications clearly far beyond the Court's purview (Landis, 1966).

Various authors have noted that the division between matters of "fact" and of "law" is not as clear-cut as it appears (Dickinson, 1927; Landis, 1966; Woll, 1963; Shapiro, 1968). Using this traditional dichotomy to anticipate whether a court will review, or should review, is not recommended by contemporary analysts. Shapiro states that the rationale of review lies at the substantive level of whether a given administrative policy does or does not need a second decision (p. 108). In this regard, Shapiro employs the term "double decision making" to capture the fundamental nature of the court-agency relationship. As he sees it, both agencies and courts are concerned with statutory intent (p. 45). In fact, "both agencies and courts engage in supplementary lawmaking as a necessary intermediate step between the statute and the determination of individual rights and duties under the statute" (p. 47). Seen in this context, courts and agencies are not natural enemies to be examined in terms of some type of predatory political ecology. Rather, they are two of several societal institutions that collectively constitute "the statute maker" (p. 18). The "statute maker" is a construct introduced by Shapiro as "a simplifying device reflecting a complex reality" (p. 20). That reality comprises the Congress, pressure groups, citizens, the president, executive departments, agencies, and the courts.

Empirically, therefore, the potential antagonism between courts and agencies becomes muted by the fact that both institutions are concerned to interpret statutes passed by the legislature. In addition, the authority of each is bounded by the statute (pp. 51, 99). Their respective interpretations of the statute differ not because judges are impartial and administrators are not. Rather, judges are generalists and administrators, specialists only of necessity. As generalists, judges' task in the division of labor is to bring perspective and proportion to the decision-making process (p. 52). As mentioned above, the task of the administrator is to "get the job done." In "getting the job done," administrators make interpretations of statutes.

Shapiro emphasizes (as do other authors—see Woll, 1963; Mashaw et al., 1978) that, by and large, courts support the interpretations made by administrative agencies (pp. 264–71). The question arises as to when double decision making "should" take place. Both courts and agencies are in the fundamental business of statute interpretation, thus, when "should" the courts do all over again what agencies have already done? Shapiro is explicit:

> Where the courts' more general perspective will yield better policy results than the more specialized views of the agency, the process of double decision is justified. . . . Judges do and should intervene when the decision to be made would benefit from the greater perspective of the generalist. They do not and should not intervene where only the specialist is capable of making the judgment. And they should not intervene where they find that the specialist has maintained sufficient perspective not to need the correction of the generalist. This last point is important. The wastes of double decision should not occur simply because a given question is of the sort that a generalist can understand and handle, but only when the specialist is not handling it well because of excessive parochialism engendered by his specialization. Thus it is not enough to examine the nature of the question. The nature and current attitudes of the agency are also crucial.
>
> This is precisely why judicial review of administrative decision

does not fall into neat and eternally fixed categories arranged by legal subject matter. The capacity of any given agency to see things in broad perspective is a crucial factor in determining judicial intervention or withdrawal, and that capacity may change from time to time. Thus courts may quite rightly intervene at one time where they have quite rightly refused to intervene at another. [pp. 98–99. This position was anticipated by Landis, 1966:152–54.]

To return, therefore, to the query, "Did *Goldberg* represent an ideal court-agency relationship?" the answer is (1) "Yes, in the degree that the Court brought a generalist perspective to the issue of citizens' rights"; (2) "Yes, in the degree that the agencies were concerned with the more narrow (but nevertheless important) issue of costs over and above the broader issue of individual rights." Baum has noted that in the Court's decision, "Fiscal considerations were not deemed to outweigh individual need. It was not that the Court denied the legitimacy of such considerations. It was simply that the Court felt that innovation and flexibility might allow the state to meet its fiscal obligations and, at the same time, serve the interest of the individual dependent on welfare" (1974:17). In turn, to the question, "Did the Court engage in judicial legislation, usurping congressional and agency prerogatives?" the answer is, "Strictly speaking, no." The Court declared benefit cutoffs without pretermination hearings unconstitutional and therefore illegal. That the effect of this decision could cost the states money is a separate issue (see below). Shapiro's stance is relevant here: "That old lawyers saw that 'hard cases make bad law' also comes down to this. Where the old law (the status quo) yields at least minimally acceptable results, it will be retained. Where a concrete case shows that the old law is yielding intolerable social results . . . courts will move from the old law even if they cannot formulate exactly what the new law should be. Hard cases make not bad law but new, and therefore frequently incomplete, law" (1968:87). Lowi's (1969, 1979) call for "juridical democracy" at the conclusion of *The End of Liberalism* reinforces Shapiro's view of the courts as a major locus of correction for laws that do not serve well. Rather than the Court's having usurped congressional or agency powers, in fact, the *Goldberg* decision was "one of principle and not implementation, which . . . requires administrative support at both the federal and state levels" (Baum, 1974:70).

The Aftermath of Goldberg. Nevertheless, such support was not entirely forthcoming. States immediately began, and continued, to oppose the HEW fair hearing regulations. They did so because they were not going to be reimbursed by the federal government for payments given to claimants who were later found to be ineligible (Baum, 1974: 22). Here is something of a gray area in which the federal government was by no means legally bound to reimburse the states (which is to say that the courts do not have the power to legislate), yet by deciding not to do so, federal policy influenced the implementation of the law at the state level. For by 1973, HEW yielded to the state requests for the establishment of local rather than state evidentiary hearings, and this permitted earlier benefit cutoffs (Baum, 1974:70).

In analyzing the issues and events that formed the aftermath of *Goldberg*, Baum, writing in the early 1970s, converged upon the general conclusion reached by Shapiro in the late 1960s: courts and agencies are both interpreters of statutes. Furthermore, "the law can accept a range for legitimate interpretation and enforcement of statute" (Baum, 1974:72). Within that range, political judgments determine the variability and direction of interpretation: "The regulations in no small measure reflect political judgments as to the nonlegal values at issue. . . . To an administration that sees welfare as a right, the determination of eligibility will likely be on the basis of claimant declaration. . . . To an administration that sees welfare as counterproductive of a vigorous society, self-declaration will not suffice. Investigation, detailed questioning, and time for analysis will all be allowed" (Baum, 1974:71). In fact, Gronbjerg's massive empirical study of the states' separately administered AFDC programs, written three years later, corroborated Baum's statement. She referred to states that see welfare as a right as having a "mass society" approach to assistance and states that see welfare as counterproductive as using a "stratification approach." She found that between 1960 and 1970 "welfare rolls rose predominantly in the states with high mass society status" (1977:155): "A state's mass society status and the selective extension of citizenship associated with it are thus important in accounting for the variation in AFDC eligibility requirements: who is granted fuller citizenship and under what conditions. The importance of these concerns is also apparent from the nature of the eligibility requirements themselves" (1977:156). Gronbjerg's results thus provide the factual basis for such statements as that made by Meenaghan and Washington (1980:232–35) that "concept selection" has much to do with the benefits received by claimants.

"Concept selection," "political judgments," "supplementary statute making"—all are ways of referring to the fact that

> the values and problems surrounding AFDC fair hearings
> will remain, whatever regulations are promulgated by HEW. . . .
> But this is not to say that the regulations on their face can go
> directly against the Constitution, as interpreted by the Supreme
> Court. . . . Nor do we mean to say that HEW willingly would
> institute administrative practices designed to subvert either the
> Constitution or statute. The point is simply that both the Con-
> stitution and statute are subject to interpretation. As the agency
> administering the statute, HEW must render the initial interpre-
> tation. The nature of that interpretation is in no small way
> dependent upon the values held by the agency decision makers.
> . . . HEW regulations in the area of fair hearings will change
> as administrations change. [Baum, 1974:72, 71]

To this Shapiro would reply that when the values of the agency decision makers are the values of the specialist, then the generalist perspective represented by the courts (that is, double decision making) is called for. Thus, the optimum relationship between agencies and courts in the United States, one that respects the function of each in the societal division of labor, one that balances individual rights against the need for, and the needs of, administrative adjudication, is undoubtedly a relationship in which the generalist perspective of the courts is available when needed. That "need" should be discoverable through an institutional framework that allows adversarial claims between agencies and clients to enter into the regular court system or any functional equivalent in which adjudication can be independent of the administrative processes.

Courts and Agencies as Uncertain Adversaries

Regrettably, the legitimation of social rights in the United States is by no means a simple matter of keeping the courts open for review so that landmark cases such as *Goldberg* might emerge. True, *Goldberg* was a decision of principle, not implementation. But other court cases in the

name of social rights to minimum standards of service delivery have
been decisions of implementation (Glazer, 1978). Such cases have
raised thoroughly disquieting questions regarding the costs of the welfare state, as well as the government institution(s) upon which responsibilities for these costs must be fixed. Leaving aside the issue
that some of these court-imposed costs may be disproportional to the
benefits received by citizens (see Horowitz, 1977; Glazer, 1978), fixing
responsibility for costs has much to do with the legitimizing of welfare
state outlays, as the literature unendingly reveals (Baum, 1974; Heclo,
1974; Heidenheimer, Heclo, and Adams, 1975; Friedman and Friedman, 1980; Meenaghan and Washington, 1980). Having established
that the court-agency relationship in the United States has had an
important effect upon the legitimation of social rights, I must now put
this limited observation in its place in a larger court-agency picture.
This larger picture will show the as yet incompletely cultivated portion
of the terrain jointly claimed by courts and agencies. This incomplete
cultivation can be inferred from the misgivings with which certain
court decisions have been greeted from the earliest days of the court-
agency relationship.

The Principled Isolation of Courts. One source of these misgivings has
to do with the fact that court decisions, in their principled isolation,
may have effects that are counter to the public good as defined by the
executive or legislature. This was immediately noted by Landis in
the aforementioned 1938 classic, *The Administrative Process.* Nor
has this point escaped contemporary analysts (Wheeler, 1965; Street,
1975; Horowitz, 1977; Glazer, 1978). If we accept Landis's (1966)
and others' (Weaver, 1978) image of the administrative agency as a
policy tool oriented toward public objectives through the discharge
of certain responsibilities, it becomes clear why the courts, at inter-
mittent junctures throughout history, have been actively proscribed by
statute from reviewing agency decisions. Shapiro (1968:261) captures
the essence of the situation that developed in the 1930s when he writes
that "regulatory statutes represent an uneasy compromise between
laissez faire and government controlled visions of the economy."
This "uneasy compromise" immediately manifested as an antagonistic
court-agency relationship:

> Courts, staffed by successful lawyers most of whom had
> been representing business interests, tended to be hostile to

administrative activity. Administrative agencies were, quite naturally, staffed largely by men with a commitment to government programs, and this was particularly true in the first years of a new agency's operation when it was likely to have to litigate most frequently. These phenomena were most marked in the New Deal period when a Democratic administration was creating a host of new agencies and reviving old ones to carry out bold, new government programs, and staffing them with a host of new men of liberal-to-radical persuasion, while the courts were largely staffed with conservative judges and the Supreme Court labored under a conservative majority. [Shapiro, 1968:92]

Shapiro is insistent that this struggle rested not upon the contradictory nature of courts and agencies, for both are concerned with statute interpretation (see above). Indeed, in time, "most of the conflict disappeared as the staffs of both courts and agencies came to share the consensus that has built up around the moderate and pragmatic liberalism of the New Deal" (Shapiro, 1968:92). Long before this conflict began to recede, however, Congress passed statutes that made certain administrative orders "unreviewable" (Shapiro, 1968:125; see also Woll, 1963:20–21). Unreviewable orders meant that courts could not tamper with public policy as formulated by the legislature or the executive. Agencies were thus given "an assemblage of rights normally exercisable by government as a whole" (Landis, 1966:15).

Though escape from the purview of the courts was attempted in the United States through the institution of unreviewable orders, still this attempt was much hampered by the federal structure of our system. Wheeler elucidates as follows:

Had the theory of the American Constitution incorporated a clear doctrine of the sovereignty of the federal legislature, for example, the self-restraint tradition of the high courts of England might have migrated to America along with the common law. However, the opposite occurred. Sovereignty was split up between executive, legislature, judiciary, states, and people. Conflicts between them could have been left unresolved. . . . But conflict over the proper order of precedence arose constantly before the Court. The fact that they were presented in adversary proceedings made it almost inevitable that the Court would "discover" the law implicit in the relations among American governmental institutions. [1965:10]

The advent of administrative law aggravated this inherent conflict among the separate elements of the sovereign U.S. government.

Indeed, observers of the British scene similarly noted that judges often "brought to statutory interpretation nineteenth century notions of the inviolability of property" (Street, 1975:6). The judges "would lean over backwards to find that a statute had not taken away an individual's property rights, even if expropriation for public purposes on payment of compensation was the aim of the Act." For this reason, "Ministers and their top civil servant advisers have in this century frequently come to doubt whether the courts are the appropriate body to decide many of these new cases. They see rightly that many of these disputes are not merely about private rights: the public good on the one hand and the interest of the particular citizen on the other must be weighed in the balance. They look at many decisions in the courts . . . and find them wanting in that they appear to disregard the social element in a problem." Thus, in Britain, there was an early "movement away from the courts" (Street, 1975:5). Nonetheless, though for reasons not identical with those that apply to the United States, the rise and expansion of administrative law is problematic in Britain as well. A clue as to the reason why administrative law is problematic lies in the nature of the circumstances that gave rise to it: "The administrative process is, in essence, our generation's answer to the inadequacy of the judicial and the legislative processes. It represents our effort to find an answer to those inadequacies by some other method than merely increasing executive power" (Landis, 1966:46). In the light of the issues just discussed, a prophetic point made by Landis takes on added importance: "The most superficial criticism which can be directed toward the development of the administrative process is that which bases its objections merely upon numerical growth. . . . Increasing their [the agencies'] number of itself need not disturb us, provided that the relationships between them, and in turn their relationship to the other departments of government, are properly resolved" (1966:24).

The relationship between agencies and courts, ambiguous at the outset, threatens to grow more snarled in the era of the welfare state. At least with regard to the Old Regulation, using Paul H. Weaver's (1978) term,[2] courts eventually came to accept that the intricacies of securities regulation, rate making, and the like required the perspective of the administrative specialist: "Incredible areas of fact may be involved in the disposition of a business problem that calls not only for legal intelligence but also for wisdom in the ways of industrial operation" (Landis, 1966:31). Judicial restraint could, perhaps, be more easily maintained with regard to a regulatory law described by Wheeler as being "technical, intricate, and detailed in statement. . . . If a new meaning, that is, a new regulation, is to be provided, it is up to the legislature or the administrative authority to do so, not the courts. Difficulties of interpretation, application, or enforcement are not met through judicial legislation, though administrative courts may call attention to the need for legislative renovation" (1965:11). Such, however, has not recently been the case with regard to the regulations promulgated by administrative units discharging the commodities and services associated with the welfare state.

Judges knew they were unwise in the ways of industrial operations and economic laws.[3] They know they are expert, however, in guarding constitutional rights. Yet Nathan Glazer has contended that, in the name of protecting such rights, the contemporary court "has moved from greater rights to smaller rights; from greater wrongs to lesser wrongs; and from rights to policy with no relation to rights" (1978:71). In turn, the ambiguity and issues surrounding judicial restraint are aggravated by the federal structure of the U.S. government. The increasing role of the U.S. courts in the matter of school desegregation provides a case in point: "Overcoming Southern state resistance to school desegregation offered judges a model justifying detailed administrative intervention in order to make constitutional rights effective" (Glazer, 1978:69). State noncompliance has inspired court orders to become more and more specific until the border was crossed between judicial orders asserting rights and detailed judicial provisions for implementation. Citing Horowitz's *The Courts and Social Policy* (1977), Glazer describes the quickening trend in which courts are moving from procedural requirements or prohibitions to administrative orders of implementation: "Horowitz points out that Judge Johnson's decision on mental hospitals was responsible for raising the state's [Alabama's] annual expenditure 'from $14 million before the suit was filed in 1971 to $59 million in 1973 after the decree was rendered'" (1978:71).

It takes very little interpretation of this rather staggering statistic to infer that the state lost a few degrees of freedom in allocating the remainder of its budget to other citizen needs. We must consider Glazer justified in wondering "whether this great increase in expenditure for mental hospitals did not have some relation to the deplorable conditions that Judge Johnson found in prisons in Alabama a few years later" (1978:71). Glazer also raises questions regarding the subsequent quality of the state's schools and colleges and its ability to police against crime or to provide welfare assistance. These are reasonable points, reinforced by Glazer's remark that "the scheduling of judicial intervention responds to lawsuits, which are ordered not in terms of greatest need, but on the basis of a variety of accidental factors" (1978:71).

This observation brings the discussion back to points made by both Blachly and Oatman (1934) and Landis (1966) that administrative apparatuses were introduced to eradicate the accidental nature of social policy and bring continuity, order, and integration to it. "Nevertheless," writes Glazer, "judicial decisions, remedies, and interventions are beginning to shape the entire structure of social policy. . . . Significantly determining how resources within any given branch of social policy are to be distributed" (1978:67). The courts have gone "beyond procedural requirements to substantive requirements: not *how* it shall be determined what prisoners need or what housing units should be built, but specifically which services prisoners should be provided with and exactly *which* housing units are to be built" (Glazer, 1978:65).

While Glazer concedes that "there is undoubtedly some difficulty in distinguishing between the rights-pronouncing decree and the administrative-intervention decree," he does suggest that "court decisions regarding school desegregation, housing, welfare, and the administration of mental hospitals and prisons seem to involve a very different kind of intervention from rulings in which a right is refined or extended" (1978:65). "Beginning with rights," Glazer contends, a judge "goes on to correct administration for the purpose of ensuring rights, and finally to correct administration that has no connection with rights at all" (1978:72). The strict constitutional constructionists to whom Wheeler refers anticipated exactly this type of dilemma: they would argue that the courts should "refuse to engage in judicial legislation and policy initiation, no matter how noble the impulse or how urgent the occasion" (1965:10).

In short, both courts and administrative units (particularly when the latter are at the state level) appear to be somewhat disoriented as they travel the ill-marked byways of the U.S. welfare state. It is not that each wishes to be the definitive cartographer, "winning" territory from the other. Rather, both courts and administrative agencies are attempting to interpret statutes whose ramifications go far beyond the territory controlled by each in the political division of labor. Protecting rights, the courts veer into policy. Far-sighted as to policy, agencies can overlook rights.

Isomorphic Features of Regulatory and Redistributive Agencies. I would here like to call attention to some parallels that apply to the sociology of administrative agencies, whether regulatory or redistributive. The first parallel has to do with the proclivity of agencies to multiply; the second, with the bases of ineradicable tension between agencies and courts. In 1938, Landis observed that "indeed, the creation of an administrative authority has attended the effort to solve almost every major economic issue of this century" (1966:26). We may here paraphrase and note that the creation of an administrative authority has attended the effort to solve almost every major social issue of this century. The agencies and their associated issues have bifurcated into the goods-and-service-oriented redistributive agencies and the New Regulatory agencies, examples of the latter being the Environmental Protection Agency, the Department of Energy, and the Nuclear Regulatory Commission. Such a service-oriented administrative unit as the former HEW has itself specialized into the current Department of Education and the Department of Health and Human Services. The creation of more and more agencies can safely be predicted for the future as more aspects of individual or family well-being (the purview of the redistributive agencies) or the well-being of the collectivity (the purview of the New Regulation) are recognized as needing the attention of specialized staffs.

A second isomorphic feature obtains between regulatory and redistributive agencies. Just as "regulatory statutes represent an uneasy compromise between laissez faire and government controlled visions of the economy" (Shapiro, 1968:261 and see above), we may think of redistributive statutes (including agency sublegislation) as representing an uneasy compromise between individual dignity and integrity and paternalistic protectionism. As regulatory statutes "are likely to embody the ambiguity and internal contradictions of contemporary economic philosophy" (Shapiro, 1968:261), so, too, redistributive statutes (including the agencies they create and the sublegislation the agencies promulgate) are likely to embody the ambiguity and internal contradictions of contemporary sociopolitical philosophy. In Chapters 2–6 of this work, I indicated just what principles may be in incongruent relationships with one another: self-reliance and individualism versus the ideal of the unity of all members of a humanitarian order. The legitimation of social rights will ever rest upon this tension between not entirely compatible values, just as government intervention into a "free market" economy is inherently anomalous.

Add to this tension the fact that a societal surplus has to be created and maintained in order for social rights to be made tangible, and the intricacies of the court-agency relationship grow ever more bewildering:

> Judicial intervention into policy and procedures on the basis of rights is in theory indifferent to ends. A right stands on the grounds of justice. . . . But this ignores the reality of the context within which rights are claimed and established. Undoubtedly, many rights are demanded simply from the point of view of justice and human dignity and independently of any contribution to or detraction from the end of a given social service or policy. Yet the fact is that we do mix together the simple-justice basis and the presumed effects basis for establishing rights. [Glazer, 1978:72]

To the specific elements of this mixture we turn in the next section.

Costs and the Legitimation of Social Rights

The availability of a societal surplus is, in contemporary parlance, "the bottom line" in the creation and legitimation of social rights. Baum has written that "people and dollars are the basic elements in the perspective on welfare. It is around these two factors that all other considerations revolve" (1974:1). Objections to this succinct statement of the issue are not to be found in the vast literature on the welfare state. Moreover, "Despite attempts to redefine 'gratuity' or 'benefit' as the 'new property,' it is the government that determines how much money will be appropriated and spent. Such appropriation and spending can be increased, and also can be decreased without violating legal rights" (Baum, 1974:1). This, too, is unarguable. What citizen of any regime has a right—legal or ethical—to the government's provision of commodities or services which the body politic cannot afford to underwrite?

Therefore, the implications of an adjudicative process that, however indirectly, forces a regime into social spending are highly problematic. *Goldberg* v. *Kelly* presented such a dilemma: "From the beginning, *Goldberg* v. *Kelly* and more particularly the implementing regulations of HEW have been an object of state concern. . . . In each and every instance the state line of attack is rooted in money costs" (Baum, 1974:62–63). As late as 1973 some of the states had refused to comply fully with the HEW regulations: "From the states' view, money cost is a primary consideration in their willingness to accept a given system for the distribution of justice" (Baum, 1974:20).

With this reference to "justice," we return full circle to the issues raised in Chapter 3 as to what, in the Western tradition, constitutes "right rule." I argued that "right rule," that is, legitimate authority, in the West rests upon impartial and impersonal rule of law. The sovereign establishes, maintains, or embellishes its legitimate authority through the rule of laws whose substantive content consists of the ideals that have been elevated by the body politic. The ideals of civil and political rights reached their apex in the eighteenth and nineteenth centuries, respectively. Throughout the twentieth century the ideal of social rights has been successively reaching new heights. The elevation of this newest ideal has rested upon the solid evidence of increasing affluence in Western nations since World War II. Unquestionably, the combination of technological advance and the institutions of an advanced market economy were central in creating a surplus and a promise of more to come unparalleled in human history.

Probably the boldest popular statement of the "more to come" point of view was Alvin Toffler's *Future Shock* (1971) with its projections of the common use of personal helicopters and the like. Toffler's statements were coincident with the idea that affluence in a society presents the possibility of a more widespread distribution and enjoyment of the good things in life. In this regard it was a description of what the "life of a civilized being according to the standards prevailing in the society" (Marshall, 1963:74) might be like in the future. Of course, Toffler's referent was the private, not the public, sector. In *Future Shock* the "prevailing standards" were envisioned as rising to "shocking" dimensions (admittedly the book was criticized by many for its overly optimistic projections regarding the future availability of resources to sustain such a sumptuous standard of living).

Others, however, have written of "future shock" in the public sector. Governments of Western regimes are already experiencing shock at their own social spending: "In the United States and Western

Europe, government spending tended to rise faster than gross domestic product of the economies between 1961 and 1972, with social transfer payments rising even faster than general government spending" (Heidenheimer, Heclo, and Adams, 1975:275). Milton and Rose Friedman write, "Britain and Sweden, long the two countries most frequently pointed to as successful welfare states, have had increasing difficulties" (1980:100). Britain's National Health Service, "once the prize jewel in the welfare state crown," has been "plagued by strikes, rising costs, and lengthening waiting lists." One dilemma associated with the affordability of the welfare state has to do with citizen satisfaction with what, realistically, can be spent from general revenues for social rights. Amitai Etzioni notes that in public (as well as in private) goods consumption, we need a new world-view "which puts ceilings on aspirations and redefines levels of satisfaction" (1973:388). This issue generates the paradoxical criticism that the welfare state should "do more," yet it is already "costing too much" (Heidenheimer, Heclo, and Adams, 1975; Wilensky, 1975; Janowitz, 1976). Or, as mentioned earlier, as Lowi states the problem, "governmental effort on a scale unknown in the Western world seems to offend more beneficiaries than it ingratiates" (1969:xiv).

The issue of costs from the standpoint of the legitimation of social rights now becomes the issue of when should the welfare state either create new rights, expand existing rights, or even cut back on rights already granted? The literature on the welfare state contains both pragmatic and philosophical replies to this query. Both bear attention here.

The Pragmatic Approach to Costs. Central to the welfare state is the existence of a societal surplus (see Lenski, 1966; Janowitz, 1976). Central to the creation and expansion of a societal surplus in Western regimes has been the market type of economy with its correlates, incentive, initiative, enterprise, and productivity. Scholars agree that the limiting factor in welfare state redistributions is that point at which initiative and enterprise are discouraged with resulting loss in productivity (see Stone, 1978:433–39). "That there is such a point, varying with each historical situation, will readily be granted" (Girvetz, 1968:516). Opponents as well as proponents of the welfare state disagree over just where that point might be.

Sheldon Danziger and Robert Plotnick (1978:5ff.) describe three antagonistically related parameters involving initiative and productivity that concern welfare state redistributions. First, there is the size of the benefit (such as an income guarantee or assistance payment) to be granted to the unit in question (this unit may be a family or an individual). Second, there is the rate at which this benefit is reduced when the individual or family raises its standard of living or income through its own work efforts (this is called the "benefit reduction rate"). Third, there is the entire cost of the redistributions, that is, the benefit payments, to the national treasury.

A high benefit reduction rate discourages individual initiative, but keeps overall program costs down. Let us say that the government provides an individual with a monthly income guarantee with a 100 percent benefit reduction rate. This means that for every dollar earned by the individual that month, the government will deduct a dollar from his income guarantee. In theory, this should reduce program costs. In practice, it could provide a disincentive to work.

Alternatively, the government might attempt to encourage work effort by institutionalizing a low benefit reduction rate: for example, an individual may be allowed to retain eighty cents of every dollar earned (that would be a 20 percent benefit reduction rate). But, until the individual earned enough to reach a cutoff point that would free the government from granting him his "socially rightful" income guarantee, program costs to the national treasury would be quite high.

Finally, the cutoff point itself determines the overall cost of the income guarantee program. Either a high cutoff point or "income guarantees that are high enough to eliminate poverty would either increase program costs dramatically, or require a benefit reduction rate so high that work would be discouraged" (Danziger and Plotnick, 1978:6). It is in these various ways that the issue of the cost of the welfare state is related to the question of individual initiative and work incentive. Philosophically, the fear that the welfare state will quell individual initiative and ultimately undermine the national economy is, in part, rooted in the tradition of classical economics. This tradition assumes a continuing interchange of individual freedoms and the spirit of individual enterprise. It sees the flourishing of democratic liberties as virtually synonymous with the flourishing of the free market that creates the economic surplus (Wilensky, 1975:115).

The Ethical Approach to Costs. A rather more philosophically oriented treatment of the issue as to when the government should expand or contract social rights is addressed by Thomas C. Grey in "Property

and Need: The Welfare State and Theories of Distributive Justice"
(1976:888ff.). Grey grapples with property theory, rights, and ethics
to the end of establishing the plausibility of the argument: "If someone could keep [a] helpless person alive by sharing some property,
at small inconvenience, he would have a duty to do so. . . . But the
[ethical argument] would weaken as the practical burden of support
became more onerous, so that what was only an inconvenience at first
might become too much to require an isolated individual or family in a
state of nature to bear over the longer run" (Grey, 1976:890). Correlatively, in the case of life, not in a state of nature, but under an
organized polity:

> The existing taxing mechanism could spread the burden
> of support over the productive taxpayers. Each of them would
> then be in the situation of the water-owner on the desert island: at
> very little cost, a sharing of his property could preserve human
> life. . . . If through catastrophe, there came to be too many
> helpless persons relative to the number of productive taxpayers,
> the cost of the rest would no longer be slight. In that case, the
> *right* to subsistence would no longer exist; the helpless would
> have to fall back on appeals to compassion and generosity.
> [Grey, 1976:890][4]

Grey notes that "the notion that A owes B a right of support only
when the burden of meeting it is relatively light will disturb some
people and even shock a few" (1976:890, n. 37). He contends, however, that nothing in the logic of the notion of a right should create any
such shock. Rather, "Promises can create rights. . . . Thus A's promise
to do B a favor 'unless it turns out to be a lot of trouble' would create
a right that would be violated if A did not do the favor though doing
it would have been only a minor inconvenience" (Grey, 1976:890,
n. 37). The critique of the welfare state from the point of view of costs,
therefore, implies that social rights are conditional.[5]

Duncan MacRae, Jr. (1979) notes that a polity ideally should be
able to "engage in 'fine tuning' of its decisions in relation to the
exigencies in which it finds itself." Namely, if the nation were being
weakened overall by the costs of welfare state redistributions, then
such redistributions would be self-defeating. The substantive rationale
that initially legitimized the social rights (a right to a civilized standard
of living for all) would be undercut by the prospect of radically lower-

ing everyone's standard of living through either the destruction of individual initiative or spreading the national treasury too thinly.

Thus, the revocation of a social right, once granted, would have to be carried out through a process of both formal and substantive rationalization of the denial of the right. A formal statute would have to be passed (but see immediately below), removing rights to certain levels of minimum income, health care, and the like. The substantive rationale legitimizing such a drastic step could only rest upon an equally drastic empirical situation: the potential for national economic deterioration or ruin. The legitimacy of social rights rests, in the final analysis, upon their economic feasibility. Ideological exhilaration must stop at the door of budgetary exhaustion: legitimation of social rights cannot overstep the boundaries of what the economy can afford.

Entitlements versus Rights: A Specification of the Pragmatic Approach to Costs. In linking notions of "right rule" with the costs of the welfare state, I have argued so far that though "right rule" in the Western welfare regime involves certain methods of redistribution (impartial and impersonal, hence "rationalized"), those methods can legitimize social rights only inasmuch as the economy can afford them. Above I noted that the revocation of social rights would involve a reversal of the steps that were taken to create them. If social rights are created by statutes that are interpreted by agencies and, upon occasion, brought before the regular courts of law for continued elaboration, then some sort of rationale would have to be elaborated to revoke the rights, and a formal procedure (such as passing a statute) would have to be followed to make this revocation "legal," that is, lawful.

At this juncture the distinction between entitlements and rights once again becomes pertinent. I have argued that the lengthy borderline between entitlements and rights is oftentimes indistinct until an entitlement case comes up for court review and a determination is made as to whether a benefit is an entitlement or a right. Entitlements can be changed through agency sublegislation alone or through the legislative budget appropriations process. Social rights, by contrast, would more likely require change by statute, as mentioned above. For example, the revocation of the right to a retirement pension (Title II of the U.S. Social Security Act) in the United States or any other Western nation would require considerable formality through law, as well as extensive explaining to the general public. By contrast, entitlements are far more vulnerable, as the following example pertaining to the U.S. food stamp program illustrates: "The federal food stamp program may run out of money this summer, depriving 260,000 persons in Washington state of food stamp benefits. . . . Hit hard by inflation and Congress' budget-balancing fervor, an additional $2.65 billion is needed if the program is to continue until Sept. 30, the end of the fiscal year. . . . One official said there is an assumption that Congress will approve the extra money eventually, but the question is when" (Sanger, 1980:1). This, of course, reinforces Baum's statement that "appropriations can be decreased without violating legal rights" (1974:1). That is true. No legal rights of food stamp recipients would be violated by a failure of additional appropriations for the program.

One conclusion that might be drawn from the differential implications of entitlements versus rights is that the entitlement allows the national treasury of a welfare state an area of latitude or flexibility. In a federal publication oriented toward residents in specific congressional districts, reference was made to the fact that

> some of the largest items in the federal budget are, by law,
> immune from specific ceilings on spending. This class of federal
> expenditures is often referred to as the "uncontrollable" part of
> the budget.
>
> The uncontrollables are composed of the so-called entitlement
> programs—social security, medicare, welfare, certain veterans'
> benefits—along with the interest on the federal debt. Together,
> the uncontrollables will account for almost 58 percent of the
> 1981 budget. Defense takes up the next largest chunk of the
> budget; 24 percent. When the cost of the uncontrollables is
> combined with the proposed defense expenditures, 82 percent
> of the budget is accounted for, leaving the responsibility
> for balancing the budget on those programs which made up
> only 18 percent of total expenditures. [Pritchard, 1980:3]

Although the government publication uses the term "entitlements" to refer to the rationalized and well-crystallized benefits that I have been calling "rights," the point is clear: benefits that reach the government category of "uncontrollable" are "rightful" in the United States. Those that fall within the other 18 percent are, in my terms, "entitlements."

Finally, it should be noted that, as if these relationships between entitlements and rights, controllable and uncontrollable parts of the budget were not enough, there is yet another factor to be considered here. That is the increasing institutionalization of "off-budget" programs. The U.S. Treasury directly funds such programs, using the tax dollar. Off-budget programs "were created in the early 1970s when the budget . . . was changed from an administrative to a unified process. The Congress did this to circumvent impoundments of congressionally appropriated funds. . . . To date [these programs] have added $41.3 billion to the national debt and will add an estimated $62.9 billion by 1983" (Hofman and Brown, 1980:A13). No one seems sure why these programs are not included in the budget, the balancing of which boils down to misleading rhetoric unless these items are taken account of, according to the authors of "Balanced Budgets and Phony Numbers." In any case, off-budget programs certainly do not embody social rights, and it is somewhat doubtful that they could be said to fund entitlements, as such. Analytically, they are clearly gratuitous. In sum, though it might be argued that off-budget programs allow latitude or flexibility in government commitment to citizen well-being, I would have to agree with Lowi (1969, 1979) that there is a point at which "flexibility" merges into pure "looseness," flatly precluding the application of law as well as the attainment of justice and fairness that laws imply. The off-budget program far exceeds that point.

In the light of the above issues, therefore, the role of the courts in transforming entitlements into rights in the welfare state is a two-edged sword. The apparent enhancement of the "rightful" material position of the citizen is inherently subject to being revealed as destructive to the initial resource base upon which the welfare state rests. Mixing "simple justice" and "presumed effects" (see above) in order to establish rights requires an expert hand indeed. If expertness is not employed, the effects of court decisions upon the costs of redistributions could be lethal: such decisions could kill both the court's own authority to elaborate social rights and the goose that lays the golden egg. More gravity and less laughter would attach to the old joke about the income tax form of the very near future: "Line 1. How much money did you make last year? Line 2. Send it in!"

In the concluding chapter I will return to issues that comprise, but go far beyond, the case of the United States. I will contrast major types of historical regimes, including the Western welfare state, in terms of the administrative-adjudicative principles that have been elaborated here. I will treat the outcome for subjects or citizens of the continued rationalization of both the civil or statute law and the administrative law that increasingly touch their lives. The relationships between the two types of law and between administration and adjudication will form the matrix against which I will compare salient features of well-known types of Western, as well as contemporary Eastern European, rule.

Chapter 11

A WEBERIAN FRAMEWORK FOR

ANALYZING THE WESTERN WELFARE STATE

AND ITS PLACE IN HISTORY

Political Alchemy and the Western Welfare State

From the thirteenth to the seventeenth centuries in Western Europe there was a belief that base metals could be transformed into gold. Alchemy was the name given to the alleged process of transformation. Though the notion of alchemy may seem absurd to the contemporary Western citizen, subjects of the medieval era would have found just as absurd the idea that their statuses could undergo a social structural metamorphosis, transmuting them from subjects into citizens. The contemporary Western welfare state represents something of a modern political alchemy in which the relatively crude and historically common status of "political subject" has been radically transformed into the precious status of "citizen" with a guarantee of minimum standards of living. We have seen here that the elixir, that catalyst through which this transformation has taken place in the West, is the continued rationalization of law in both formal and substantive directions.

I have depicted the Western welfare state as a sociopolitical organization unique for its guarantee to citizens of a highly sophisticated notion of rights. The sophistication to which the right to legal equality has been raised in the Western welfare state comprises civil, political, and social rights. Moreover, the law that guarantees these rights has become increasingly rational in Weber's deliberate sense of the term. Law has both a formal structure and a substantive content and thus has two aspects or features that may undergo rationalization. Rationalized law is, accordingly, both formally and substantively rationalized.

Formal rationalization of law entails the following: (1) precise specification of the concepts or principles through which the law is articulated; (2) generalization of the law's concepts or principles; (3) the construction of legally relevant relationships involving these principles; (4) logical synthesis of the legally relevant relationships, such that they are mutually consistent; (5) determinateness regarding the applicability of the law over a particular range of empirical events. Substantive rationalization of law entails the unceasing search for, and clarification of, the law's "real intent." This search takes place through logical sublimation of the law's meaning. Part of the logical sublimation process involves elaborating the consequences, implications, and ramifications of the law as it stands. Namely, does the law lead to absurd or contradictory consequences? Can such inappropriateness be the law's real meaning? If the answers to these questions are, respectively, yes and no, then reinterpretation of the law's quintessential objective(s) is necessary. Substantive rationalization of law, therefore, is the logical analysis of the law's "spirit," including elaboration of that spirit.

Substantive rationalization of law must be a continuing process because the citizen-sovereign relationship, which it is the task of the law to make legally relevant, is ever in flux. To avoid ossification, therefore, the law must achieve an ongoing synthesis of the rationalization of both its form and content. As the law's concepts become more abstract, the law's form becomes more rationalized, for it then encompasses more fact situations. In turn, the extension of the relevance of the law's authority to more social situations often needs elaboration so that the advance of the state's force into new territories is seen as legitimate. Archibald Cox refers to this process when he writes in "Constitutional Adjudication and the Promotion of Human Rights" that the "ability to rationalize a constitutional judgment in terms of principles referable to accepted sources of law is an essential, major element of constitutional adjudication. It is one of the ultimate sources of the power of the Court—including the power to gain acceptance for the occasional great leaps forward which lack such justification" (1966:98).

Therefore, one of the major features of the analysis I have presented has been to call attention to both the theoretical and empirical importance of the complementary relationship between the law's form and its substance.[1] Weber, emphasizing the antagonism between the two, called close attention to the ways popular demands for a more concretely meaningful justice tended to corrode the law's formality.[2]

This can and does happen, to be sure. The perspective advanced here, however, makes possible a clearer understanding of the bases upon which the Western welfare state's legitimacy rests, given the seemingly insurmountable presuppositions surrounding the legitimate uses of state authority after the democratic revolutions. I have shown that, far from having sacrificed the formality of the law, the development of the welfare state has corresponded with the increasing rationalization not only of the civil or statute, but also of the administrative law. In short, the addition of new substantive content (social rights) to the law's already "formalized" principles did not destroy the form of those principles. The principles of impersonality and impartiality, far from being eroded, were raised to new levels of abstraction. Continuity of the law's form was maintained while the law was adjusted to meet new circumstances to which it would be applied. Thus, my central concern in Part I of this work was to offer an explanation for the legitimacy of the explicitly redistributional state in the West.

Part II, in turn, was an examination of the importance of the distinction between administration and adjudication, including the process of the rationalization of the law associated with the administrative mode of exercising authority. I applied insights gained from this examination to concrete problems faced by the United States in particular and the Western welfare state in general. Refining the notion of "administration" through reference to contemporary writings, I elaborated connections among gratuities, entitlements, and administrative law. I then related these connections to social rights and the civil or statute law. This, in turn, led to an explication of the relationship between administrative adjudication and adjudication in the regular courts of law, including the problems posed for the welfare state by institutional disjunctures between these two formats for adjudication. I emphasized that both formats join citizen and sovereign in legally relevant relationships, but regular adjudication is far superior for guarding the citizen's rights vis-à-vis political authority. Finally, I examined the ramifications of these several relationships for the legitimacy of the redistributions made in the name of the welfare state, giving special emphasis to the importance of the costs of such redistributions to the society.

A Framework for Analyzing Salient
Regime Traits throughout History

In this final chapter, I would like to apply the Weberian framework developed here to an examination of some broad historical trends, as well as to a comparison of regime types throughout Western history. In constructing Figure 11–1, I attempted to note which types of regimes or regime activities were associated with epithets. Epithets can be informative: they can communicate rather pointedly what aspects of regimes are interpreted by "publics" (usually scholars or other analysts) as salient. Too, because epithets carry a judgmental note regarding the regime's salient activities, they hint at the degree of acceptability or legitimacy accorded the regime from the standpoint of those using the labels. Finally, lack of an epithet associated with a particular type of regime or regime activity may also be of information value. Absence of an epithet may denote (1) that the activities are/ were not well recognized as taking place, (2) that the nature or implications of the activities are/were not well understood, (3) that the activities are/were not controversial and therefore, do/did not call attention to themselves, (4) that the activities may actually be/have been shielded from publicity by those in charge of them. Inappropriate epithets may similarly inform, suggesting a disparity between images and facts.

Regime Activities and Characteristics. Figure 11–1 is organized around two major types of regime activity as represented by the columns labeled administration and adjudication. The rows denote broad divisions of rule by eras or centuries and indicate one major regime characteristic. That characteristic is the degree to which the regime activities take place within a framework of law (whether civil, statute, or administrative) that has undergone rationalization. Figure 11–1, thus, expands upon Figure 7–4.

The civil or statute law may progress from being either formally irrational (as in charismatic justice) or substantively irrational (as in primitive formalism) to being rationalized both formally and substantively (as discussed in Chapter 4). Administrative law may progress from being merely the word of the ruler or the reglementations by which his officials administer the realm, to the legalized and judicialized type of law analyzed in Chapter 7. Figure 11–1 shows a gradual but by no means linear movement from irrational to rationalized law for both column categories, administration and adjudication. It will be seen that the movement has been more linear and the ideal more closely approximated for civil or statute law than for administrative law. It should here be noted that all phenomena (both cells and margins) represented in Figure 11–1 are ideal typical. For example, cell 15, the welfare state, more closely approximates a regime whose civil or statute law is rationalized, both formally and substantively, than any other regime type throughout history. But this is not to say that the ideal has been reached.

Adjudication Activities. Within the category of adjudication (column C), regimes or regime activities are classified according to the single criterion of the character of the judicial system, including the distinctive type of right created or protected by the regime in question. I will make some comments here about terminology. I have assigned the epithet "the liberal state" to the regime whose unique judicial feature was the institutionalization of civil rights, "the democratic state" to the regime that institutionalized political rights, and "the welfare state" to the regime that institutionalized social rights. Moreover, I characterized the liberal state as "negative" government: the institutionalization of civil rights essentially removed restrictions upon geographic, social, economic, and occupational mobility. In turn, I characterized the welfare state as "positive" government: the institutionalization of social rights essentially creates minimally favorable conditions for the individual to affirm his integrity as a member of society. The term "affirmative action," popular in the United States, captures the essence of positive government as that which acts to bring about conditions that will enhance the self-affirming or self-actualization potential of the individual.[3] Thus, negative government removed restrictions from "above" and positive government creates a floor "below" the individual as a citizen under a particular regime.

Administration Activities. I have chosen two activities associated with administrative authority throughout this work. In column A I call attention to the side of administration that is largesse-dispensing and, by implication, discretionary, as depicted in Chapter 2. In column B I call attention to the side of administration emphasized in Chapter 7—administrative activity as the task-oriented merging of all three government functions to "get the job done." Column B, therefore, lists regime types according to the objective in terms of which the regime

FIGURE 11-1
Epithets Associated with Salient Aspects of Rule by Administration and Adjudication

WEBER'S POLAR CONSTRUCTS FOR THE EXERCISE OF AUTHORITY

		ADMINISTRATION		ADJUDICATION
		The Word of the Ruler	Reglementations	Formally or Substantively Irrational Law
Century	Broad Category	Type of largesse characteristic of the regime (A)	Type of objective in terms of which regime defines its effectiveness and for which it establishes administrative apparatus(es) (B)	Character of the judicial system or the rights created or protected by the regime (C)
6th–15th	MEDIEVAL RULE	Favors/Gratuities (PATRIARCHALISM) (1); Offices/Benefices (PATRIMONIALISM); Fiefs/Titles (FEUDALISM)	Hydraulic Agriculture (ORIENTAL DESPOTISM) (6a); Taxation (PATRIMONIALISM) (6b) (FEUDALISM)	CHARISMATIC JUSTICE (11); PRIMITIVE ADJUDICATION; PRIMITIVE FORMALISM
16th–19th	PRE-REVOLUTIONARY RULE	Royal charters: direct subsidies to manufacturers (MERCANTILISM) (2)	Keeping internal order; fighting wars (ROYAL ABSOLUTISM) (7) The patrimonial codifications: Law governing rights and duties becoming more systematized (ENLIGHTENED DESPOTISM)	Particularized (PATRIMONIALISM; rights of law ABSOLUTISM) communities (12a) (12b)
16th–19th	POST-REVOLUTIONARY RULE (THE RULE OF LAW)	Dispensation of lands; aid to railways; corporate charters (LAISSEZ-FAIRE STATE) (3)	Keeping internal order; colonial expansion; establishing transportation, communication, banking, credit and tariff systems (LAISSEZ-FAIRE STATE) (8)	Civil rights (THE LIBERAL STATE) (13) (NEGATIVE GOVERNMENT); Political rights (THE DEMOCRATIC STATE)
20th	EASTERN EUROPEAN RULE	Gifts; privileges (THE NEW CLASS) (4)	Matching labor force to requisites of a command economy (TOTALITARIANISM) (9)	Socioeconomic rights articulated with polity to achieve "an association in which the free development of each is the condition for the free development of all" (Marx) (SOCIALISM) (14)
20th	WESTERN RULE	Contracts; licenses; subsidies; franchises; use of public resources (THE CONTRACT STATE) (5a); Social welfare entitlements (?) (5b)	Presuming responsibility for the ruled and enforcing their strict conformity "for their own good" (AUTHORITARIANISM) (10a); Regulating private activity in the public interest (THE PUBLIC INTEREST STATE) (10b)	Civil rights (THE LIBERAL STATE) (15); Political rights (THE DEMOCRATIC STATE) (POSITIVE GOVERNMENT); Social rights (THE WELFARE STATE) (POSITIVE GOVERNMENT)
		Rationalized Administrative Law via Legalization and Judicialization		Formally and Substantively Rationalized Law

Degree of Rationality of the Law — Low (top) ... High (bottom)

BROAD CATEGORIES OF RULE BY CENTURY

defines (defined) its effectiveness and for which, thus, the regime will establish (established) an administrative apparatus.

Administration versus Adjudication: Effectiveness versus Legitimacy. It is clear from the most casual glance at column B that, from the standpoint of those committed to civil liberties, the most uncomplimentary epithets fall into this column. The reason is close at hand: with regard to those tasks that define a regime's effectiveness, its authoritative decisions are open to little or no appeal. Appeal, of course, is the very hallmark of authority exercised in terms of the adjudicative principle; never, in the primeval case, is it the attribute of administrative authority. Even in the modern case this distinction persists: Weber (1968:644–45), who fully recognized the "remedies" offered the citizen through appeal to administrative tribunals "formally identical with those existing in the field of the administration of justice," nevertheless was emphatic when he stated, "but none of these guarantees can eliminate the basic contradiction between adjudication and 'government,' "[4] by which Weber meant the administrative realm (see 1968:644).

Contemporary scholars retain Weber's association of appeal with "juridical" rule and the absence of "effective challenge of decisions" with "tyranny" (Lasswell and Kaplan, 1963:232). Seymour M. Lipset's (1960) "legitimacy" and "effectiveness" as the two criteria essential to regime stability similarly reduce to Weber's "adjudicative" and "administrative" categories. Adjudication, the application of rules to achieve an outcome acceptable to disputing parties, is oriented toward the elaboration and, hence, the justification or legitimacy of the grounds used to settle claim disputes. The rule of law, accordingly, has to do with the justification of the claim settlement between citizen and sovereign as much as between citizen and citizen. Column C, therefore, depicts a progressive rationalization of the adjudicative principle through which the settlement of claims between citizen and sovereign are accorded legitimacy by each party. By contrast, administration, the alignment of executive, legislative, and judicial functions into a set of roles to accomplish an objective, is inevitably related to regime effectiveness. Just as legitimacy and effectiveness are both necessary to regime stability, so, too, administration and adjudication are complementary regime activities, as I have argued throughout.

The major division between columns C and B, therefore, portrays the long-noted tension between regime legitimacy and regime effectiveness.[5] It would seem that the sovereign must be effective when it is oriented toward the needs of the collectivity at large, as when defending the realm from outside enemies. But the sovereign must be legitimate when it is oriented toward the application of law to the individual case.[6] Hobbes's argument for the leviathan state is the prototypical argument for the indispensability of regime effectiveness, the ultimate argument for the sovereign to merge all three functions of rule to achieve quintessential efficacy. Hobbes reduces legitimacy to effectiveness, thereby underemphasizing the importance of individual rights in relationship to the sovereign. Hobbes did not solve the problem of how regimes might reconcile the tension between the need to be legitimate and the need to be effective, the need for adjudication, the need for administration.

When Administrative Authority Scowls

In this and the following sections I will lend concreteness to the general points above through a consideration of various regime types. Figure 11–1 shows that regimes have always established administrative apparatuses for task implementation. Such apparatuses, however, reveal a persistent tendency to become organs of domination. This happens because with regard to the task at hand the regime merges the three functions of rule in order to increase its effectiveness. As indicated above, there is far less, if any, chance for appeal from the citizenry against regime decisions made by the administrative apparatus with regard to that task which the regime has defined as the measure of its effectiveness. Thus, the regime is "tyrannical" in that area of its authority.[7] When, therefore, the job to be accomplished by the administrative apparatus requires that the latter increase the scope of its effective power to include more and more areas of subject or citizen life, the society becomes "regimented" (Lasswell and Kaplan, 1963:221). In turn, "totalitarianism is the form of rule with maximum regimentation" (Lasswell and Kaplan, 1963:221–22).

By this logic, the three entries in column B that imply the severest degrees of tyranny, administration at its most unchallengeable, that is, administration's darkest face, are the ones in which the regime's objectives are so vast in scope that in order to achieve them the regime regiments the populace under the authority of a powerful administrative apparatus. These are oriental despotism (cell 6a), totalitarianism (cell 9), and authoritarianism (cell 10a). The first involves harnessing the labor power of entire societies to the task of conducting large-scale irrigation (or hydraulic) agriculture. The second involves matching the societal labor force to the requirements of a command economy. The third entails the assumption by the sovereign of all responsibility for the ruled and the correlative suppression of opposition to bring about conformity and obedience "for their own good."

Oriental Despotism. "Oriental despotism," Karl Wittfogel (1957) points out, is a somewhat misleading label, for it is an organizational phenomenon that has been found far beyond the borders of the Orient. It refers, in fact, to the development of government bureaucracy without bureaucratization (Delany, 1963:487). This analytic feature makes oriental despotism an appropriate phenomenon to discuss within the general context of administration as task-oriented role organization that merges all three rulership functions to become political domination. William Delany writes that

> large-scale irrigation agriculture has two characteristics that
> are very important and directly relevant for the development of
> administration. First, it involves a specific type of division of
> labor. . . . The second characteristic, and key organizational
> need, is large-scale co-operation in performing these specialized
> operations. Whether the irrigation civilization covers a small
> region or an empire, co-operation is necessary. In order to
> achieve it, leadership, planning, co-ordination, control, and
> supervision—in a word, administration—emerge. Of course, the
> extent to which administration develops depends upon the scope,
> complexity, and stability of the operations involved.
>
> Wittfogel sees the management of these projects as leading to
> political control. The state fulfills significant economic functions
> in the agricultural sector, but also in large construction. The
> operation of these large-scale irrigation and construction
> enterprises (to say nothing of the immense armies) necessitated
> regular sources of government revenue and a variety of fiscal
> organizations, administrations, and systems of transportation,
> communications, and (since most of these taxes were in kind),
> storage. [1963:486]

Administration of the economy became domination of the political economy.

Totalitarianism. In a similar vein, administration of the economy became totalitarian domination in the U.S.S.R. The command economy of the U.S.S.R. is one whose planners attempt to synthesize the goals of maximizing citizen well-being with various economic and planning objectives. In the course of administering the economy, therefore, regulations governing the enjoyment of benefits by citizens become "an indispensable tool for social engineering" (Rimlinger, 1971:325). By controlling the sources of security and the benefits citizens receive, the government can control incentives to increase the supply, efficiency, and distribution of the Soviet labor force to unattractive geographic areas (Rimlinger, 1971:325). Rimlinger (1971:326) writes that "the only sources of economic security . . . are wages or salaries and social security, and all of them are controlled by the state."

Nevertheless, the Soviet regime, theoretically representing the "right" of the collectivity, puts forth the logic that "there is presumably no conflict between the rulers and the ruled" (Rimlinger, 1971:255). By this casuistry, of course, the need for adjudicative procedures to resolve citizen-sovereign conflicts becomes irrelevant. Administration is here free to become domination, not merely an organizational apparatus associated with a domination to achieve a specific and limited objective defined by the sovereign. In terms of Figure 11–1, we may think of this situation as the utter absorption of cell 14 into cell 9 and thus the obliteration of socialism as it was envisioned by Karl Marx (see Heilbroner, 1980) and has been envisioned by others (see Fromm, 1965).

Authoritarianism. Finally, when the sovereign presumes that "it knows best" what is good for the citizen, and takes upon itself the extensive task of effectively assuming all responsibility for citizen well-being, rule is authoritarian.[8] Coercion of citizens and the demand for obedience and conformity are characteristic (Lasswell and Kaplan, 1963:228).

Authoritarianism, of which Italian fascism and German nazism were prime historical examples, typically extends the scope of its administrative purview through incorporation of important segments of the private sector into the centralized government. These sectors remain privately owned. Accordingly, "corporatism" or "the corporate state" are names for varieties of authoritarian rule or approximations thereof. As with oriental despotism and totalitarianism, so with authoritarianism, the administrative apparatus discourages appeal against its decisions. Suppression of differences with the sovereign is extreme. Administration shows its most scowling face.

When Administration Assumes a Benign Countenance

To reiterate, regimes within column B receive their labels according to the outcome of their having established an administrative apparatus for the achievement of particular objectives. Depending upon the nature and scope of the objective(s) so sought, the regime as a whole comes to be characterized by an epithet pointing to a distinguishing feature of the enforcement-obedience configuration spawned by its administrative apparatus. It is in this connection that Charles Reich (1966) applies the label of "the public interest state" to the aspect of U.S. administrative authority that defines as its purview the enforcement of the conformity of private activity (public activity, too, where applicable) to its authoritative directives "in the public interest." The regulation of large-scale activities, in particular, through such U.S. agencies as the Environmental Protection Agency and the Consumer Product Safety Commission, is the prototypical manifestation of the public interest state. Weaver (1978) uses the term "the New Regulation" to refer to what Reich calls the public interest state.[9]

Both authors voice certain objections to the phenomenon they analyze; neither uses the term "authoritarianism" in connection with his criticisms, but the invidious comparison is implicit. Weaver (1978:60) writes that "a cardinal principle of the New Regulation is that of 'internalizing the externalities'—making manufacturers and consumers pay the social costs of modern goods and services." In noting that the environment does get cleaner and products do get safer through such regulation, Weaver is in agreement with Reich (1966:83), that, indeed, there is a "public interest" that can benefit from government regulation.[10] Yet, Reich (1966:89, 83) observes that "'the public interest' is all too often a reassuring platitude that covers up the sharp clashes of conflicting values, and hides fundamental choices." This, he avers, distorts the high purposes of the early reformers who argued that the commonweal needed government protection. Weaver is in agreement with Reich's view that the rationale of "the public interest" is, at times, used to suppress legitimate societal interests that deserve a voice.[11] In order to better convey the implicit connections between authoritarianism and the public interest state (or the New Regulation),

I shall present a short composite of Reich's and Weaver's respective statements of the problem. I shall then proceed in terms of Reich's analysis. Both authors address only the U.S. case, and I, too, refer only to the U.S. case as illustrative of the analytic category represented by cell 10 of Figure 11–1.

The Public Interest State. The public interest state came about through a gradual institutionalization during this century of a transfer of private responsibility to the realm of government. This transfer was stimulated by efforts to reform the abuses of private property. The steps involved in this transfer were, first, "the displacement of the old bourgeois class by the corporate managerial class, and a corresponding shift from purely private economic institutions to quasi-public institutions like the corporation" (Weaver, 1978:59). Corporations, in turn, became "private governments" and "the defense of private property" became "almost entirely a defense of its abuses—an attempt to defend not individual property, but arbitrary private power over other human beings" (Reich, 1966:81).[12]

Reform followed. The "second managerial revolution" transferred power from the managerial class to a "new class—that rapidly growing and increasingly influential part of the upper-middle class that . . . tends to make its vocation in the public and not-for-profit sectors" (Weaver, 1978:59; see also Stone, 1978:436). At the same time, power was transferred from quasi-public institutions to fully public ones, that is, to government (Weaver, 1978:59). Thus, the reform of the abuses of private property "took away some of the power of the corporations and transferred it to government. In this transfer there was much good, for power was made responsible to the majority rather than to the arbitrary and selfish few. But the reform did not restore the individual to his domain. What the corporation had taken from him,[13] the reform simply handed on to government.[14] And government carried further the powers formerly exercised by the corporation" (Reich, 1966:81). In turn, the specific device through which the government was able to further its powers over the individual turned out to be none other than administrative law.

Administrative Law, Largesse, the Public Interest State, and the Contract State. Although I have dealt (in Chapter 8) with the effect of administrative law in its various stages of rationalization upon the rights of those receiving assistance, Reich's concern is far broader. In the terms used here, Reich's argument covers and integrates the connections among the public interest state, the contract state, and social welfare entitlements (cells 10, 5a, and 5b) with implied references to authoritarianism (cell 10a) (1966:79). Thus, it is worth examining Reich's argument in greater detail. Reich (1966:61) casts his argument in terms of the effects upon individual rights and freedoms of "the unique legal system that is emerging" as an adjunct of the largesse-dispensing state. That unique legal system is administrative law. The largesse-dispensing state manifests in the form of the contracts, licenses, subsidies, and the like, which the state gives out. The connection between the largesse-dispensing state, to which I have assigned the epithet, "the contract state,"[15] and the public interest state is that the latter regulates the beneficiaries of the former through administrative law "in the public interest." I refer now to Reich's elaboration of connections among these phenomena.

Reich (1966:78–79) states that as an outcome of the reform of private property we have been turning wealth and rights over to government, which, in turn, reallocates and redistributes them in the many forms of largesse. "Largesse" is the generic term Reich uses to refer to a wide variety of governmentally dispensed forms of wealth, and under this rubric he categorizes contracts, subsidies, franchises, occupational licenses, government jobs, the use of public resources, services (such as postal and public transportation), as well as the income and benefits typically associated with the welfare state. In turn, the connection between the public interest state, on the one hand, and the contract state and social welfare entitlements, on the other, is that "when government—national, state, or local—hands out something of value, whether a relief check or a television license, government's power grows forthwith; it automatically gains such power as is necessary and proper to supervise its largess. . . . Objections to regulation fade, whether in the minds of the general public or legal scholars, before the argument that government should make sure that its bounty is used in the public interest" (Reich, 1966:66, 67). Reich's explication shows what, in my terms, is the commonality between the two types of administrative activity portrayed in columns A and B: they both use administrative law to join citizen and sovereign in legally relevant relationships. Moreover, a characteristic of administrative law with which we are already familiar from the material I presented in Part II is reiterated in Reich's assertion that "the administration of the system has given rise to special laws and special tribunals, outside the ordinary structure of government" (1966:79). In short, there is a gap between the administrative law and the civil or statute law. There is a gap between benefits enjoyed by dint of administrative largesse and benefits enjoyed by dint of "right."

To fill this gap Reich advocates the institutionalization of a "new property" in which "rights in largesse" are guarded in the same way that private property is guarded by civil rights or, more specifically, the U.S. Bill of Rights. At this juncture Reich's argument and mine are parallel: his call for a "new property" is a call for an institution to bridge the gap between what I have called entitlements and rights, between the respective effects upon the citizen of the application of administrative law and the application of the civil or statute law. But Reich's special concern is the modern state, one of whose distinguishing features is that it makes vast redistributions within the context of the contract state as well as within the context of explicit social welfare redistributions. I am concerned with the welfare state, and I will be saying more about the differences between it and the modern state below.

As for the scope of the effects of the redistributions made by the modern state, an analytic subcategory of which may be said to be the contract state, we may turn to a statement made by Kleinberg (1973). Kleinberg wrote of the contract state in a context quite different from Reich's (1966) analysis of rights in largesse. Nevertheless, Kleinberg reinforces Reich's observation that the scope and effects of modern government redistributions are vast and that they take place outside the system of rationalized civil or statute law:

> As the economy's largest consumer today, government is
> no longer a passive referee of the rules of the economic game. The
> government contract, an improvised, inadequately understood,
> but basic instrument of the new political economy, has become an
> increasingly important device for intervention in the economy
> and in the larger society. . . . The government contract serves not
> only the ends of economic stability and growth; it becomes a
> basic means of achieving important ends of government policy,
> involving the allocation of major resources and the mobilization
> of manpower for specific programs of development deemed vital
> to the national well-being. Concomitantly, it has become an
> important means for the distribution of wealth and the reordering

of social status and power in various states and regions of the country. [1973:82–83]

Kleinberg's reference to "an improvised, inadequately understood" government contracting process may be taken as an oblique reference to an inadequately rationalized administrative law within whose ambit the contracting falls.[16]

On Rationalizing Administrative Law. By 1966, when "The New Property" appeared in *The Public Interest*, Reich had amassed a chilling list of empirical examples in which he showed, essentially, the low degrees of legalization and judicialization of the administrative law within which the largesse-dispensing system had been taking place. His suggestions for how this "unique legal system" can be improved reveal the nature of the flaws of administrative law and administrative adjudication to be similar to the flaws I treated in connection with social welfare entitlements. He calls for "procedural safeguards" to be incorporated into administrative law. These correspond to greater degrees of legalization and judicialization.

> Procedure offers a valuable means for restraining arbitrary action. . . . The grant, denial, revocation and administration of all types of government largess should be subject to scrupulous observance of fair procedures. Action should be open to hearing and context, and based upon a record subject to judicial review. The denial of any form of privilege or benefit on the basis of undisclosed reasons should no longer be tolerated. Nor should the same person sit as legislator, prosecutor, judge and jury, combining all the functions of government in such a way as to make fairness virtually impossible. . . . Even higher standards of procedural fairness should apply when government action has all the effects of a penal sanction. [Reich, 1966:87]

In connection with this latter, Reich notes that "administering largess carries with it . . . the power to inflict many sorts of sanctions not classified as criminal punishments. The most obvious penalty is simply denial or deprivation of some form of wealth or privilege that the agency dispenses" (1966:71). In short, the welfare recipient (who popularly might be thought of as getting a government "handout") and the important government contractor or the owners of an industrial enterprise (who receive the much less stigmatizing "subsidy") ironically find themselves to be equal in the eyes of the law: in the eyes of an insufficiently rationalized administrative law applied to them all, all are vulnerable. None have "rights."

Moreover, Reich suggests several "substantive" limits within which the administrative law should operate. A careful reading of these indicates that he is referring to the same issues raised by other scholars and discussed earlier, namely, that administrative law itself is not formally capable of dealing with "substances" or "ultimate values." Wheeler's discussion of how the application of administrative law may be legally correct even if it destroys national parks and forests (see n. 3, Chapter 9) is a case in point. Accordingly, Reich suggests some rules for making the rules. He names some "substantive" criteria or ultimate values or principles that should guide the making of the administrative rules and regulations in the first place:[17]

> The first type of limit should be on relevance. It has
> proven possible to argue that practically anything in the way of
> regulation is relevant to some legitimate legislative purpose. . . .
> Courts sometimes manage, by statutory construction, to place
> limits on relevance. One example was the negative judicial
> reaction to attempts to ban "disloyal tenants" from government
> aided housing projects.
>
> Besides relevance, a second important limit on substantive
> power might be concerned with discretion. To whatever extent
> possible, delegated power to make rules ought to be confined
> within ascertainable limits, and regulating agencies should not
> be assigned the task of enforcing conflicting policies. Also,
> agencies should be enjoined to use their power only for those
> purposes for which they were designed. . . . A final limit on sub-
> stantive power . . . might be a principle that policymaking
> authority ought not to be delegated to essentially private or-
> ganizations. . . . [This] adds to the feudal characteristics
> of the system. [1966:86]

With this reference to the merging of the public and the private sectors within the ambit of administration, we are now ready to link the larger discussion of the public interest state, the contract state, and social welfare entitlements to the earlier discussion of authoritarianism and totalitarianism.

The Authoritarian Connection. Two comments by Reich suggest that there is an authoritarian undertone to the relationship between citizen and sovereign within the present context of insufficiently rationalized administrative law. First, he states that "the recipients of largess themselves add to the power of government by their uncertainty over their rights, and their efforts to please. Unsure of their ground, they are often unwilling to contest a decision. The penalties for being wrong, in terms of possible future loss of largess, are very severe." (1966:68). In short, the system reinforces obedience and conformity beyond what those interested in the protection of civil liberties think it ought to. His second comment draws an even more explicit connection between the emergent U.S. system and authoritarian rule: "According to one scholar, national socialism regarded property as contingent upon duties owed the state" (1966:79). And from here, an invidious comparison to totalitarianism is inevitable: "In Soviet Russia, the trend reportedly has been somewhat similar, although starting from a different theoretical point" (Reich, 1966:79).

The Totalitarian Connection. The vast scope of citizen life that comes under government control in the public interest state, the contract state, and through social welfare entitlements invites comparison with the case of the U.S.S.R. regarding the government's control of the major forms of security. Reich writes that "the valuables dispensed by government take many forms, but they all share one characteristic. They are steadily taking the place of traditional forms of wealth— forms which are held as private property" (1966:57). In the degree that these transfers are taking place "outside the ordinary structure of government," that is, in terms of an administrative law not articulated with the civil or statute law, citizens have benefits without rights, just as they do in the U.S.S.R. Stated otherwise, as the government increases the scope of its effective power, but not the area within which citizens may appeal, society becomes "regimented." It is for these reasons that analysts such as Reich and Weaver are skeptical of the public interest state or the New Regulation. They are alarmed, rather, at the administrative ambit within which the commonweal is being "protected," not at the idea that the commonweal could benefit from the institutionalization of protections that did not exist under the laissez-faire state. It is in this context that Weaver makes the acerbic observation that the New Regulation seems to be directed "not merely at those in business who . . . 'go around making things without permission,' but also, and perhaps especially, at the mass of Americans who go around doing and enjoying things without permission" (1978: 60). He may well have used overstatement, but analytically, his point is well taken.

The Feudal Connection. The lack of clarity in the relationship between citizen and sovereign, particularly as regards the border between private society and the public realm, has inspired various scholars (Lowi, 1969, 1978; Kleinberg, 1973; Wolfe, 1977) to use the terms "corporatist" and "feudal," in addition to the implied "authoritarian" and "totalitarian" or "regimented" mentioned above, to describe contemporary conditions. Reich observes: "The holder of government largess is expected to some extent, to act as the agent of 'the public interest' rather than solely as that of his own self-interest. . . . The 'mix' of public and private and the degree to which the possessor acts as the government's agent, varies from situation to situation. . . . The result of all this is a breaking down of distinctions between public and private and a resulting blurring or fusing of public and private" (1966:65).

An examination of the entries in column B of Figure 11–1 must dispel any impression that a comparison of certain contemporary government features with feudalism is a mere figure of speech. Quite the contrary, a fundamental continuity with the administrative form of exercising authority, not superficial resemblance, is revealed in carefully drawn comparisons of modern regime features with the generic attributes of feudalism:

> The comparison to the general outlines of the feudal system
> may best be seen by recapitulating some of the chief features of
> government largess. (1) Increasingly we turn over wealth and
> rights to government, which reallocates and redistributes them in
> the many forms of largess; (2) there is a merging of public and
> private, in which lines of private ownership are blurred; (3) the
> administration of the system has given rise to special laws and
> special tribunals, outside the ordinary structure of government;
> (4) the right to possess and use government largess is bound
> up with the recipient's legal status; status is both the
> basis for receiving largess and a consequence of receiving it;
> hence the wealth is not readily transferable; (5) individuals hold
> the wealth conditionally rather than absolutely; the conditions

are usually obligations of loyalty to the government; the obligations may be changed or increased at the will of the state; (6) for breach of condition the wealth may be forfeited or escheated back to the government; (7) the sovereign power is shared with large private interests; (8) the object of the whole system is to enforce "the public interest"—the interest of the state or society . . . by means of the distribution and use of wealth in such a way [as to end up creating and maintaining dependence]. [Reich, 1966:78–79]

Indeed, this point is reinforced by Lowi's (1978) analysis of general revenue sharing which, in addition to special revenue sharing, was enacted in the United States during the Nixon administration. Through the two kinds of revenue sharing, local governments were tied more closely to the federal government than previously. This came about as follows: "Under traditional grant-in-aid programs, there is a moderate limitation to discretion inherent in the fact that each grant-in-aid program was tied to a particular subject matter category. This is why we came to call them 'categoric aid' to distinguish them from general bloc grants" (Lowi, 1978:21). Under revenue sharing, however, the federal government provided grants-in-aid to local government units with no categorical strings attached. Discretion was thus increased at the local level. The important point for purposes of this discussion is:

From the other side, this means that the federal government is all that much more able to use grant-in-aid appropriations on a patronage basis to buy the support of mayors, governors, and urban lobbies. In the very short run, this . . . will produce "client relationships" between the national center and the 39,000 local principalities. . . . In this sense, the national presence has been extended, and the direct national-local relationship has been cemented. Thereby our positive national state has been perpetuated in virtually the same manner as earlier national states cemented and eventually perpetuated the relationship between the central prince (*primes inter pares*) and all of the other feudal lords. [Lowi, 1978:21–22]

If revenue sharing reinforces dependency of smaller governmental units upon the national unit, the activities that transpire according to Lowi's (1979) notion of "permanent receivership" reinforce dependency of private institutions in society upon the U.S. government. According to Lowi, "*Receivership* refers to the method of maintaining social order during a crisis involving the bankruptcy of an individual or an enterprise. . . . *Permanent receivership* would simply involve public or joint public-private maintenance of the assets in their pre-bankrupt form and never disposing of them at all" (1979:279). In turn, "The state of permanent receivership is a state whose government maintains a steadfast position that any institution large enough to be a significant factor in the community may have its stability underwritten. It is a system of policies that sets a general floor under risk" (Lowi, 1979:280). Thus, through either regulation or planning the government may enmesh private sector institutions and activities within its official ambit by actions analogous to the principle of receivership (Lowi, 1979:280ff.). This analysis would certainly be compatible with Reich's statement that perhaps the "feudal philosophy of largess and tenure may well be a characteristic of collective societies, regardless of their political systems" (1966:79).

In sum, the notions of "permanent receivership," "the contract state" or, as Titmuss has called it, "the pressure group state," have all emerged to express an awareness of "a shift from contract to status; from open social rights to concealed professional syndicalism; from a multiplicity of allegiances to an undivided loyalty" (Titmuss, 1969: 231). I would, therefore, paraphrase Reich's above description of the "feudal philosophy of largess and tenure" in these terms: Keeping the adjudicative principle or the rule of law from being absorbed into the ambit of administration may well be a characteristic task of any society, regardless of its political system. I will say more about this in the immediately following section.

For now, however, I would like to recall the images I have used to introduce the last two major sections—the dark and scowling face of administration and the benign countenance of administration. With regard to the latter, we have seen that when largesse is dispensed within the ambit of an administrative law neither well rationalized nor well integrated institutionally with the regular system of civil or statute law that guards rights, the benign countenance is nothing more than the indulgent smile of a dangerously benevolent paternalism. This smile is centuries, indeed, millennia, distant from the modern welfare state. It is a smile that fades successively as it is countered by the adjudicative principle, the ultimate expression of which is the rule of law that has undergone rationalization.

Confronting the Chasm

It is clear that the epithets hurled at regimes or regime activities to which column B calls attention rise steamily from the chasm that opens up between administration and adjudication once the adjudicative principle emerges within a legal order. As Weber indicated, administration is the oldest form of government. It is, in a sense, what "comes naturally" to politically organized society. Primitive adjudication emerges at first between kin groupings only. At later junctures, adjudication emerges by degrees within an order that is first and foremost administrative. As the adjudicative principle undergoes more and more rationalization (indeed, *if* it does), a point may be reached, as was the case with the democratic revolutions in the West, when the principle itself becomes the source of legitimately exercised authority. This is Weber's "legal authority."

Once this point has been reached, the chasm between administration and adjudication may be interpreted yet another way: the fissure between the two becomes more pronounced because regimes exercising legal authority (the rule of law) establish administrative apparatuses to achieve objectives by which those regimes measure their effectiveness. The administrative units, in their turn, incline toward reaching their objectives with as little opposition as possible, and thus without effective means of appeal against their decisions and actions. Regimes exercising the rule of law will invariably have certain essential objectives that administrative units will be established to reach; thus, it is inevitable that at the core of these regimes will actually be a gulf with administration and adjudication on opposite sides.

What to do about this gulf is the reigning question from the standpoint of the legitimate exercise of sovereign authority within the Western tradition. Let us pursue to its logical conclusion the point that there are two sources that can cause a chasm to open, deepen, and widen between administration and adjudication. Those two sources are (1) the introduction and enhancement of the adjudicative principle into an administrative order, and (2) the expansion of administration within a political order that has reached the point where the grounds for the legitimate exercise of authority is the rule of law (the adjudicative principle itself). First, one can quickly see that under patriarchal authority no disjuncture (and therefore, no problem) will arise, for only the right of the patriarch exists. Regardless of the scope of the administrative objectives set by the patriarch, no subject "rights" will be violated, for none exist. By the same token, no disjuncture will arise within any political order in which either the rights of subjects (citizens) or the right of the ruler(s) is somehow eliminated, for there cannot be a chasm if one "side" is missing.

By contrast, the chasm will be deepest and widest in those regimes in which (1) the rule of law is the most highly developed, and (2) administrative objectives are not only crucial to regime effectiveness, but extensive in scope. First, in a regime in which the adjudicative principle is highly developed, the rights of citizens in relationship to the sovereign are sharply defined. Second, in such a regime, the "right" of the citizen actually refers to the width of the legally relevant space surrounding the citizen which the regime's administrative staffs cannot, with legitimacy, enter.[18] The more highly developed the rights of citizens, the greater the width of this space. Under a regime in which the citizenship right comprises civil, political, and social rights, the legally relevant space surrounding the individual vis-à-vis the sovereign authority is generous in comparison with that surrounding a mere "subject." This means that the administrative apparatuses established by the regime to carry out a diversity of objectives have less "room" to move around in relative to citizenship rights. If and when, therefore, the objectives important to regime effectiveness successively increase in scope, eventually administrative activities will reach the borders of the legally relevant space which adjudication has awarded exclusively to the citizen.

Here is where the split between administration and adjudication, tyranny and juridicality, will become manifest. The regime, through its administrative arm, will be "tyrannical," that is, will brook no appeal regarding its decisions concerning the objective by which regime effectiveness is measured. If, however, the regime, through application of the rule of law, upholds its commitment to the legally relevant space surrounding the citizen, the regime will be ineffective in an area it has defined as the measure of its worth. The prototypical example, of course, would be the sovereign's right to exercise administrative authority to conscript the citizenry to defend the collectivity at large in the event of an invasion by enemy forces. Rarely are the issues so clear-cut, however. As indicated in the sections on oriental despotism, totalitarianism, and authoritarianism, tyranny tends to overtake juridicality when the scope of the objectives sought by the administrative apparatus is vast and the objectives themselves have been defined by the rulers as the measure of the worth of the regime. We might here say the more crucial the objective, the deeper the split between the administrative and the adjudicative principles. In turn, the more extensive the scope of the objective, the wider the split between the two and the more regimented the society. Thus, a split can be deep, but if the objectives of the administration do not overlap into the territory of the rights of citizens, the disjuncture, though latent, will not be problematic. I will be showing that this was the case with the laissez-faire state (cells 3 and 8, Figure 11–1).

The case of the welfare state (cell 15, Figure 11–1) represents, possibly, the most interesting variation upon the theme of adjudication's counterpoint to administration. Here, both sources of the split emerge in clear form. On the one hand, from the adjudicative side of the gap, citizen rights are sharply defined vis-à-vis the political authority, and they are extensive. The addition of social rights to the other two has increased by just that much more the legally relevant space around the citizen that cannot, with legitimacy, be entered by administrative staffs associated with the regime. On the other hand, from the administrative side of the gap, the very measure of the effectiveness of the regime as a welfare state rests upon the degree to which the administrative units succeed in making the redistributions, which, by statutory authority, they are authorized to make. Thus, in the name of raising the citizen's standard of living, regimes under the rule of law actually allow the monumental arms of administrative staffs to embrace the citizen to the bounteous body of the sovereign. This is simply a restatement of the paradox to which I have been referring throughout this work. Consider, by contrast, the case of the laissez-faire state to which I referred in Chapter 5. There, the narrow definition of citizenship rights and the narrow scope of their distribution throughout industrializing Britain, for example, made it comparatively easy for the regime to abide by the rule of law (honor citizen rights) while simultaneously accomplishing administrative tasks defined by the regime as central to its effectiveness (see below).

In sum, regime efforts to confront the chasm fall into several definable categories. First, there is no chasm unless each of rulers and ruled have rights vis-à-vis one another. Thus, one solution to the disjuncture would be to assume away the rights of one "side." I will argue that this has been the solution chosen by the U.S.S.R. Second, an attempt to fill in the chasm can be made by amalgamating the attributes of the two separate sets of legally relevant relationships between citizen and sovereign, the administrative and the adjudicative. I will illustrate this by a recapitulation of Weber's analysis of the patrimonial codifications. Third, administration and adjudication can "change costumes," that is, one can assume the form of the other. I will refer to Weber's observation in this regard and then argue that this solution applies to the administrative activities carried out under that aspect of prerevantionary rule represented by mercantilism (cell 2, Figure 11–1), on the one hand, and the administrative activities of the laissez-faire state, on the other. Fourth, and finally, a regime can attempt to acknowledge the unique character of each principle, of each set of legally relevant relationships generated between citizen and sovereign, and then build institutions to bridge the gap in a way that compromises neither the rights of citizens nor the effectiveness of administrative activities. In connection with this last alternative I will discuss the welfare state (cell 15) and its analytic relationship to social welfare entitlements (cell 5b), on the one hand, and the generic phenomenon, the modern state, on the other. The modern state comprises the contract state, social welfare entitlements, the public interest state, and the welfare state, in addition to other administrative and adjudicative activities not implied by these specific labels.

The Soviet Solution. The Soviet solution to the potential dilemma posed by administrative prerogative versus the rule of law was a potent solution indeed: it literally dissolved the grounds for citizenship rights. This dissolution was both theoretical and, in the degree that the rule of law did exist in czarist Russia, empirical. However imperfectly approximated by concrete rulerships, the principle of adjudication through appeal to law was nevertheless a feature of prerevolutionary Russia. In *A History of the Russian Secret Service* (1972) Richard Deacon writes:

> While the Ochrana [czarist secret police] . . . did many things that were illegal, they adopted a curious stance of bureaucratic correctitude in dealing with the trainees. They referred each case to the Public Prosecutor and, ironically in a country where law and justice so often had little meaning, the Public Prosecutor's Department decided that no legal measures could be taken against the arrested persons because they had not committed any offence on Russian Territory. For once the law took precedence over even the Ochrana's jurisdiction.
> Perhaps this typified the essential difference between the

Czarist regime and the Communist terror which followed. Harsh
deeds, brutal punishments and criminal acts occurred frequently
under the last Czars, but there was in the background a façade of
respect for the law: there were some cases when justice was seen
to be done. Under the Communist terror there was no mercy, no
respect for legality, a cynical refusal ever to be bound by laws
if the laws did not suit the purpose of the rulers. [p. 201]

In the name of the ideals embraced by Karl Marx's philosophy of
humanism, socialism, and communism, the Russian Revolution of
1917 took place. Ostensibly, the revolution represented a step in the
direction of socialism (cell 14), but this destination was never reached.
As a concrete phenomenon, socialism is as elusive as the fabled uni-
corn. As an ideal construct, it is rich and varied. I would be stepping
far beyond the boundaries of my own expertise to attempt to fully
describe or analyze Marx's as well as others' treatments of socialism.
Nevertheless, for purposes of this discussion of alternative regime solutions to the administration-adjudication gap, I have tried to capture analytically a few pertinent dimensions of an ideal about which
writings have ranged from prosaic to lyrical.

In the scheme I have been presenting here, socialism represents a
regime in which a unique type of citizenship right would be guaranteed
by the sovereign. We might call this a "humanistic" right, namely, the
type of right Marx might have had in mind when he envisioned an
allocative system that would embody the principle "from each according to his ability, to each according to his need." Yet Marx was concerned with the whole person, not just material needs. Ivan Svitak
(1965) summarizes the core of Marx's *Economic and Philosophical
Manuscripts* (1844) as conveying the idea that "communism without humanism is no communism and humanism without communism
cannot be humanism." Too, in the tradition of Ludwig Feuerbach's
Principles of the Philosophy of the Future, Marx saw man as a relationship, as a creature of social belonging (Svitak, 1965:20). That is,

Marx held that free and independent man could exist only
in a social and economic system that, by its rationality and
abundance, brought to an end the epoch of "prehistory" and
opened the epoch of "human history," which would make the full
development of the individual the condition for the full
development of society, and vice versa. Hence he devoted the

greater part of his life to the study of capitalist economics and the organization of the working class in the hopes of instituting a socialist society that would be the basis for the development of a new Humanism. [Fromm, 1965:viii–ix]

We might, therefore, think of humanistic rights under socialism (and ultimately communism) as having these characteristics: (1) They would embody the ethical principle that humans are of equal worth and dignity regardless of the specific task they perform in the division of labor. (2) The economically oriented content of the right would capture the principle that material wealth is the outcome of collective activity and it should therefore be shared according to the dictum, "from each according to his ability, to each according to his need." The socioeconomic implication here would be that regardless of the variability of form that a person's productive labor takes, all types of labor are needed in society and, therefore, have value to the collectivity. The social recognition of this value would be tangibly expressed through communal ownership of society's resources and the sharing of the fruits of communal labors. (3) The politically oriented content of the right would embody the notion that the individual in society achieves a sense of efficacy as the direct outcome of affirming the self through productive labor in a setting in which the value of all work and the unity of all people are paramount principles. The political expression of the individual, therefore, would be the outcome of these institutionalized socioeconomic relationships among people and between the people and the factors of production. (4) Finally, these rights would be truly universal, belonging to each person in society.[19]

Absent from Marx's depiction of socialism, as well as from many pre- and post-Marxist treatments of socialist utopias, is a clear enunciation of the mechanisms by which rights would be protected.[20] Analysts have long noted the peculiar assuming away of the bases of societal conflict in the portrayal of ideal social orders.[21] Marx's portrayal of the citizen-sovereign relationship under socialism is not elaborate: rule is at first by the proletariat, after which, eventually, the state withers away. He leaves the nature of the legal system in his ideal society indeterminate, though Marx was no stranger to sophisticated notions of law, including relationships linking citizen, sovereign, and administration in the modern state.[22] The absence of a clearly articulated ideal to characterize legally relevant relationships between citizen and sovereign (even though the citizens were to be the sovereign) in Marx's socialist society left the issue open to interpretation by others.

Empirically, the most historically significant "others" to presume to interpret and implement the Marxist ideal turned out to be the 1917 Bolsheviks and their successors to the present day.[23] Not surprisingly, the interpretation they gave to the mode by which socialism would be attained was consistent with the long and tumultuous political history of Russia (see Guins, 1954; Hazard and Shapiro, 1962; and Berman, 1950, 1963). The political culture that had developed in Russia from, in particular, Ghengis Khan, to the czars was not one in which the adjudicative mode of exercising authority flourished. Marx himself would have named Russia as one of the last nations on earth in which his idea of humanism could successfully take root. Deacon writes that

> for two and a half centuries the Mongols and Tartars
> dominated Russia. Throughout this period the people were
> conditioned to accept rule through an efficient but ruthless in-
> ternal police, aided by informers. It was not until 1492 that Ivan
> the Great expelled the intruders and formed something approach-
> ing a Muscovite empire. Yet the pattern of terror and informers,
> of counter-espionage and police rule, imposed by the Mongols
> was not to be changed. Indeed, the Russian people and especially
> the Soviet thinkers of today, put most of the blame for Russian
> backwardness on the Mongols. The pre-Revolution Russian
> scholar, B. J. Vladimirtsoff, is at one with the Marxists in
> accepting this thesis. This explains much of the theoretical
> antagonism of the Russian Marxists for Maoism today. Karl
> Marx said that "the bloody mire of Mongolian slavery forms the
> cradle of Muscovy," meaning that the Mongols made Russia
> ignorant, semi-Asiatic and possessed of a slave mentality. . . .
> The pattern of terror they introduced remained in greater or
> lesser degree the lot of the Russian people throughout
> their history. [1972:7]

What this means for the argument at hand is that advancement toward the socialist ideal was carried out within the context of the administrative mode of exercising authority. The economy was collectivized; political authority became more centralized within an administrative apparatus than was the case under the last czar, Nicholas II. The citizen-sovereign relationship became enmeshed in a larger matrix of economic planning (see above). The presuming away of conflict between the rulers and the ruled effectively presumed away any distinction between adjudication and administration, resulting in the obliteration of the former by the latter. Although, therefore, the U.S.S.R.'s postrevolutionary leaders announced that they would build an order having the analytic traits that I have summarized in cell 14, in fact, the political order they and their successors built, absorbing the nations of Eastern Europe into their administrative ambit, has the characteristics represented by cell 9. This situation is described by Weber when he writes:

> A legal system may assume a character. . . . [in which]There exist no norms having the character of right-granting laws. In such a situation, the entire body of norms consists exclusively of "regulations." In other words, all private interests enjoy protection, not as guaranteed rights, but only as the obverse aspect of the effectiveness of these regulations. This situation . . . has never prevailed anywhere in its pure form, but in so far as it obtains, all forms of law become absorbed within "administration" and become part and parcel of "government." [1968:644]

Rheinstein's footnote to this observation of Weber's states, "This description of the 'ideal type' of the totalitarian state was written before it emerged in its modern form" (1967:44, n. 7). The outcome of the Soviet solution could be described as "tragedy in the grand Russian style, a conflict between mind and fist in which power prevails."[24]

In turn, for cell 4, which indicates the type of largesse characteristic of Eastern European rule, that is, the Soviet bloc, I have chosen the term "the new class" to refer to the chief context within which gifts and privileges are enjoyed. Milovan Djilas's (1957) *The New Class* links the enjoyment of regime largesse to the emergence of a "special stratum of bureaucrats" who enjoy the privileges of administration. It is worth recapitulating a few of Djilas's major points here, for they tie in with the general outlines of the argument I have been making with regard to Figure 11–1 in general:

> When Communist systems are being critically analyzed, it is considered that their fundamental distinction lies in the fact that a bureaucracy, organized in a special stratum, rules over the people. This is generally true. However, a more detailed analysis will show that only a special stratum of bureaucrats, those who are not administrative officials, make up the core of the new class.

This is actually a party or political bureaucracy. Other officials are only the apparatus under the control of the new class; the apparatus may be clumsy and slow, but no matter what, it must exist in every socialist society. . . .

It is important to note the fundamental differences between the political bureaucrats mentioned here and those which arise with every centralization in modern economy—especially centralizations that lead to collective forms of ownership such as monopolies, companies, and state ownership. . . .

Bureaucrats in a non-Communist state have political masters, usually elected, or owners over them, while Communists have neither masters nor owners over them. The bureaucrats in a non-Communist state are officials in modern capitalist economy, while the Communists are something different and new: a new class.

As in other owning classes, the proof that it is a special class lies in its ownership and its special relations to other classes. In the same way, the class to which a member belongs is indicated by the material and other privileges which ownership brings to him.

As defined by Roman law, property constitutes the use, enjoyment, and disposition of material goods. The Communist political bureaucracy uses, enjoys, and disposes of nationalized property.

If we assume that membership in this bureaucracy or new owning class is predicated on the use of privileges inherent in ownership—in this instance nationalized material goods—then membership in the new party class, or political bureaucracy, is reflected in a larger income in material goods and privileges than society should normally grant for such functions. In practice, the ownership privileges of the new class manifests itself as an exclusive right, as a party monopoly, for the political bureaucracy to distribute the national income, to set wages, direct economic development, and dispose of nationalized and other property. . . .

The ownership privileges of the new class and membership in that class are the privileges of *administration*. This privilege extends from state administration and the administration of economic enterprises to that of sports and humanitarian organizations. Political, party, or so-called "general leadership" is executed by the core. . . .

Other systems, too, have their professional politicians. . . .
However, there are fundamental differences between professional
politicians in other systems and in the Communist system. In
extreme cases, politicians in other systems use the government
to secure privileges for themselves and their cohorts, or to favor
the economic interests of one social stratum or another. The system
is different with the Communist system where the power and
the government are identical with the use, enjoyment, and
disposition of almost all the nation's goods. . . .

Now that the party has consolidated its power, party membership means that one belongs to a privileged class. [Djilas,
1957:42–47 passim]

More than two decades later, observers such as David K. Shipler
(1979) reiterated Djilas's theme, namely that it is typical in the Soviet
type of regime for the enjoyment of largesse to rest upon politically
conditioned relationships, not money per se. These relationships are
distinctly premodern in nature; the discretionary element looms large.
Shipler's comparison between the games of Monopoly and chess is
particularly à propos:

"Making it" in the Soviet Union does not necessarily mean
acquiring money, for cash does not guarantee access to roomy
apartments, good books, excellent schools, vital medicines,
stylish clothes, automobiles, pleasant vacation resorts or even
meat and vegetables. These items and others are either available
to employes of select factories, farms, scientific institutes and
other establishments, or they are obtained through the influence
of friends and connections, or, they are bought in the West by
those whose jobs authorize such travel, or they are accessible to
people who have permission to live in cities that are favored with
good stores, schools and housing. . . . To the extent that success is
measured in terms of a materially comfortable and cultured life,
then, it means positioning oneself strategically rather than just
accruing income. It is not a game of Monopoly, but of chess, and
those who play with cunning and alertness live well. Like money,
the access to privilege can often be passed to heirs; unlike
money, it can be taken away at the whim of the state.

Finally, that the citizen-sovereign relationship in the U.S.S.R. takes
place within a purely administrative ambit accompanied by the proto-

typically patriarchal mentality is underscored by Rimlinger's observation that "Soviet ideology stresses that social security benefits are a *gift* from the state—a genuine act of governmental benevolence. . . . Hardly an occasion is missed to underline the state's and the party's concern for the welfare of the workers and to remind them of the debt of loyalty they owe the rulers" (1971:254).

The Patrimonial Codifications. The patrimonial codifications, of which Weber was entirely skeptical, were the outcome of a recognition by "enlightened despots" of the gap between the administrative legal system and the adjudicative one. Because the codifications attempted to confront the gap by amalgamating the two systems to form one homogeneous body of law, I have placed them on the border (represented by the broken line) between cells 7 and 12a of Figure 11–1. Weber writes: "The ideal was to deprive the law of its specialist character and to formulate it in a way that would not only instruct the officials, but above all, would enlighten the subjects about their rights and duties exhaustively and without outside aid" (1968:856). We might, therefore, think of the following statement as coming straight out of Weber's analysis of the codifications: "Modern law has become a series of instructions to administrators rather than a series of commands to citizens." Rather, it was made by Lowi (1969:144) in description of a U.S. trend.

Writing a decade later in the Preface to the second edition of *The End of Liberalism* (1979), Lowi reinforces his initial insight. Referring to the increasing homogenization of congressional with executive and administrative authority in the United States, he describes the outcome in terms of the construct, the "Second Republic." As part of that Republic's "unwritten constitution" he cites such principles as these: "the separation of powers to the contrary notwithstanding, the center of this national government is the presidency. . . . Congress must take care never to draft a careful and precise statute because this would interfere with the judgment of the president and his professional and full-time administrators. . . . In no instance should Congress or the courts attempt to displace the judgment of the administrators with their own" (Lowi, 1979:xii). Observing that "the only redeeming feature of the Second Republic constitution is that it does not correspond fully to reality" (1979:xii), Lowi nevertheless emphasizes that there has definitely been a fundamental change in the nature of rulership in the United States from the "Roosevelt Revolution" to the present

(1979:271–79). The change Lowi describes closely parallels Weber's depiction of the patrimonial codifications, including their devastating effects upon law formation and the position of the ruled in relationship to sovereign authority:

> It was not until the era of fully developed "enlightened despotism" that, beginning with the eighteenth century, conscious efforts were made to transcend the specifically formal legal logic of the Civil Law. . . . The decisive role was played . . . by the general rationalism developed by bureaucracy in line with its growing self-confidence and its naive belief of "knowing better." Political authority with its patriarchal core assumed the form of the welfare state and proceeded without regard for the . . . desires of the groups interested in the law and the formalism of the trained legal mind. [Weber, 1968:856]

Moreover, "Nobody could feel stimulated to undertake a scholarly treatment of a law which created neither formally precise norms nor clearly intelligible institutions, as neither of these was intended by this utilitarian legislation. As a matter of fact, patrimonial substantive rationalism has nowhere been able to provide much stimulation for formal legal thought" (Weber, 1968:857). In short, Weber was wary of the smile of a dangerously benevolent paternalism represented by the codifications under which "patriarchalism could act more freely" (Weber, 1968:856). In this Weber (once again) anticipated the concerns of contemporary analysts over rulership approaches that either turn the "citizen" into an "administré" (Lowi, 1969, 1979) or that otherwise compromise the adjudicative principle in the interest of "knowing better" (see above on "the public interest").

Changing Costumes: The Laissez-Faire State. A third type of resolution involves administration "assuming the form of judicial procedure" and conversely (Weber, 1968:645–46). Changing costumes is different from the case of amalgamation above, where a blend of the distinctive characteristics of administration and adjudication is attempted. Here, rather, the format of the one is used to address the issues of the other. To illustrate adjudication assuming the form of administration Weber (1968:635) notes that judges may be instructed (presumably by the executive branch of a regime) to render decisions on the basis of ethics, equity, or expediency. With regard to administration assuming the form of adjudication, Weber writes that this practice began early in English history, was practiced on the Continent as well, and carries over in certain matters to modern times:

> [In England] Parliament deals with "private bills," i.e., with such purely administrative acts as licensing, etc. in exactly the same way that it treats public bills. The failure to distinguish between the two types of legislation has been a general feature of older parliamentary procedure; for the English Parliament it was, indeed, a decisive factor in the establishment of its position. Parliament arose originally as a judicial body, and, in France, it became such to the exclusion of all other activities. This confusion between legislative and judicial functions was conditioned by political circumstances. In Germany, too, the budget, which is a purely administrative matter, is treated as a legislative act, in adherence to the English pattern as well as for political reasons. [1968:645–46]

The confusion to which Weber refers gives us a useful perspective for approaching the roles assumed by these two principles in the laissez-faire state as well as under mercantilism.

I have already mentioned that, in accomplishing its objectives, the administrative arm of the laissez-faire state did not elbow its way into the legally relevant space within which citizens enjoyed rights. I indicated that citizen rights were comparatively narrow, both in content and distribution, so that there was "room" for administration to administer without violating rights. The labels "laissez-faire" or "noninterventionist" state might suggest that the state was not doing much in the line of administration anyway, and for this reason the regime did not violate citizen rights. Numerous scholars from a diversity of viewpoints, however, have converged upon the conclusion that the noninterventionist state was by no means administratively idle (Ward, 1881; Neumann, 1966; Tonsor, 1973; Wolfe, 1977; Lowi, 1978): "The liberal state has always been as strong as the . . . situation . . . demanded. It has conducted warfare . . . protected its investments . . . defended and extended its boundaries. It has been a strong state precisely in those spheres in which it had to be strong and in which it wanted to be strong" (Neumann, 1966:22). Thus, it had objectives in terms of which it measured its effectiveness and for which it established administrative apparatuses. Yet, curiously enough, there are no epithets of excoriation to describe the exercise of administrative authority by the laissez-faire state, as such.[25]

Wolfe offers this explanation:

> It is almost a sociological law that those in power will
> deny that power exists and that those who control the state will
> argue that the state is unimportant, for such ideas will make
> control easier to maintain. . . . Far from being natural, laissez
> faire, as Antonio Gramsci once wrote, was "introduced and
> maintained by legislative and coercive means. . . . Consequently,
> laissez faire liberalism is a political programme, designed to
> change—in so far as it is victorious—a State's leading personnel,
> and to change the economic programme of the State itself." Proof
> of this was the difficulty of establishing the ideal of no state
> intervention; even those who were most committed to the
> principle were willing to go along with some violations in fact.
> If laissez faire had indeed been natural, it would never have
> needed the passion and eloquence of a Summer or a Spencer
> to justify it. [1977:53][26]

Thus, on the one hand, political opinion leaders throughout the nineteenth and well into the twentieth century set afoot the idea that the laissez-faire state was the best thing that had happened in the West since the disappearance of bubonic plague. On the other hand, who would cast aspersions upon such administrative objectives as the establishment of transportation, communications, banking, credit, and tariff systems (see cell 8, Figure 11–1) from which nineteenth- and early twentieth-century societies ruled by laissez-faire regimes ultimately reaped such wealth (see Wolfe, 1977:13–41)?

As much validity as I think there is in Wolfe's predominantly Marxist explanation of how it came about that misleading labels have been attached to activities undertaken by the laissez-faire state,[27] further light can be shed upon this issue through the approach I have been pursuing here. Matters that had ordinarily fallen into the purview of administration assumed the costume of adjudication during the laissez-faire and mercantilist eras and so acquired the legitimacy reserved for societal institutions wearing that venerable cloak. This shows up especially in the statutory manner selected by these regimes to disburse largesse, classically a discretionary and "administrative" activity.

Wolfe's mention of the way corporate charters were obtained is illustrative: "In the United States, a state legislature had to pass a bill . . . while in England a private Act of Parliament was necessary" (1977:21). Using statutes to bring about objectives ordinarily administrative in nature was common to both the mercantilist and laissez-faire states:

> Originally a corporation had been a mercantilist notion, referring to an exclusive grant by the state to a private company for the purpose of providing something that was in the common interest of the whole society.[28] . . . In pre-Civil War America, the only significant corporations were in areas like banking and transportation. . . . In Peel's England, railroads were incorporated because of the general understanding that they had a public as well as a private nature. [Wolfe, 1977:21]

The disbursement of land and resources, however, is the most telling example of how an adjudicative format was used to engage in a traditionally discretionary activity. Here, citizen and sovereign are joined in a legally relevant relationship under the rule of law, but the content of the relationship is the classic content of ideal typical administration, namely, giving away something of value: "Between 1789 and 1839, 370 different laws dealing with land were passed by Congress (and signed by Presidents), a fact that does not say much for the existence of laissez faire, even at the national level. The effect was, as Rohrbough noted, as follows: 'Through control of the public domain, the federal government touched the lives of thousands of remote citizens, who had previously neither known nor acknowledged its existence'" (Wolfe, 1977:38, citing Rohrbough, 1968:300–301). Reich's account concurs: "Some land was the gift of the sovereign under laws such as the Homestead Act. Many other natural resources—water, minerals, and timber—passed into private ownership under similar grants. In America, land and resources all were originally government largess" (1966:84). And Lowi's description leaves no doubt: "The domestic policies of the federal government were almost entirely concerned with subsidies, bounties, and claims. Land grants were piled upon land sales at low prices, and these were piled upon still additional land grants until the frontier ran out. Subsidies in the form of money and privilege were granted to the coastal trade, the railroads, and other common carriers. Tariffs were handed out to virtually any manufac-

turer or producer who could gain effective representation in Congress"
(1978:16).

I would suggest that an absence of aspersions cast upon the administrative activities of the laissez-faire and mercantilist states has had much to do with the adjudicative format within which they were carried out. The adjudicative format was used to patronize without eroding citizen rights. "Rights in largesse" were created in the very narrow sense that the right to claim land under the terms of the Homestead Act, for example, would be protected in a regular court of law. Moreover, the grant would not easily be reversible; repeal of the Homestead Act would be necessary. By contrast, the "right" to claim a portion of the radio or television spectrum under today's administrative regulations put forth by the Federal Communications Commission is far more tenuous. The potential homesteader would likely be put on the regular court calendar far ahead of the potential broadcaster (who would first have to exhaust his administrative remedies), and the claim of the latter could well become obsolete the day that the FCC rewrote its regulatory code. It is by no coincidence that the degree of reversibility of a claim to largesse and its disbursement within either the administrative or the adjudicative format correlate. This is what Weber meant by the definition of a right "as being no more than an increase of the probability that a certain expectation of the one to whom *the law* grants the right will not be disappointed" (1968:666–67; italics mine).

To summarize, the laissez-faire and mercantilist states were never forced to confront the chasm between administration and adjudication. It was not that these states had a body of administrative law that was well rationalized and well integrated with the civil or statute law. Indeed, the lack of a clear body of administrative law governing citizen-sovereign relationships was probably the reason why statute law was often selected as the mode to accomplish such clearly administrative tasks as the building of railroads and the disbursement of largesse in order to make the economy ultimately more productive. True, the laissez-faire state engaged in administrative activities (the maintenance of armies and navies, colonial expansion). But these took place within the context of administrative laws that did not directly clash with the notion of citizenship rights as those rights were defined at that time. With the coming of new administrative activities—regulation and redistribution—administrative law was to emerge in its contemporarily recognizable form to join citizen and sovereign in legally relevant ways unprecedented in Western history. It is for these reasons that excoriating epithets were not affixed to the administrative activities of the laissez-faire and mercantilist states. These activities were in the very respectable costume of statute law, and when they were in their own dress, as with the activities related to colonial expansion, they did not threaten citizen rights. The "changing costumes" alternative however, resting upon an illusion as it did, would be far too flimsy to sustain the realities of the modern redistributional era: "In an era of comparatively circumscribed administrative powers, the restriction of official discretion by reference to the common law and statute was a workable and satisfying concept. Given the enormous expansion of governmental activity, not only in the regulation of private activity but also in the provision of goods, services, and advantageous opportunities, it is no longer an adequate or even coherent model" (Stewart, 1975:1811).

Reality Testing: The Western Welfare State

To put the Western welfare state in historical perspective, we may now examine the major dimensions and relationships that have been shown in Figure 11–1. First, the poles of the main diagonal—cells 1 and 15—have shown the two extremes of conditions that may surround the enjoyment of benefits by subjects or citizens. Under primeval administration (patriarchalism), law is the word of the ruler; benefits are favors discretionarily bestowed by the person of the patriarch. Under the rule of law, which has undergone formal and substantive rationalization, benefits are social rights, impersonally and impartially guaranteed as legitimate aspects of the citizenship status. The other cells of Figure 11–1 have represented successive approximations of either one or the other of these two poles.

The poles of the off-diagonal—cells 5b (social welfare entitlements) and 11 (primitive adjudication, primitive formalism, charismatic justice)—have also called attention to strategic junctures within the larger scheme (this was seen clearly in Figure 7–4, where only the four poles of the two continua were depicted). The larger scheme has been formed by two continua that have shown the gradual transition of the degree to which (1) legally relevant regime activity is reglementative or right-creating in relationship to the ruled (Weber, 1968:641–47, 667), and (2) law is rationalized (Weber, 1968:654–58, 809–15). The poles of the off-diagonal have shown the points at which respective quantum leaps on the two continua have occurred both analytically and historically. Cells 5b and 11 show the following two qualitative changes with respect to the two continua.

First, social welfare entitlements (cell 5b) fall within the analytic purview of administration, yet the administrative law from which they flow is rationalized. These entitlements, accordingly, are at the nexus at which irrationalized (administrative) law becomes rationalized. Though analytically they stand within the heritage of the gratuity, they share the analytic trait with social rights that both stem from a type of law that has undergone rationalization. Empirically, this has, in effect, made the entitlement far more similar to the social right from the standpoint of the recipient. Entitlements save the recipient from having to curry favor of a possibly capricious personalized ruler in order to receive a benefit.[29]

Second, primitive adjudication, primitive formalism, and charismatic justice (cell 11), in turn, fall within the purview of adjudication. Yet the law from which they stem is either formally or substantively irrational. Nevertheless, these phenomena stand at the nexus at which the adjudicative function is initially differentiated from the purely administrative mode of rulership. The nature of rulership is here qualitatively changed into one in which rudimentary rights have emerged. These rights stem from the application of a norm, and that norm, ultimately, is capable of undergoing rationalization to create the rights of the welfare state. Empirically, these primitive rights may be a good deal more tenuous than a gratuitous relationship between patriarch and toady, for these early rights stem from the application of law whose irrational nature makes the outcome unpredictable. Yet, a right is analytically more tenable than a gratuity (Weber, 1968:667).

Finally, Figure 11–1 has revealed one other strategic point: there occurred a qualitative change in the status of the ruled from "subject" to "citizen" once the law underwent that quantum leap in rationalization marked by the democratic revolutions (cell 12b to cell 13). The movement from pre- to postrevolutionary rule, that is, from the absolutist to the liberal state, however, was unequivocally predicated upon the change in the quality of the civil or statute law that henceforth characterized rulership in the West. That change is of interest because, within the realm of administrative law, there has been no counterpart to the definitive transition that took place with regard to the civil or statute law.

Within the adjudicative realm, subjects became citizens. But within the administrative realm, what did (have) subjects become? Citizens hold rights. But what is the unique label for the holders of entitlements? The liberal state has been associated with civil rights, the democratic state with political rights, and the welfare state with social rights. But with what pithy catch phrase do we label the aspect of the contemporary Western state that is associated with entitlements? I have deliberately refrained from coining an epithet to represent cell 5b of Figure 11−1. I have remained true to the awkward and unparallel usage of social welfare entitlements to emphasize that no summary way has yet emerged, equivalent to the contract state or the public interest state, to refer to this specific aspect of modern administrative activity.

The empirical events, activities, and outcomes represented analytically by cell 5b are implicitly included in generalized discussions of the welfare state. My argument throughout this work has shown, however, that this lack of recognition of the distinctive nature of cell 5b obscures important issues related to the legitimation of redistributional activity undertaken by welfare regimes. As I mentioned above, the absence of an appropriate epithet to summarily capture a particular category of regime activity may indicate that the nature of the activity or its implications are not well understood. It may indicate that the activity's outlines are not sufficiently clear to suggest a categorical identity. Even Reich's analysis, which I have followed closely, does not draw a fine distinction between the types of largesse that government devolves upon incorporated units, organizations, and the like, on the one hand, and individuals and families, on the other. For purposes of my argument, the distinction is very important: once social welfare entitlements have their own analytic category, a vantage point is gained from which the several relationships among the modern state, the welfare state, and social welfare entitlements may be analyzed and interpreted. Namely, the legitimation controversies that have surrounded redistributions made in terms of social welfare entitlements as well as the welfare state can be contrasted with comparatively noncontroversial redistributions made by the modern state.

The Modern State. I will here make explicit what I mean by the modern state as distinct from the various other states I have been analyzing throughout this chapter. For purposes of this discussion, the modern state includes not only the adjudicative and administrative activities that I have explicitly listed and discussed here, but also all of the other activities, either adjudicative or administrative in orientation, that a contemporary Western regime undertakes: defense, foreign policy, comprehensive planning, fiscal and monetary policy, applying criminal, civil, and statute law involving claims among citizens, and the like. It has become essential to separate the notion of the modern state from the others because I will now show that the modern state engages in much redistributional activity outside the contexts of social welfare entitlements, the welfare state, and even the contract state. Legitimation controversies attach differentially to these differing contexts of redistribution.

The modern state engages in activities that are obliquely redistributional, that is, redistributional not in intent, but in outcome. Yet, these activities do not face the same types of legitimation controversies reserved for explicitly redistributional policy as carried out through social welfare entitlements and the welfare state. Indeed, Heidenheimer, Heclo, and Adams (1975:188) have specified that it is social insurance and public assistance that "have been identified with the welfare state and its controversies," They (1975:187–88) note, however, that "less obvious forms of income support" include a complex tax system, public employment, and publicly subsidized private employment, as well as government intervention into the labor market to affect basic earning levels (such as through minimum wages, equal opportunity employment, and fair labor practices).

The theme that redistribution takes place under rubrics less value-laden than those associated with "welfare," "poverty," "guaranteed annual income," "the needy," and the like has been repeated throughout the literature. Elsewhere Heidenheimer, Heclo, and Adams return to this point (I would, however, eliminate the word "welfare" from their opening statement):

> The modern welfare state intermingles benefits, dispensations and transfers to such an extent that it is practically impossible to separate dependents and non-dependents. One group of social policies may affect the single mother receiving public assistance, free medical care, welfare milk and public housing. Another range of policies may affect the "rugged individualist" who is dependent on the tax law to subsidize interest payments on his otherwise too costly home, on state-enforced credit regulations to multiply his purchasing power, on tax indulgences for his

lucrative "private" retirement plan and expense account, and on government planning services to make others bear the social costs of urban renewal, private transportation, and deflationary fiscal policies. Considering only cash transfer payments in the United States, in 1970 approximately two-fifths of American families benefitted from them; in fact, 22 percent of the families with incomes over $25,000 received some type of transfer grant from the government. [1975:276–77]

Danziger and Plotnick similarly observe of the United States that "the existing transfer system is so broad that 42% of all households received some form of cash transfer, which averaged $2803 in 1974 (when mean household income from nontransfer sources was about $11,000)" (1978:2). Janowitz concurs: "The influence of social welfare clearly extends in a significant and pervasive fashion upward through the social structure. Social welfare benefits are in their own right essential for wide segments of the middle class" (1976:xviii).

Indeed, the "Introduction" to the *Encyclopedia of U.S. Government Benefits* (Grisham and McConaughy, 1975) is utterly unequivocal in pointing out the degree to which we are all beneficiaries of the welfare state:

A woman turns on a light, sees her children off to school, drops a letter into a mailbox, drives to a bank, listens to an account of a satellite launching, all the while totally unaware that in all these things there are direct government benefits. Her husband may be the recipient of a Small Business Administration Loan, her brother of veterans' compensation, her father of social security, her son of a National Defense Education Loan for his college education. Her home mortgage may be FHA-insured. Her grandchildren's health may someday be dependent on fresh water made possible by a government-developed desalinization plant; the life expectancy of her entire family is much greater than was that of her grandparents, largely through the efforts of the public health service; the food she eats has been carefully inspected for safety and quality; her vacation may be a trip with her family to a National Park or Forest; her future, and that of all her descendants, is being vitally affected by the forward-looking space program that will open avenues undreamed of a generation ago.

This same woman, however, hardly considers herself a

ward of a welfare state. . . . She and a large majority of Americans tend to lose sight of the fact that . . . the services provided by government are in reality investments in the effectiveness and future of all of its citizens, not simply gifts of the moment.

This disparity between feeling and fact, this lack of complete information on the part of the people, is . . . the reason for this work.

Titmuss made one of the earliest statements with regard to the multiplicity of formats within which identical objectives have been sought by modern welfare regimes: "Considered as a whole, all collective interventions to meet certain needs of the individual and/or to serve the wider interests of society may now be broadly grouped into three major categories of welfare: social welfare, fiscal welfare, and occupational welfare" (1969:42). Yet fiscal and occupational welfare policies have generated nowhere near the degrees of controversy that social welfare policies have. This requires explanation, for, as Titmuss notes,

when we examine them in turn, it emerges that this division
is not based on any fundamental difference in the functions of the
three systems (if they be so described) or their declared aims. It
arises from an organizational division of method, which, in the
main, is related to the division of labor in complex, individuated
societies. So far as the ultimate aims of these systems are
concerned, it is argued that their similarities are more important
than their dissimilarities.[30] The definition, for most purposes,
of what is a "social service" should take its stand on aims; not
on the administrative methods and institutional devices employed
to achieve them. [1969:42]

The existence of sundry administrative purviews with nevertheless similar aims is partially the outcome of the fact that as new "states of dependency," both natural and man-made, have come into definition, new administrative units have appeared in piecemeal fashion to respond to them (Titmuss, 1969:34–55 passim).

Finally, if Titmuss has noted that a series of very specific aims can spawn a series of policies administratively diverse, Lowi (1969) has noted that vague, ill-defined aims can produce the identical result. Analyzing the U.S. War on Poverty in terms of the broadness of its aims, Lowi wrote of the Kennedy administration that "they set themselves the heroic task, among many others, of eliminating poverty. Alleviation was for sissies. . . . More than 100 distinct proposals were made. However, each agency tended to see a new war waged by expansion of its own programs" (1969:227, 231). By creating the impression that it was willing to "do everything," the Kennedy administration opened up new territories for the advance of conspicuous administration and its inevitable sidekicks, program duplication and fragmentation. In sum, although the degree to which redistribution occurs within a regime may be heavily obscured by the multifarious administrative rubrics under which it transpires, the ultimate connection between redistribution and legitimacy does not dissolve. For a time—and this may even be for an indefinite time—it merely remains invisible.

The Deficient Legitimacy of the Oblique Redistribution. Once the premise is accepted that redistribution is the outcome of a collective political act (see Janowitz, 1976) and is, therefore, bound to imply questions regarding the legitimacy of the contingencies that surround redistribution, it then becomes extremely important for a regime's governing apparatus to be aware of both the explicit and oblique redistributional effects of its official activity. In this section I will argue that the oblique redistribution—that which occurs as a by-product of fiscal, monetary, environmental, trade, defense, transportation, urban, or other policies of the modern state—by its very nature cannot measure up to the criteria of legitimation which explicit redistributions must meet to achieve, retain, and enhance their legitimacy, as discussed in Part I.

Figure 11-2 shows the types of redistribution that are at issue. We have seen that explicit redistribution generates controversy at some stage before it either gains legitimation as a social right or, at least, formal recognition as an entitlement under administrative law. Oblique redistributions initially avoid legitimation controversy upon grounds of redistribution, although disagreement may attach to the immediate policy objectives. If and when, however, the redistributional effects of these latter policies become publicized, there are several mutually reinforcing reasons why they fall short in terms of the criteria of legitimation treated earlier in this work. Briefly, the chief characteristics of oblique redistributions are their relative invisibility,

FIGURE 11-2

Types of Redistributions

		Nature of the Redistributions	
		Explicit	Oblique
Realm Exercising Sovereign Authority	Adjudicative	(1) Social rights of THE WELFARE STATE	(2) By-products of statutes, if any are needed, formalizing diverse policies of THE MODERN STATE, as listed in cell (4)
	Administrative	(3) Social welfare entitlements	(4) By-products of diverse policies of THE MODERN STATE: fiscal, foreign trade, defense, urban, transportation, etc.

unchallengeability, inequitability, unjustifiability, and probable un-affordability to the society in question. The administrative origin of these redistributions accounts for these traits, as I will now show.

With regard to the invisibility of oblique redistributions, Figure 11-2 indicates that, in fact, we have no name for redistributions that are by-products of other policies of the modern state. Because re-distribution is not the aim, but only the unintended effect, of these policies, there can be no meaningful label for these redistributions, collectively considered. Neither, of course, is there a meaningful label that summarily refers to the beneficiaries of these diversely initiated redistributions. Some people are just lucky. Thus, although invisibility attaches to these redistributions, this by no means precludes their various effects being felt by those whom they touch.

Next, the redistributional outcomes of these policies are not, if at all, easily challengeable by the ruled. Wage-price controls would here be an example. Once again, Lowi's (1969) distinction between the coercive but elusive nature of policy and the coercive but self-cor-rective nature of law becomes pertinent. He emphasizes that "policy" and "police" have the same roots, a fact that must gain increasing recognition with respect to "the new, positive national state" (1978:17).

Third, as the outcome of diverse policies, oblique redistributions are bound to fall inequitably upon individuals whose status as citizens of the modern state gives them the right to be ruled impartially. Thus, whereas explicitly redistributional authoritative acts achieve their legitimacy through association with impersonal and impartial law, these oblique redistributions are impersonal without being impartial.

Fourth, explicit redistributions attain legitimation through accompanying rationales, as I showed earlier. By contrast, no rationales are offered to accompany oblique redistributions because the chief aims of the authoritative directives from which they stem are not redistributional. We think of rationales and justifications, as such, as accompanying intended effects, whereas unintended effects and trade-offs may be only acknowledged. This is a subtle but important distinction where matters of legitimation are concerned.

Finally, Figure 11-2 gives an intimation of one other reason why oblique redistributions can be found wanting in ultimate legitimacy: their fragmentation makes virtually impossible a comprehensive, meaningful consideration of their costs and hence, affordability, to the society in question. If the "bottom line" for the legitimacy of redistributions is their effect upon a society's economic health, then a diversity of hidden drains under misleading rubrics cannot be what the doctor ordered. In sum, therefore, the characteristics of the oblique redistribution are such that they could not gain legitimation were their ramifications to be made explicit, if we accept that legitimation rests upon impersonal, impartial, and challengeable law whose rationale is publicly acceptable and whose outcomes do not incur costs that the society cannot ultimately afford.

The following excerpt from the column of U.S. journalist Jack Anderson (1980) illustrates the comparative invisibility, unchallengeability, inequitability, unjustifiability, and potential unaffordability to the United States of an oblique redistribution: "The Pentagon spends more than $350 million a year to operate cut-rate food commissaries across the country. Service families buy food and other items at a 25 percent discount, thanks to this taxpayer subsidy. Congress intended that commissaries serve military posts that were remote from civilian shopping centers, but the Pentagon wordsmiths have gotten around this by coming up with a unique definition of the word 'remote.' In the brass hats' view, a post is remote if it is more than 10 minutes' drive from a supermarket." It is clear that Anderson is scorning the lack of legitimacy that attaches to the administratively manipulated, particularistically oriented, costly, redistributional effects of an official objective that was not initially intended to be redistributional, as such. The above, of course, could be classified as a highly sophisticated form of "welfare cheating." By redefining the word "remote," the letter of the law was adhered to while its spirit was abandoned. "Legalism" dissolved legitimacy. As with all "welfare cheating," once transfers are revealed as taking place outside the agreed-upon criteria, a sense of failed legitimacy immediately characterizes them.[31] This illustration is particularly poignant because the initial aim of the congressional act that brought the institution of the commissary into existence was not redistribution, as such, but compensation in kind for the inconvenience suffered by military families in truly "remote" districts.

Limits and Legitimation. The weight of my argument for the legitimation of social rights, for the legitimacy of the redistributions of the Western welfare state, has rested heavily upon the underlying notion of the "boundary." The boundary between administration and adjudication conditions the degree to which law will be challengeable by those under its authority. Law provides the boundary between rights and nonrights. Formally rational law adheres to the boundaries of logic. Substantively rationalized law specifies value boundaries. Impersonalization of law establishes an institutional boundary between those who exercise the law and those who obey it. Impartiality of law removes boundaries that divide and exclude and substitutes a new boundary that includes and unites the body politic under citizenship. The rights associated with citizenship—civil, political, and social— establish different types of boundaries around the individual which the sovereign or other members of society cannot legitimately transgress. Explicit redistributional policy marks the boundaries at which skirmishes and major battles may occur over the criteria (that is, boundaries) of redistribution within a society. Finally, oblique redistributions arrive at their boundaries either indiscriminately or particularistically. Their boundaries (scope) are potentially limitless, their costs potentially bottomless, and their effects uncontrollable and elusive. Their legitimacy is nil.

In turn, I have drawn analytic boundaries around the notion of the "welfare state," distinguishing it and its unique purview from the activities of other types of states throughout history, as well as from the activities of the modern state. I have shown that upon certain boundaries—namely, the formal and substantive rationalization of law that creates the social rights of citizenship—rests the legitimacy of the redistributions undertaken by the welfare state. By contrast, re-distributions—either gratuitous, oblique, or approximations thereof —that transpire outside these boundaries have suffered, do suffer, and will always suffer insurmountable legitimation problems. In the ideal typical welfare state, boundlessness and indiscriminateness are not mistaken for comprehensiveness or universality. This mistake is avoided because the ultimate feature of formally rationalized law is its determinateness (see Chapter 4). The formal rationality of law that pertains to redistributions thus sets the upper limits of those redistri-butions at any one historical point. In turn, the substantive rationality of the law justifies those limits, absolving the sovereign from illimitable responsibility for citizen well-being. At the theoretical level, therefore, cost-related controversies surrounding welfare state redistributions are resolvable through the mechanism of formally and substantively rationalized law.

This depiction of the welfare state is reinforced when examined from the vantage point of Weber's notion of rational action in which action becomes increasingly subject to guidance by the conscious ar-ticulation of ideas. In Ann Swidler's discussion of Weber's concept of rationality she states that it is "deliberateness which is the crucial feature of rationality. The wider the area over which conscious ideas have influence, the more rational a culture, society, or institution" (1973:39). Thus, the redistributions of the welfare state as they have been analyzed here are those that are the most consciously articulated, both formally through law and substantively through a justifying ra-tionale. They represent the deliberate subjection of action (sovereign assumption of responsibility for citizen well-being) to ideas (the social right to a civilized standard of living as a legitimate component of citizenship).

Social welfare entitlements, in turn, have been somewhat less con-sciously, less deliberately articulated than have been redistributions that are social rights. The connection between ideas and action has been more tenuous. In the United States, court review has helped to make the connections between ideas (ultimate agency objectives, con-stitutional ideals) and action (what agencies do, how agencies orient themselves toward citizens) more explicit and more compatible. The rationalization of administrative law and the increasing willingness of the regular courts to review agency-client cases are two indicators of the increasing rationality of legally relevant action that characterizes redistributions that take place within the context of social welfare entitlements.

Finally, the oblique redistributions of the modern state are the least consciously articulated, if at all, of the types of redistributions considered here. The match between ideas and action is ill fitting if the ideas behind the policies are other than redistributional, but policy implementation is redistributional in outcome. This does not mean that the modern state ought not to implement policies if they have redistributional effects. It only means that the redistributions that obtain cannot be defended as redistributions. They cannot be defended by the same criteria that justify explicit redistributions. At most, they can be defended as justifiable trade-offs in combination with the diverse goals of the modern state. Thus, the greatest legitimacy attaches to redistributions that are the product of rational action as represented by the deliberateness of formally and substantively rationalized law. The least legitimacy attaches to redistributions that are the product of ideas that bear no relationship to the redistributional outcomes which, in fact, may follow from them.

In the degree that redistributions are made within the context of explicitness/rationality/legitimacy as against the context of obliqueness/nonrationality/deficient legitimacy, the welfare state is able to exert that capacity of self-regulation which is central to the classical notion of social control. In his review and analysis of this sociological concept, Janowitz states that social control rests upon a value commitment to "procedures of redefining societal goals in order to enhance the role of rationality" (1975:84). Such rationality staves off the possibility of coercive control, of which social control is the antithesis, for "social control involves the capacity of constituent groups in a society to behave in terms of their acknowledged moral and collective goals" (Janowitz, 1975:84). By rational choice, society's constituent groups establish boundaries for themselves, boundaries that have acceptability because they have meaning to those who chose them. These self-imposed boundaries constitute the self-regulation that precludes the necessity for externally imposed boundaries, that is, coercion.

Janowitz's discussion of social control parallels the distinctions I have drawn here between the administrative and adjudicative principles, for social control also rests upon a value commitment to "the reduction of coercion, although it recognizes the irreducible elements of coercion in a legitimate system of authority" (1975:84). In this regard, social control is the analogue of the adjudicative principle and coercion the analogue of the administrative principle. That is, the adjudicative principle, whose highest expression is the rule of law which has undergone formal and substantive rationalization, allows a society the greatest degree of social control as conscious and deliberate self-regulation. By contrast, the administrative principle, whose purest expression is the absence of appeal in the face of the need for sovereign effectiveness, allows a society the least degree of self-regulation; rather, the administrative apparatus assumes responsibility to regulate, to coerce, and to enforce in the name of effectiveness.

It is from this point of view that the failure of a society to regulate itself through rational action may generate a backlash of authoritarian coercion. Namely, society's wealth is always limited in the sense that choices as to its disposition unavoidably include some and exclude others. These choices may originate in the impersonal market, or in either the administrative or adjudicative realms of sovereign authority, or in some combination of these sources. Nevertheless, if a society's always-limited wealth is inadvertently squandered, either through the market or through legally relevant actions whose ultimate outcomes are ill considered, fewer choices subsequently remain open to that society as to future dispositions of wealth and, by implication, the general running of the society as an effective social organization. This situation—the increasing lack of choice open to a society—implies that a "crisis" stage has been reached, a stage classically associated with the call for authoritarian effectiveness.

In his *Social Control of the Welfare State* Janowitz emphasizes that we must ask "whether authoritarian solutions can be avoided—for even a limited increase in authoritarian sanction would destroy the moral basis and the goals of the welfare state" (1976:5). In turn, such authoritarian sanction may well spring from a failure of the redistributional state to draw boundaries, to regulate itself from within: "Any effort at institution building for social welfare must . . . assess whether a materialistic hedonism and a consumer-oriented format of social welfare can implement the transcendental goals of the welfare state" (Janowitz, 1976:xix). Herein lies the importance of the parallel between the adjudicative principle and the notion of social control as the capacity for the welfare state to explicitly make and defend choices as to the grounds upon which redistribution shall take place. For it is the use of the adjudicative principle, the use of rationalized law, which can avoid authoritarian solutions. Rationalized law achieves temporary closure, but closure nevertheless, with regard to these crucial questions that confront every welfare state: When is enough, enough? What is the defensible upper limit of sovereign responsibility for citizen well-being? What is the justifiable lower limit of a civilized standard of living for citizens under a regime given the level of its surplus?

In turning to the literal meaning of "transcendental" as "transcending human experience, but not knowledge," it becomes clear that the term captures the essence of the welfare state as both rational and humanitarian. The welfare state ideally regulates itself through rationalized law that limits and justifies sovereign responsibility at the same time as it elevates its citizens to a new experience in human history: the experience of enjoying the social right to a minimum standard of living, a standard whose explicit relationship to the society's level of wealth does not leave the legitimacy of that standard in doubt.

NOTES

Chapter 1

1. All references to Max Weber's *Economy and Society* are to the first edition by Guenther Roth and Claus Wittich (New York: Bedminster Press, 1968). Since I began this work a second edition has been published: (Berkeley: The University of California Press, 1979). Initially, Weber's work appeared as *Wirtschaft und Gesellschaft* and was published by Verlag von J. C. B. Mohr (Paul Siebeck) in Tubingen, Germany, 1922. In 1925 an enlarged, second edition was published (noted in Rheinstein, 1967:xvii).

2. Bendix (1962:291) specifies that "for Weber, 'domination' was identical with the 'authoritarian power of command.'" Weber's "domination" (*Herrschaft*) derives "from *established authority* that allocates the right to command and the duty to obey." This is distinct from the power (that is, the possibility of imposing one's will upon others) that derives from a constellation of interests that develops on a formally free market (Bendix, 1962:290).

3. For brevity, I will refer loosely to reglementations as emanating from the administrative staff of the patrimonial ruler, though, in the pure case, the ruler himself issues the rule ordering the affairs of the realm.

4. See Chapter 3, n. 4, for the specific senses in which the terms "authoritarian" and "libertarian" are used throughout this work.

5. "Civil" law refers either to Roman law, especially the part applied to Roman citizens, or to the body of law relevant to private rights; statute law means law established by a legislative body (Webster, 1970:1028). I use both terms together throughout this work because my analysis applies in particular to statute law, which is also civil law, that is, law creating citizenship rights.

6. In Chapter 7 I elaborate on why the categories "formal" and "substantive" do not transfer directly to an analysis of administrative law; rather, the notions of legalization and judicialization are more apt. Calling attention to some specifying concepts used by today's analysts does not mean that Weber did not deal with the rationalization of the law used by administrative officials. Indeed, this is covered in his treatment of bureaucracy and referred to in his analysis of the patrimonial codifications (1968:856–59); see Chapter 11.

7. Rules dealing with the public may be classified, broadly, under the rubric of "public law." Weber (1968:641–44) discusses distinctions between "public" and "private" law, emphasizing that "the exact criteria of this distinction are surrounded by controversy." One general distinction defines public law as regulating state-oriented conduct, whereas private law (though issuing from the state or the political authority) regulates other types of conduct (for example, of citizens toward one another). Public law may be thought of as the law of subordination, private law as the law of coordination, such that when several parties are confronting each other, their legal spheres are correctly allocated relative to one another. Of relevance to the present discussion is that the first form of "public law" is the reglementation, which is also the law reg-

ulating the behavior of the administrative staff: "Public law might be regarded as identical with the total body of the 'reglementations,' i.e., those norms which only embody instructions to state officials as regards their duties, but, in contradistinction to what may be called 'claim norms,' do not establish any 'rights' of individuals" (Weber, 1968:641–42). In Weber's depiction of modern bureaucracy (1968:217–26, 956–1005), however, it is clear that there is a sharp distinction between the rules that orient its activities to those outside itself (a "public," as it were, be they citizens or some other type of client) and the "housekeeping" rules that orient the staff to one another. This comes with the rationalization of reglements into adminsitrative law. The reglement, thus, is the precursor of both administrative law and the (housekeeping) internal staff rules of today's administrative units.

8. The term "sublegislation" is also used to refer to administrative law. Sublegislation specifically means referring to rules and regulations made by agencies using authority delegated them by legislative bodies to "fill in" the meaning of statutes passed by those bodies. Blachly and Oatman's (1934) discussion of sublegislation is classic, and Shapiro's (1968) is an informative contemporary statement.

9. In using the term "administrative law" I do not presume rationality. Indeed, in Part II, I will show the effects of varying degrees of legalization and judicialization of administrative law oriented toward granting assistance to citizens throughout this century. Accordingly, the continuum to which I refer is bounded by the reglementation (by definition irrational) and rationalized administrative law.

10. Hereafter I will refer to this continuum as "the rationalization of administrative law," with the "reglementative" understood.

11. This statement does not ignore that under traditional authority the ruler is not free to make all the rules, for "the commands of such a person are legitimized in one of two ways: (a) partly in terms of traditions which themselves directly determine the content of the command . . . (b) partly in terms of the master's discretion in that sphere which tradition leaves open to him; this traditional prerogative rests primarily on the fact that the obligations of personal obedience tend to be essentially unlimited. Thus there is a double sphere. . . . In the latter sphere, the master is free to do good turns on the basis of his personal pleasure and likes. . . . So far as his action follows principles at all, these are governed by considerations of ethical common sense, of equity or of utilitarian expediency" (Weber, 1968:227). Within the second sphere the ruler is free to rule in terms of motives that reflect themselves in his reglementations.

12. The reader might assume that if rationalized statute law creates social rights to benefits and then delegates the tasks of delivering the benefits to administrative agencies, entitlization of claimants will be straightforward. In Part II, I show how and why the history of the welfare state, especially in the United States, defies such crisp categorization.

13. I do not imply that when agencies turn down applicants for benefits they are ipso facto turning down eligible individuals (see Chapter 7).

14. Proponents of the negative income tax (NIT) would largely disagree that administrative apparatuses are necessary, at least to the extent that they have been used. They argue that waste and confusion could be done away with by substituting an NIT for administration (see n. 5, Chapter 9). Nevertheless, because the welfare state has come into being through the establishment of ad-

ministrative units that have the besetting characteristics treated here, I must address the empirical situation as it exists.

15. The U.S. daily newspapers easily confirm that Western welfare regimes view this as a legitimate citizen expectation. Here is a typical statement: "The economic slump is making people physically as well as emotionally sick and could lead to 19,443 additional deaths in Michigan, including more suicides, murders and heart attacks, a report said yesterday." This report was prepared by the University of Michigan for that state's human services cabinet ("Recession: It's Enough to Make You Sick").

16. I am following Lenski's definition of the societal surplus as "the goods and services over and above the minimum required to keep [the society's members] alive and productive" (1966:44). Janowitz (1976:41–71) gives a detailed account of the specific variables that have contributed to the decline of the economic surplus in the West during these last decades, for, in fact, "the welfare state has . . . been accompanied by an expansion of the propensity to consume more than is produced" (p. 48).

17. The legitimation literature is vast, the more so because issues concerning the legitimate use of authority are often the implied referent of discussions ostensibly oriented toward other substantive areas (social control, social change, political modernization, revolution, the nature of legal systems, political ethics and ideologies, and the like). Implicit references to the processes of legitimation (or delegitimation) and the elements of legitimate rulership ubiquitously pervade an interdisciplinary literature. Below, therefore, I simply list a sampling of works that have led me to form the generalization that legitimacy is the outcome of a relationship of congruence between two sets of politically relevant variables, theory and practice, and rulers and ruled (see also note 19 below): Bendix, 1977, 1978; Benn and Peters, 1959; Bottomore, 1964; Braybrooke, 1968; Brinton, 1959; Cotgrove, 1975; deJouvenel, 1963; Eisenstadt, 1963; Friedman, 1977; Friedman, 1975; Friedrich, 1972; Friedrichs, 1979; Gurr, 1971; Habermas, 1970, 1975; Hacker, 1972; Huntington, 1968; Janowitz, 1976; Jones, 1958; Kleinberg, 1973; Lenski, 1966; Lindenfeld, 1968; Lipset, 1960; Marx, 1971; Michelman, 1967; Moore, 1967; Mosca, 1939; Nonet and Selznick, 1978; Pareto, 1935, 1966; Parsons, 1951, 1961; Shils, 1965; Tonsor, 1973; Tussman, 1960; Weber, 1968; Welch and Taintor, 1972; Wilensky, 1975; Williams, 1960; Wolfe, 1977. Many of these works, of course, build upon such classical statements as Bodin's *Republic* (1576), Hobbes's *Leviathan* (1651), Locke's *Two Treatises of Government* (1690), Rousseau's *The Origin of Inequality* (1754–55) and *The Social Contract* (1762), Burke's *Reflections on the Revolution in France* (1790), Hegel's *The Philosophy of Right* (1821), Bentham's *Principles of Morals and Legislation* (1789), Austin's *Province of Jurisprudence Determined* (1832), J. S. Mill's *Considerations on Representative Government* (1861), and Kelsen's *General Theory of Law and State* (1945).

18. Lenski's definition of a "regime" is à propos: a regime refers to "the members of a particular political elite who come to power by force and to all their successors who come to power by legitimate means. Thus a regime governs from the time of its victory in one revolution until its defeat or overthrow in a subsequent war or revolution" (1966:59, n. 16). For variety, however, throughout this work I will loosely interchange the terms "regime," "rule," "political authority," "nation," "the sovereign," "government," and "the

state." Williams, for example, distinguishes between "*government*, which is the particular group of persons that at any given time mans the apparatus of the state" and the state as "the *structure* by which the group's activity is defined and regulated" (1960:217). I recognize these distinctions, but I do not here want to grind them to too fine a point.

19. The legitimation literature treats regime legitimacy as the outcome of events that take place on one or more of the following eight continua which could alternatively be expressed as a 2 × 2 table with political principles and political practices forming the columns and the respective orientations toward them of the rulers and the ruled forming the rows. Thus, the literature summarizes legitimacy as correlating with the following combinations of judgments: (1) Judgments made by rulers or competing elites upon the degree of congruity that exists between political principles and political practices. (2) The degree of congruity that obtains between judgments made by both rulers and ruled with regard to political practices. (3) Judgments made by the ruled upon the degree of congruity that exists between political principles and political practices. (4) The degree of congruity that obtains between judgments made by both rulers and ruled with regard to political principles. (5) The degree to which rulers or competing elites are in accord among themselves with regard to political principles. (6) The degree to which rulers or competing elites are in accord among themselves with regard to political practices. (7) The degree to which the ruled are in accord among themselves with regard to political practices. (8) The degree to which the ruled are in accord among themselves with regard to political principles. There are, of course, permutations on these eight themes. For example, we would not expect all of the ruled to hold the same views of political practices vis-à-vis all of the rulers. There will be variation within categories.

20. Faint echoes of this criticism can be heard to the present day: Friedman writes that "most of the present welfare programs should never have been enacted. If they had not been, many of the people now dependent on them would have become self-reliant individuals instead of wards of the state" (1980:119). See also Freeman (1975).

21. This criticism has been applied (not without justification) to the social legislation instigated by Otto von Bismarck in Imperial Germany. See n. 1 Chapter 8.

22. It would be unwise to think of law as utterly impersonalized and impartial, however, for Lenski warns that after a revolution, "by virtue of its coercive power, a new elite is in a good position to rewrite the law of the land as it sees fit. This affords them a unique opportunity, since by its very nature law is identified with justice and the rule of right. Since legal statutes are stated in general and impersonal terms, they appear to support abstract principles of justice rather than the special interests of particular men or classes of men. The fact that laws exist prior to the events to which they are applied suggests an objective impartiality which also contributes to their acceptance. Yet laws can always be written in such a way that they favor some particular segment of society. . . . In short, laws may be written in such a way that they protect the interests of the elite while being couched in very general, universalistic terms" (1966:52). See also n. 12, Chapter 11.

23. That is, they went "out" at the formal (legal) level. They certainly went "out" compared to prerevolutionary practices. Never, however, and nowhere are these types of political arrangements absolutely "out."

24. Weber (1968:695–98, 880) discusses this particularism in his treatment of the special or private law communities. I make reference to this in Chapter 2. With regard to the extreme fragmentation of the sociopolitical order associated with special laws, Sabine's (1952:461–62) description of pre-revolutionary France is without parallel (Sabine notes that he has based this upon R. R. Palmer's "Man and Citizen: Applications of Individualism in the French Revolution" in *Essays in Political Theory*, edited by Milton R. Konvitz and Arthur E. Murphy [1948], pp. 130ff.): "For the revolutionist of 1789 the abolition of feudalism meant relief from very galling realities of his everyday political experience. Everywhere he found himself confronted by the fact that his legal rights and his political privileges depended not at all on the fact that he was a Frenchman but on his membership in some group to which custom or royal grant assigned a special place in the society and the economy and the government. Affiliations of this sort determined his social standing, his place in the army, his position in the economy, his taxes, and the part in politics that he might hope to play. If he belonged to the nobility, he had substantial privileges but he was debarred by law from engaging in many occupations. If he were a professional man, a lawyer for example, his position was fixed by membership in a professional association, and such membership was costly and hard to get, for the association held a monopoly of some branch of practice and membership conveyed the right to take part in the affairs of some municipal corporation. The same was true if he were a skilled artisan and the member of a guild. And if he were a peasant, he shared privileges in common land controlled by his village but he shared also a communal responsibility for taxes and road work. If he were an official, his office was likely to be property which he must inherit or buy, and he was irremovable. In 1789, when the government revived the obsolete practice of electing a States General, everyone voted with the group where his station in life placed him, for according to the constitutional theory what was represented was not the individual but the corporations which composed the estates of the realm. French society was a maze of corporate bodies that were at once legal, vocational, and political and that were endowed with privileges and monopolies and duties. Whatever rights a Frenchman possessed he had as a member of one or more such groups; his rights were privileges in the etymological sense of the word, that is, private laws. In French politics there were hundreds of liberties, corresponding to the hundreds of positions or ranks or stations, but there was no liberty conceived as the civil or political attribute of men as citizens. It was this fact that gave force to revolutionary slogans like the 'Rights of Man and Citizen.'"

25. Bell (1973) is known for his articulation of the construct "postindustrial society," a notion far broader than that of the welfare state. He writes: "In descriptive terms, there are three components: in the economic sector, it is a shift from manufacturing to services; in technology, it is the centrality of the new science-based industries; in sociological terms, it is the rise of new technical elites and the advent of a new principle of stratification. . . . The post-industrial society means the rise of new axial structures and axial principles: a changeover from a goods-producing society to an information or knowledge society; and in the modes of knowledge, a change in the axis of abstraction from empiricism or trial-and-error tinkering to theory and the codification of theoretical knowledge for directing innovation and the formulation of policy" (1973:487). Bell believes that "the major orders, or realms,

of societies can best be studied by trying to identify *axial* institutions or principles, which are the major lines around which other institutions are draped, and which pose the major problems of solution for the society. In capitalist society the axial institution has been private property and in the post-industrial society it is the centrality of theoretical knowledge. In Western culture in the last one hundred years the axial thread has been 'modernism' with its onslaught on tradition and established institutions" (1973:115).

But when Bell continues that "in the Western political systems the axial problem is the relation between the desire for popular participation and bureaucracy," I disagree. Rather, and more along Weberian lines, I believe the axial problem for Western political systems is to resolve the mutual antagonism between administration and adjudication, an antagonism that seemed to abate during the laissez-faire era (see Chapter 11, this work) but has been revived by welfare state redistributional efforts. The axial problem is to institutionally acknowledge some very real points of complementarity between these two processes, which are fundamentally antithetical.

26. The term "affirmative action" arose to popular usage in the United States in connection with this practice. Affirmative action can mean government enforcement of "reverse discrimination," that is, discrimination in favor of previously discriminated against minorities. The government may make the availability of federal funds contingent upon "quota representation" as referred to by Bell. An excerpt from an item in *Time* (10 December 1979, p. 99) entitled "How Far Can Congress Go?" suggests some of the difficulties presaged by Bell in connection with quota representation: "For the third time in two years, the Supreme Court is deciding a major reverse discrimination claim. The issue this time is not the permissibility of racial quotas for professional school admissions . . . or of company job-training programs . . . but of a congressional award of a share of federally financed local public works contracts to minority-controlled businesses. The case . . . should help to further define the still murky limits to which affirmative-action programs may go in redressing racial imbalances.

"The case, called *Fullilove vs. Kreps*, focuses on a 1977 federal law authorizing grants to local governments for public projects with $4 billion to be allocated by Dec. 31, 1978. Noting that minority-controlled companies had been getting only 1% of all Government contracts, Maryland Democrat Parren Mitchell proposed an amendment guaranteeing such firms 10% of the $4 billion. The amendment passed, to the distress of the construction industry. All told, 27 suits were filed charging that the 10% set-aside was unconstitutional. . . .

"In last week's arguments, the plaintiffs' lawyers maintained that the 10% set-aside was wrong because Congress should order quotas only when it had made 'detailed findings' of past discrimination, which it had not done in the case of construction contracts. Moreover, they insisted, the size of the set-aside itself was arbitrary. 'Why 10%?' asked one of the attorneys. 'Why not 4%—the number of black contractors in the United States?' Fullilove himself is fearful about the lack of restraint on quota setting. A 10% set-aside might conceivably be tolerable, he says, but the problem is that 'next time around it might be 15% or 25%.'

"Arguing for the Government, Assistant Attorney General Drew Days maintained that Congress had no need to provide a detailed justification for the 10% set-aside, since it had 'unique competence' to right past wrongs as it saw fit."

See also Chapter 11, n. 3, for further references to affirmative action, as well as Chapter 11 for my distinctions between the negative and the positive or affirmative state.

Chapter 2

1. Selznick (1969:18–26) briefly summarizes Durkheim's, Mead's, and Weber's treatments of morality as integral to social life. Phillips (1979) applies a sociological perspective to a wide range of philosophical works, including Rawls (1971) and Nozick (1974), among others, to treat the general notion that society is a moral order. Mommsen's (1965) treatment of Weber's philosophy of world history shows Weber's continuing concern with this issue.

2. As the norm becomes more general, the adjudication process becomes more "rational" (Weber, 1968:654–58; see Chapter 4). Also, a type of adjudication exists in which it is not, strictly speaking, a norm that is applied, but a fixed procedure: for example, a specific technique for consulting an oracle falls under that type of "irrational" adjudication called "primitive formalism" (Weber, 1968:758–65, 656–57).

3. The utter flexibility of interpretation of the elements in natural law is noted by Sabine who writes, "The theory of contract, taken in the large, need not be used as a means of limiting the power of government or of defending resistance, though of course it frequently was so used. Hobbes and Spinoza bent it, or perhaps distorted it, to a defense of absolute power" (1937:431).

4. This figure of speech is not meant to reify the political authority of the market.

Chapter 3

1. In fact, they did so intervene. See Chapter 11.

2. The "liberal state," as such, was more of an ideal than an empirical reality of lengthy duration (see n. 27, Chapter 11). Rather, it would be on firmer ground to say that certain nineteenth-century government acts capture the essence of the liberal state, the initial failure to institute social protections for citizens being a case in point.

3. MacRae's (1976) analysis of the various issues surrounding old and new welfare economics illuminates the nature of this transition. See especially Chapters 5 and 6 (1976:107–202). Marshall (1972) and Myrdal (1972) also treat this transition.

4. Lasswell and Kaplan (1963:228–30) define a continuum of rule according to assumption of responsibility as follows: when all responsibility for citizen security and welfare is assumed by the political sovereign, rule is authoritarian. When, instead, rights and freedoms are instituted so that the individual in society may assume responsibility for his own well-being, rule is libertarian. I, in turn, have added the notion of humanitarian rule to account for that gradation of possibility offered by the Western welfare state.

5. Weber lists the following "mutually dependent ideas" implied by acceptance of the validity of legal authority: that any given legal norm may be established by agreement or imposition, on grounds of either or both of expedience or value-rationality; that every body of law is essentially a consistent

system of abstract rules established, for the most part, intentionally; that those in authority are themselves subject to an impersonal order and orient their actions to it as they issue commands; that those who obey are obeying "the law" and that this law is obeyed only in the capacity of a member of the organization to which the legal authority applies; that incumbents may not appropriate offices, and "rights" of officials are strictly for the purpose of their orienting their actions to the relevant norms of the legal order; that administrative acts, decisions, and rules are formulated in writing and are a nexus for the "office" or bureau; that the forms according to which legal authority is exercised may be multifarious (Weber, 1968:217–19).

6. McIntosh (1970:906) similarly notes this connection: "If we are speaking of pure types of *legitimacy* . . . The third member of the Weberian trilogy [in addition to tradition and charisma] is not bureaucratic authority, nor even strictly speaking rational (positive) legal authority, but rather, natural law."

7. Wilensky (1975) and Weed (1979) specify such variables. Janowitz (1976), Leichter (1979), and Myrdal (1969) provide excellent comprehensive views. Bowler (1974) and Burke and Burke (1974) deal with the "brass tacks" of specific social legislation in the United States during the early 1970s. Danziger, Haveman, and Smolensky (1977) treat the practical parameters conditioning the Carter administration's proposed welfare reforms.

8. See, however, Benn and Peters (1959), Brecht (1959), and Sabine (1937) for accounts of how Hobbes and the utilitarians differed with this interpretation of natural law.

9. Sabine notes, "The criticism of Louis XIV's government which began at the end of the seventeenth century was not at first the product of any political philosophy but merely the reaction of conscientious men to the shocking effects of bad government." But "Criticism of the absolute monarchy urgently needed a philosophy . . . and the philosophy of the English Revolution [natural law/natural 'rights'] was ready to hand" (1937:545, 546).

Chapter 4

1. But see n. 22, Chapter 1.

2. The "special law" as treated in Chapter 2 detached a legally relevant trait (such as occupational or religious affiliation) that was narrow, not general, and thus constricted the law's impersonality and impartiality.

3. Swidler's (1973:36–38) summary of Weber's treatment of rationalization is concise and I have used it as the basis for my enumeration. See also Eisen (1978) and especially Kalberg (1980) for comprehensive treatments of Weber's types of rationality.

4. This discussion has necessarily been simplified to show the essentials of the argument regarding how the law can be rational. The complexities of the contemporary welfare state will be successively introduced throughout ensuing chapters.

5. Selznick (1969:8–18) treats the distinction between the law's ultimate objectives and its formal character in terms of, respectively, the law's "civilizing potential" and "intimate association with the realization of values," on the one hand, and the law's "legal correctness," which can "degenerate into legalism" (the divorce between means and ends), on the other. Like Weber, Selznick notes the inherent tension between the form and substance of the law:

"When the law is conceived as a functional necessity, the focus tends to be on order and control. . . . This might be called the *minimalist* view of what law is and does. For it, 'justice' is not a compelling symbol and at an extreme may even be scorned as the refuge of hopelessly muddled men" (Selznick, 1969:8).

Chapter 5

1. The democratic revolutions to which Sabine (1952:453) refers are the Puritan Revolution during the mid-seventeenth century, culminating in the "bloodless" English Revolution of 1688, and the French Revolution (1789).

2. It is not especially clear from Weber's account just how freedom of contract and the inviolability of individual property became "joined to" freedom of conscience. As a historical fact, though, this conjunction did take place.

3. Milestones in the history of Britain's poor laws include the Elizabethan Poor Law (1601) and the Act of Settlement (1662). In 1832 the Royal Commission embarked upon an inquiry that resulted in the 1834 Poor Law Reform Act Amendment (Rose, 1976, cited in Fraser, 1976:25–27).

4. I invite the reader to note the circularity of nineteenth-century logic regarding issues of dependency: "Citizenship at first excludes all socially and economically dependent persons" (Bendix, 1977:90). If women and children were working in the factories, they were demonstrating at least economic independence. Yet, their (arbitrary) legal status as dependents entitled them to protection by way of the Factory Acts, which, nevertheless, did not technically compromise the liberal regime's fidelity to the rule of law.

5. Marshall (1963:83) specifies that by law persons were classified as paupers and were disenfranchised by accepting help under the terms of the Poor Law. Also, in practice, they forfeited their civil right of personal liberty by internment in the workhouse.

6. Their works were, respectively, *Poverty: A Study of Town Life* (1901) and the seventeen-volume *Life and Labour of the People of London* (see Briggs, 1961:252–53).

7. Briggs (1961:253) concurs, noting that "sharp turns of thought about poverty" and "signs of fundamental re-thinking" were evident not only in Britain, but throughout Europe and the United States.

8. To alleviate primary poverty, Rowntree advocated what today would be recognized as the redistributional objectives of the welfare state. He called for old-age pensions, family allowances, public housing, and supervised factory working conditions as citizen rights (see Briggs, 1961:253).

9. Bismarck's social legislation of the 1880s was of this type (Wilensky, 1975).

10. Heidenheimer, Heclo, and Adams (1975:194–95) note that in Sweden the pension was based on contributory insurance, provided little income redistribution, and covered virtually the entire population rather than only the manual workers. In Britain, by contrast, the first pensions were "simple grants to the poorest of the aged" and because they were noncontributory, "they were not a policy approach capable of sustained development." Rather, contributory social insurance (see later in this chapter) became the ultimate mechanism through which the British were able to justify the liberation of citizens from the stigma of the Poor Law.

11. In turn, the government contributed from general taxation to the insur-

ance fund in order to pay out unemployment benefits under specific conditions that precipitated the unemployment of the insured (Heclo, 1974:89).

12. The clarity of the relationship between categories of dependency, justifying rationales, and legitimately assumed government responsibility for citizen well-being can also be seen in the case of Sweden, which echoed the British response. The first national expenditure in Sweden on behalf of the unemployed came from the argument that "the wartime origin of unemployment dictated a presumption of state responsibility to help prevent those newly unemployed from falling upon poor relief. . . . In this situation, unemployment insurance seemed the obvious palliative, subject neither to the disgrace of the poor law nor the harsh regulations and patchy coverage of relief work" (Heclo, 1974:93, 99).

13. Goodin (1976:106–24) provides a stimulating philosophical treatment of social insurance, noting that "everyone benefits from the insurance provided . . . anyone might some day be down on his luck, and when he is, governmental programmes . . . help to guarantee a certain minimal standard of living" (p. 115n.). His treatment is compatible with those who view the welfare state as a boon to citizens at specific, vulnerable points in their life cycle. This is to be distinguished from the view that welfare statism is aimed only at a "lumpenproletariet," as it were, the unremittingly needy.

Chapter 6

1. The "universalism" which welfare state scholars see as characteristic of new plans for social rights after the war is slightly different, but by no means inconsistent with Parsons's usage. Parsons's "universalism" (see Chapter 2) refers to the use of general (abstract) and even cognitive (mental) criteria in orienting the self toward others. Postwar universalism similarly implied the use of the most general criteria in articulating the rights of citizenship: equality of humanness and equality of circumstance (particularly of sacrifice due to the war).

2. Such unification of objectives and administrative apparatuses yet remains to be achieved (see Chapter 11).

3. The British use the term "the welfare services" to refer to those programs of the social services oriented to "problem cases" that fall through the net of the other social services, as well as through the nets of social insurance and social assistance. The welfare services of the British welfare state are oriented toward the sick, the disabled, children, and the families of these persons (see Sleeman, 1973:30–31).

4. A note on terminology may be helpful. The literature on the welfare state indicates that certain terms have been used interchangeably, such as "social insurance/national insurance" and "social assistance/national assistance." Next, Rimlinger (1971) uses the term "social security" in a generic sense to refer to programs affecting the well-being of the citizen, and his usage should not be confused with the narrower one spawned in the United States, which refers to the terms of specific titles of the Social Security Act (1935). Also, Heidenheimer, Heclo, and Adams (1975:200) speak in terms of "income maintenance programs" of which income support through either social insurance or public assistance are only a part—other parts being taxation policies and the like. Titmuss (1969) similarly recognizes that what is often labeled "the welfare state" refers to only one division of a three-part division

of social welfare policies: social, fiscal, and occupational (see Chapter 11). Heclo (1974), in turn, considers "social policy" to be that "myriad of interventions aimed at redistribution."

Chapter 7

1. For treatments of administrative law see Pound, 1942; Carrow, 1948; Schwartz, 1954, 1962; Prettyman, 1959; Landis, 1966; Davis, 1969, 1976; "Administrative Discretion" (1972); Stewart, 1975.

2. Reasons can be found in Blachly and Oatman, 1934; Leys, 1943; Woll, 1963; Crozier, 1969; Lowi, 1969, 1979; Handler, 1979. See also this chapter and Chapters 8–10 passim.

3. But see Leys, who cogently argues that definiteness alone is not a sufficient criterion for the limitation of discretion. He argues that the "fundamental distinction is not between definite and indefinite standards. The philosopher is mainly concerned with the distinction between general (or abstract) standards, on the one hand, and specific standards, on the other hand. He wants to know whether you act on a general principle or only on an immediate, concrete rule" (1943:15). Indeed, judicialization can help reveal the absence of a general principle in rule application and thus, by indirection, bring about a change in the rule so that it is more in line with the general principles of the statute that initially authorized the agency's objectives.

4. "Internal procedures" are "housekeeping rules" rather than "public law" (see Chapter 1, n. 7).

5. In comparing the French bureaucratic system to U.S. practices, Crozier (1969:231–36) has noted that the United States relies more heavily upon due process of law than upon peer control to control administrative discretion.

6. The "legalistic" arbitrary criterion is the one in which the official adheres to the letter of the law, though doing so is not related to officially determined objectives. Exceeding the speed limit by one mile per hour does not really endanger the drivers' or others' safety, for example, but a "legalistic" decision could result in an arrest or a traffic citation for the driver. Thompson (1961) refers to legalistic behavior as "bureaupathic" (cited in Jowell, 1975:14).

7. Jowell goes on to say, "The requirement that a decision be justified, and the justification be published, implies that the justification is open to public criticism. Thus adjudication normally provides an opportunity for scrutiny and thus for the accountability of the decision makers to their clientele and to the public" (1975:27). I argue in Chapter 9 that this is more true of regular adjudication.

8. I discuss these phenomena in Chapter 11.

9. This is consistent with my earlier point that the authority of agencies is derivative authority; the legitimacy of its objectives is derivative legitimacy.

10. Lowi writes that "the Interstate Commerce Act of 1887 reflects all of the problems and all of the concerns that have plagued government regulation ever since. In this famous Act, Congress (1) delegated its own power to regulate an aspect of interstate commerce (2) to an administrative agency (3) designed especially for the purpose" (1969:129–30).

11. See Wolfe (1977:38, 66). See also Chapman (1959) for a comparative approach to public administration throughout Europe, as well as for an extensive bibliography on this subject.

Chapter 8

1. In this regard Weed's "Industrialization and Welfare Systems: A Critical Evaluation of the Convergence Hypothesis" (1979) makes excellent discriminations cross-nationally. His conclusions not only support the argument I have advanced here, but go beyond it: "Most Western European nations, along with Canada and the United States, were already advanced urban industrial societies before they developed their first modern welfare programs between 1883 and 1935. These programs were designed to solve political-economic problems in advanced societies. The underdeveloped or semideveloped nations today are developing welfare systems before they are industrialized nations. These programs are bound to reflect a different set of political-economic problems such as granting economic security in the form of welfare benefits to an administrative class in return for the political security they provide (Bottomore, 1964). The segments of society that get covered by welfare programs tend to be those segments whose compliance is necessary for the continual exercise of political-economic control. The fact that welfare systems tend to develop in a variety of political structures and may often serve to benefit the economically privileged more than the economically underprivileged groups needs further understanding" (p. 291). Weed's reference to Bottomore (1964) is to T. B. Bottomore's "The Administrative Elite," in Irving L. Horowitz, ed., *The New Sociology* (New York: Oxford University Press). Weed also observes in a note that "a classic example of this kind of economic trade-off would be Bismarck's Germany in the 1880's where the granting of increased rights in the form of welfare was intended to prevent having to grant enlarged political rights (Rimlinger, 1971:112)." Others (Briggs, 1961; Dahrendorf, 1969; Heidenheimer, Heclo, and Adams, 1975; Wilensky, 1975; and Wolfe, 1977) have similarly commented upon the conservative intent of Bismarck's social legislation. By the early 1880s conditions in Germany had ripened for the establishment of new rights for citizens; the pressure came from below. Bismarck's justification for his social legislation, however, came from above, "from the patriarchal conception of the duties of the state" (Rimlinger, 1971:112). His social legislation was, therefore, oriented toward preserving a medieval hierarchy of the social protection of one class by another.

2. The Social Security Act was amended in 1961 to arrange for the federal government to reimburse states for aid to families with unemployed fathers, the Aid to Families with Dependent Children and Unemployed Fathers program (AFDC-UP) (Piven and Cloward, 1972:126). "As of early 1969, however, only twenty-four states made use of the new option, and the eligibility restrictions were so severe that very few families with unemployed fathers actually got on the rolls . . . 5 percent of the AFDC rolls" (Piven and Cloward, 1972:126–27).

3. Formally speaking, these were "legislative initiatives," because bills must be introduced by the legislature, but, in fact, the respective executive staffs of Presidents Nixon and Carter formulated the programs to be discussed in this section.

4. Various other sources have detailed the character of PBJI thoroughly ("Carter, Congress, and Welfare," 1977:471–78; Danziger et al., 1977; Danziger and Plotnick, 1978; Storey et al., 1978; American Enterprise Institute for Public Policy Research, 1979).

Chapter 9

1. A right is less reversible than an entitlement in that the former may be guaranteed directly by statute or perhaps the court may already have elaborated, loudly and clearly, a rationale the society accepts. Entitlements, by contrast, are ever vulnerable to rule changes within the administrative ambit. And yet, such clear-cut analytic distinctions may vanish in the face of empirical situations. The following is an excellent illustration of the mutual interaction of the two principles of the rule of law and administrative regulation: "More than a million jobless Americans face the prospect of reduced unemployment benefits in 1980 and 1981 because of a rule change by the Labor department. At President Carter's instruction, the department this month tightened a formula that determines which states are eligible for money to pay up to 13 weeks of extended unemployment benefits to those who have exhausted their regular 26 weeks of insurance. . . . Essentially, Mr. Carter has changed the rule in a way that will produce lower unemployment rates in states at the time they are eligible for extended benefits. As a result, the benefits would shut off sooner than under the old rules for calculating jobless rates" ("1 Million May Lose Jobless Benefits"). The key word in the passage above is "extended." This extension is at the discretion of the executive branch. By it the content (level or degree) of a social right (unemployment insurance benefits under Title III of the Social Security Act) is open to modification. I will argue in Chapter 10 that such discretion is desirable to the extent that it allows needed flexibility of choice relative to the state of the economy.

2. This is a typical account: "The United States Supreme Court today unanimously upheld Labor Department regulations prohibiting an employer from discriminating against a worker who refuses to perform a task he believes would endanger his life. The court said the regulations promulgated by the labor secretary are in line with the intent of the Occupational Safety and Health Act of 1970 to provide a hazard-free workplace. . . . A lower court found . . . that the labor secretary had exceeded his authority in issuing the regulations. The 4th U.S. Circuit Court of Appeals overturned that decision, ruling the 'right to a hazard-free workplace' is implicit in the 1970 law" ("Worker's Right to Refuse Dangerous Task Upheld").

3. The broader public interest, for example, can escape the purview of administrative law. Wheeler asks whether, in the case below, such extensive commercialization and near destruction of the wilderness is really in the public interest: "Individual administrative actions that taken singly are reasonable and proper may in the aggregate run counter to the deeper public interest. . . . National park authorities, proceeding under clear statutory authority, seem bent on the progressive conversion of the nation's parks into paved and redesigned tourist centers indistinguishable from the motel enclaves that dot the nation's highways. Nothing is illegal about this. . . . The issue of whether, or to what extent, this should occur cannot be confronted under the present mode of administrative hearings. . . . The question is beyond the competence of an administrative tribunal, and one that our legal order as presently constituted cannot adjudicate at all" (Wheeler, 1965:13).

4. Spindler's *Public Welfare* (1979) is highly illuminating, as is, in a quite different way, Meenaghan and Washington's *Social Policy and Social Welfare* (1980), which summarizes a wide variety of issues associated with governmental service delivery, whether direct or indirect (see especially the latter, pp. 114–15). See also Marmor (1971).

5. Friedman and Friedman (1980:91–127) are highly critical of the costs associated with social welfare administration, advocating instead the replacement of "the ragbag of specific programs with a single comprehensive program of income supplements in cash—a negative income tax linked to the positive income tax" (p. 120). The main purpose would be to "provide a straightforward means of assuring every family a minimum amount, while at the same time avoiding a massive bureaucracy" (p. 121). In the early 1960s, both Friedman (1962), who is known as a "conservative" economist, and Theobald (1963), who is reputed to be a "radical" economist, converged upon the principle of the NIT. Experiments with limited applications of the principle have been conducted in the United States, but interpretations of the results of these experiments have by no means been in agreement (Pechman and Timpane, 1975; Rossi, 1976; Kershaw and Fair, 1976–77; see also Williams, 1972; Organization for Economic Cooperation and Development, 1974; Gordon, 1977).

Burns, by contrast, has recommended a system of "universal taxable demogrants" to overcome the flaws of excessive administration and other defects in the present system. A demogrant distributes a benefit to an individual on the basis of a demographic characteristic held by the individual. Though not themselves without problems (Burns, 1977:14), the demogrants could eliminate what Burns calls our penchant for relentless investigation in the name of fairness. Our present system "tries to ensure that all people in similar circumstances are treated precisely alike, while also giving additional assistance to those who have special needs. This sounds admirable, but . . . has resulted in an incredibly and fussily detailed system that takes account of every conceivable resource of each individual case, in determining eligibility (Burns, 1977:8). She also alludes to "the disgusting spectacle of millions of people having to come with rent receipts, bank books and other records in hand, to prove that they are indeed poor and entitled to some assistance" (1977:13).

Thus, detailed information gathered in the name of fairness can become the object of attack of those concerned with the administrative costs of the welfare system as well as with the effects of the information-gathering process upon the integrity of individuals seeking assistance. To illustrate the nature of these concerns I present the following list of documents required of an applicant for an eligibility interview for Medicaid assistance in the state of Washington (Medicaid is a program created by Title XX of the U.S. Social Security Act; different states have different conditions, within a particular range of latitude, for offering the service):

Documentation Required for Eligibility Interview

1. Personal identification & address verification (driver's license, military I.D., letters addressed to you, etc.).
2. Marriage certificate(s). NOTE: PLEASE INCLUDE ALL PREVIOUS MARRIED NAMES & MAIDEN NAME ON THE APPLICATION FORM.
3. Birth certificates for all members of the household.
4. Social Security cards for each member of the household. If anyone in the household (including children) does not have Social Security numbers, you are required to apply for one for each person and provide verification of the Social Security application.
5. Verification of pregnancy (if there are no other children under 18 years of age in your family).

6. Information related to child support (court order or divorce decree).
7. Insurance policies (life & health) and burial plans.
8. Registration for all vehicles (cars, trucks, boats, cycles, etc.).
9. Stocks, bonds, sales contracts or other resources of value you own or have an interest in. If you are currently selling property, documents as to progress of sale.
10. Property purchase or sales agreements. Documents or papers regarding any other property you own, are buying or have a share in.
11. If you are employed, or have been employed during the past month, wage stubs are required. Information and documents on income you have received or are receiving from Social Security, Veterans, Retirement, child support, dividends, insurance payments, income tax refunds, rentals, contracts, etc.
12. Unemployment Compensation book or verification as to whether or not you are currently receiving, have received, will receive or are not eligible to receive Unemployment Compensation.
13. Current bank statements (savings and checking accounts).
14. Current receipts for rent and utilities. If you plan to move, bring a statement from a landlord verifying agreement to rent, amount of rent, if utilities are included, and landlord's name, address and telephone number.
15. Receipts for house payments or proof of home ownership, along with tax statements.
16. If you and/or your spouse are ill (unable to work) bring in a doctor's statement to that effect, indicating length of time of unemployability and reason for unemployability.
17. If someone is paying for your rent, utilities or other items, bring in signed statements from them indicating their address and telephone number.
18. If you recently quit a job or refused a job offer, bring a statement including full details explaining the circumstances. A statement from your former employer may be required.
19. If husband (in home) is able to work, provide verification that he has earned $50.00 or more in 6 out of the last 13 work quarters . . . OR that he has drawn Unemployment benefits within the past year.
20. Verification of last day you and/or your spouse worked and any pay received or expected.
21. Medical receipts for expenditures *over* $10.00 per month.
22. Verifications of payments of child care to other persons when it is necessary in order for a family member to accept or continue employment, training or education.
23. Tuition and mandatory fees for education.
24. Verification of expenses for disasters, such as fire, flood, etc.

Chapter 10

1. The question may well arise, "When 'should' entitlements be created instead of social rights?" Apart from allowing budgeting flexibility, do entitle-

ments serve any useful purposes that rights do not? I can think of one: as I have shown, the creation of social rights, that is, the legitimation of redistribution of societal wealth, has rested consistently upon the premise that certain states of dependency are unavoidable. Ergo, social rights can hardly accompany states of dependency that are avoidable. But what is the appropriate government response to citizens who, comparatively speaking, create their own social dependencies?

What of the individual who, under his own volition and through genuine laziness, drops out of school, thereby consigning himself to a lifetime of substandard earnings or utter unemployability? What of the unattached female who, through carelessness, uses no form of contraception and has several children with no one but herself to support them? Do they have the same right to benefits that represent redistribution of the societal surplus as do the unavoidably dependent members of the body politic? Most people would be forced to answer "no" to this question, feeling, substantively, that something would be "unfair" about not differentiating between the careless and the blameless. At the same time, most of those answering "no" to the question would also feel vaguely uncomfortable or callous about the prospect of denying some type of help to innocent children and even their devil-may-care parents. Should people who, after all, are only fallible and human starve or suffer simply because they could have avoided their dependency? The weight of Western tradition, complete with a continually rationalized natural-law legacy, forces a negative answer to the above question. Yet what form of government help can be justified?

The entitlement would here be a defensible government response to the ethical problem of socially protecting those who refuse to protect themselves, though "opinion" alleges that they could do so if they tried. As argued in Chapter 7, entitlements are, analytically, within the tradition of persons helping persons through gratuities. Entitlements, as rationalized gratuities, allow institutions to help persons in as equitable and efficient a manner as possible. Entitlements, by this logic, can also serve as a modern form of charity, the twentieth-century institutional expression of compassion. Entitlements are, if such an apparent anomaly of terms will be allowed, impersonalized patronization.

Redistribution, the essence of the welfare state, has never, and can never, be justified in the name of charity. Redistribution is firmly connected to unavoidable dependency. Entitlements, however, represent redistributions whose status as "socially rightful" is always tentative unless explicitly so deemed by a court. Thus, entitlements can be justified on grounds of charity, whereas social rights cannot. The dilemma of the welfare state, therefore, is resolvable at the analytic level, as regards the creation of social rights over entitlements: only create social rights (legitimate redistributions) when considerations of costs and retaining individual initiative can be accommodated. Create entitlements when charity is needed and when seemingly avoidable dependency precludes the "fairness" (the "legitimacy") of redistributing what others have worked for.

Entitlements, as such, are a new bottle for an old wine, the wine of pure human decency. Social rights are a new wine altogether: they are the wine of equity, that is, giving each person his "due" or compensation for it, in the form of minimum standards of living, when he was denied his "due" by contingencies beyond his control.

2. Weaver writes: "The Old Regulation is an expression of a . . . movement in American social history—the effort, which began in earnest around the turn

of the century, to create a modern economy that would deliver the enormous economic growth and other social benefits made possible by large-scale, technologically-progressive, corporate capitalism without sacrificing the benefits of traditional, bourgeois "small business"—its economic efficiency, its natural legitimacy, and above all its capacity to make the ideal of individualism an economic reality" (Weaver, 1978:57–58).

3. They are inclined to leave to others the technical issues raised by the hard sciences as well. In a controversial case involving the patenting of genetic creations, the court ruled that new forms of life created through "genetic engineering" can be patented. The Carter administration had opposed the granting of such patents on the grounds that there were significant economic implications given the vast area that the ruling opened to patentability. Nevertheless, though divided 5–4, the Supreme Court ruled that Ananda Chakrabarty's microorganism fit the definition of "manufacture" and "composition of matter" covered by federal patent law. The Court's majority opinion was that "Congress is free to amend (the applicable patent law) so as to exclude from patent protection organisms produced by genetic engineering. Or it may choose to craft a statute specifically designed for such living things. But until Congress takes such action, this court must construe the language of (the law) as it is. The language of that section fairly embraces (Ms. Chakrabarty's) invention." Yet the temptation to interpret the statute was quite clear in the dissenting opinion written by Justice William J. Brennan, Jr.: "Congress plainly has legislated in the belief that (patent law) does not encompass living organisms." Quoted in "Genetic Creations Can Be Patented."

4. In short, the possibility of a "welfare state" rests upon the availability of a societal surplus; in times of scarcity, "compassion and generosity" become the major avenues of redistribution, such as it is. These latter traits are associated with the Christian duties of medieval rule.

5. Grey (1976:890) cites Thompson, "A Defense of Abortion," *Philosophy and Public Affairs* 1 (1971):47, 61, as approaching the conditionality issue through the use of the notions "Minimally Decent Samaritan" versus the proverbial "Good Samaritan." It would not be defensible to coerce people to be Good Samaritans, that is, "to take substantial risks or bear substantial burdens" on behalf of strangers, but it may be defensible to enforce a duty to be a Minimally Decent Samaritan. This distinction "makes the question of whether a right applies in a given situation turn on how difficult it is to accord the right. The point recurs constantly, in ethics as well as law."

Chapter 11

1. If it is accepted that the rationalization of the law's formality and its substance stand in a complementary relationship, the tendency toward constructing a fourth authority type in Weber's work must then dissipate. Several authors have attempted to turn "value rationality" or "substantive rationality" into the basis for a fourth authority type, paralleling the formal rationality of rule represented by impersonal law. Blau implies this as follows: "At one point, Weber outlines . . . a fourth type of belief that legitimates a social order, namely, 'rational belief in an absolute value. . . . Natural Law.' This fourth type of legitimate *order*, however, is not included in the subsequent more detailed analysis of legitimate *authority*, while the other three are. Does this imply that Weber considered a *wertrationale* orientation toward natural rights

a possible basis of political institutions but not a basis of political authority? He makes no explicit statements to help us answer this question" (1963:308). Willer (1967) and Spencer (1970) similarly seize upon Weber's mention of four types of legitimate order as implying a fourth authority type. Willer (1967:234) labels it the "ideological type" and derives it from one of Weber's four types of action, that is, value-rational action (see Weber, 1968:24–26). Of the possibility of ideological authority, Willer writes: "Ideological authority, like legal rational authority, implies a bureaucratic administrative structure. It too, has the characteristics of authority of the expert, separation of the administrator from the means of his administration, impersonality of relationships, and the like. The newly formulated bureaucratic type differs, however, from its legal-rational counterpart in that action, though at times based on rules, is ultimately legitimated by ideological norms, not by laws" (1967:237). I have argued, however, that Weber's third type of authority has indeed been legitimated by natural law, that is, by ideological norms. In addition, bureaucratic administration serves such authority. Thus, there is no need to identify legal rational authority with "laws" and ideological authority with "ideological norms." Rather, the authority that accompanies administration becomes more rationalized through legalization and judicialization. And, in turn, administrative authority is ultimately legitimated by the ideological norms that legitimate the authority the administration serves.

Spencer, in turn, calls upon a "supervening principle" to locate the source of legitimacy of political authority bounded by a rationalized legal system: "the authority of these offices [president, judges, congressmen, or governors] rests to a considerable extent upon a supervening principle—the consent of the governed—and the constitution is the embodiment of that principle. The authority of office is thus not merely defined, certified and bounded by specific laws, but by a *general principle* which underlies these laws and which may be appealed to (and generally is) when the exercise of office appears to violate that principle," (1970:129). Spencer then elaborates a fourth type of authority, value-rational authority. Having already said that there is a general principle that "supervenes" the sheer legality of the law, however, Spencer's position is untenable when he makes "legal-rational" authority parallel to "value-rational" authority. This shows up in his explanation of where each type of authority can be found in political organization: "Legal-rational authority is typically located in bureaucracies and exists in relation to specific laws that define its precincts. Value-rational authority is typically found in the higher realms of political office—president, prime minister, chancellor or even constitutional monarch, and exists in relation to principles. Thus, if legal rational authority is celebrated as an administration of laws, not of men, value-rational authority is a government of principles, not men" (1970:130). Spencer has let one type of authority (legal-rational) apply to the administrative realm and the other (value-rational) to the "higher realms" of what I have called legislation and adjudication pertaining to civil law. In so doing, he has, essentially, compared apples and oranges. My own treatment, which, following Weber, links the administrative realm with regulations and entitlements, and the adjudicative realm with laws and rights, seems theoretically more serviceable.

2. Weber writes: "New demands for a 'social law' to be based upon such . . . ethical postulates as 'justice' or 'human dignity,' and directed against the very dominance of a mere business morality, have arisen. . . . By these demands legal formalism itself has been challenged. Such a concept as economic

duress, or the attempt to treat as immoral and thus as invalid, a contract because of a gross disproportion between promise and consideration, are derived from norms which, from the legal standpoint, are entirely amorphous and which are neither juristic nor conventional nor traditional in character but ethical and which claim as their legitimation substantive justice rather than formal legality" (1968:886). A discussion with Guenther Roth has enabled me to understand that in the above passage Weber was not simply in the business of apologizing for capitalistic interests, disregardful of the ideals represented by the welfare state. Rather, at the time Weber wrote, the welfare state had not come into being and, therefore, *Economy and Society* contains references to the modern state in terms of the liberal state. Elsewhere in *Economy and Society* (1968:729–31), Weber makes clear that he is aware of the substantive disadvantage the law crystallizes for workers versus employers (see n. 12, this chapter).

In a similar vein, Jones (1958) offers a critical analysis of the archetypal connection between democracy and capitalism as initially stated in 1944 in Friedrich A. Hayek's *The Road to Serfdom*. In analyzing the generic attributes of "the rule of law," Jones essentially argues that the welfare state may enforce ethical postulates such as social justice without compromising the formality of the law.

3. Hennig and Jardim (1977:187–207) give an excellent interpretation of "affirmative action." They discuss its formal meaning in using government coercion to bring about equitability, as well as its substantive objectives. They also summarize the various effects, past and potential, both immediate and long term, of affirmative action on women, minorities, men, the private firm and the private economic sector, and the larger social order.

4. Rheinstein (1967:44, n. 8) mentions that "Weber's term 'government' has been retained [in the translation] . . . although the term 'executive' might better correspond to American parlance."

5. This tension is also the implied referent of the classical notion of social control as societal self-regulation as discussed by Janowitz (1975; 1976).

6. This would be true of all three types of legitimate authority.

7. The effect of the Hundred Years' War upon the centralization of authority in France provides a case in point. DeJouvenel writes, "The Hundred Years' War was needed to accredit finally a permanent tax, which made possible a standing army and the development of an executive to carry out the royal will. The history of sovereignty is linked with the history of administration" (1963:179).

8. Herein lies the basis of Dahrendorf's (1969:60) criticism of "the authoritarian welfare state" in which social legislation is used to defend paternalistic protectionism, rather than to extend citizen rights. Dahrendorf (1969:60) emphasizes that the subjects of the authoritarian welfare state are treated "like children of the patriarchal family," which, most certainly, is "not a condition of liberalism." Such a state does not permit the development of subject into citizen, for a citizen has rights that are "incompatible with the very foundation of authoritarianism." Heidenheimer, Heclo, and Adams (1975:193) point out that with regard to the authoritarian welfare state established by Bismarck's social legislation, the protections were created by administration as an antisocialist device for building working-class loyalty to the state, with parliament and interest groups playing a far secondary role.

9. The National Environmental Policy Act (1969), a copy of which follows,

is the ideal typical expression of the public interest state. The implementation of its seemingly impeccable principles has been accompanied by the types of criticisms highlighted by Weaver (1978) and Reich (1966).

The National Environmental Policy Act

PURPOSE

Sec. 2. The purposes of this Act are: To declare a national policy which will encourage productive and enjoyable harmony between man and his environment; to promote efforts which will prevent or eliminate damage to the environment and biosphere and stimulate the health and welfare of man; to enrich the understanding of the ecological systems and natural resources important to the Nation; and to establish a Council on Environmental Quality.

TITLE I

DECLARATION OF NATIONAL ENVIRONMENTAL POLICY

Sec. 101. (a) The Congress, recognizing the profound impact of man's activity on the interrelations of all components of the natural environment, particularly the profound influences of population growth, high-density urbanization, industrial expansion resource exploitation, and new and expanding technological advances and recognizing further the critical importance of restoring and maintaining environmental quality to the overall welfare and development of man, declares that it is the continuing policy of the Federal Government, in cooperation with State and local governments, and other concerned public and private organizations, to use all practicable means and measures, including financial and technical assistance, in a manner calculated to foster and promote the general welfare, to create and maintain conditions under which man and nature can exist in productive harmony, and fulfill the social economic, and other requirements of present and future generations of Americans.

(b) In order to carry out the policy set forth in this Act, it is the continuing responsibility of the Federal Government to use all practicable means, consistent with other essential considerations of national policy, to improve and coordinate Federal plans, functions, programs, and resources to the end that the Nation may—

(1) fulfill the responsibilities of each generation as trustee of the environment for succeeding generations;

(2) assure for all Americans safe, healthful, productive, and esthetically and culturally pleasing surroundings;

(3) attain the widest range of beneficial uses of the environment without degradation, risk to health or safety, or other undesirable and unintended consequences;

(4) preserve important historic, cultural, and natural aspects of our national heritage, and maintain, wherever possible, an environment which supports diversity and variety of individual choice;

(5) achieve a balance between population and resource use which will permit high standards of living and a wide sharing of life's amenities; and

(6) enhance the quality of renewable resources and approach the maximum attainable recycling of depletable resources.

(c) The Congress recognizes that each person should enjoy a healthful environment and that each person has a responsibility to contribute to the preservation and enhancement of the environment.

Sec. 102. The Congress authorizes and directs that, to the fullest extent possible: (1) the policies, regulations, and public laws of the United States shall be interpreted and administered in accordance with the policies set forth in this Act, and (2) all agencies of the Federal Government shall—

(a) utilize a systematic, interdisciplinary approach which will insure the integrated use of the natural and social sciences and the environmental design arts in planning and in decision-making which may have an impact on man's environment;

(b) identify and develop methods and procedures, in consultation with the Council on Environmental Quality established by title II of this Act, which will insure that presently unquantified environmental amenities and values may be given appropriate consideration in decisionmaking along with economic and technical considerations;

(c) include in every recommendation or report on proposals for legislation and other major Federal actions significantly affecting the quality of the human environment, a detailed statement by the responsible official on—

(1) the environmental impact of the proposed action,

(2) any adverse environmental effects which cannot be avoided should the proposal be implemented,

(3) alternatives to the proposed action,

(4) any irreversible and irretrievable commitments of resources which would be involved in the proposed action should it be implemented.

Prior to making any detailed statement, the responsible Federal official shall consult with and obtain the comments of any Federal agency which has jurisdiction by law or special expertise with respect to any environmental impact involved. Copies of such statement and the comments and views of the appropriate Federal, State, and local agencies, which are authorized to develop and enforce environmental standards, shall be made available to the President, the Council on Environmental Quality and to the public as provided by section 552 of title 5, United States Code, and shall accompany the proposal through the existing agency review processes;

(d) study, develop, and describe appropriate alternatives to recommended courses of action in any proposal which involves unresolved conflicts concerning alternative uses of available resources;

(e) recognize the worldwide and long-range character of environmental problems and, where consistent with the foreign policy of the United States, lend appropriate support to initiatives, resolutions, and programs designed to maximize international cooperation in anticipating and preventing a decline in the quality of mankind's world environment;

(f) makes available to States, counties, municipalities, institutions, and individuals, advice and information useful in restoring, maintaining, and enhancing the quality of the environment;

(g) initiate and utilize ecological information in the planning and development of resource-oriented projects; and

(h) assist the Council on Environmental Quality established by title II of this Act.

Sec. 103. All agencies of the Federal Government shall review their present statutory authority, administrative regulations, and current policies and procedures for the purpose of determining whether there are any deficiencies or inconsistencies therein which prohibit full compliance with the purposes and provisions of this Act and shall propose to the President not later than July 1, 1971, such measures as may be necessary to bring their authority and policies into conformity with the intent, purposes, and procedures set forth in this Act.

Sec. 104. Nothing in Section 102 or 103 shall in any way affect the specific statutory obligations of any Federal agency (1) to comply with criteria or standards of environmental quality, (2) to coordinate or consult with any other Federal or State agency, or (3) to act, or refrain from acting contingent upon the recommendations or certification of any other Federal or State agency.

Sec. 105. The policies and goals set forth in this Act are supplementary to those set forth in existing authorizations of Federal agencies.

In addition, see Lowi (1978:19) for a list of important but "not necessarily exhaustive" regulatory laws enacted by Congress since 1970, as well as Anderson (1978:62) for a list of national regulatory agencies in the United States in 1977, broken down by (1) independent regulatory commissions, (2) independent agencies, and (3) bureaus in executive departments.

10. In his discussion of what constitutes "just" compensation Michelman (1967) gives a thorough treatment of ethical questions surrounding the use of government coercion to defend the public interest. Strong and Rosenfeld (1976) raise various ethical questions in "Ethics or Expediency: An Environmental Question."

11. Garvey (1975) offers a completely different point of view centered around the notion that "a person's interest in a decent environment may be treated as a vested right virtually in the classical constitutional sense, on a par with . . . economic and property interests." Reich (1966) and Weaver (1978) would independently argue that the right to a decent environment could be quite incompatible with a person's economic and property interests.

12. Weber (1968:729–30) himself was unrelenting in his detailed analysis of the capitalist arrangement and its potential for coercion. Less flamboyantly than Karl Marx, with whose ghost he entered into frequent debate, Weber nevertheless saw through the "seeming" fairness of a law stated in general terms, but favorable to a certain class: "The development of legally regulated relationships toward contractual association and of the law itself toward freedom of contract . . . is usually regarded as signifying a decrease of constraint and an increase of individual freedom." Weber refers to the correctness of this opinion as "relative," for "the formal right of a worker to enter into any contract whatsoever with any employer whatsoever does not in practice represent for the employment seeker even the slightest freedom in the determination of his own conditions of work, and it does not guarantee him any influence on this process. It rather means, at least primarily, that the more powerful party in the market, i.e., normally the employer, has the possibility to set the terms, to offer the job 'take it or leave it,' and, given the normally more pressing economic need of the worker, to impose his terms upon him. The result of con-

tractual freedom, then, is in the first place the opening of the opportunity to use, by the clever utilization of property ownership in the market, these resources without legal restraints as a means for the achievement of power over others. The parties interested in power in the market thus are also interested in such a legal order. Their interest is served particularly by the establishment of 'legal empowerment rules.' This type of rule does no more than create the framework for valid agreements which, under conditions of formal freedom, are officially available to all. Actually, however, they are accessible only to the owners of property and thus in effect support their very autonomy and power positions."

13. Baran and Sweezy's *Monopoly Capital* (1966) is one of the classic statements of what the corporation took from the individual.

14. Within the context of his critical analysis of the notion of "the end of ideology," Kleinberg (1973) treats issues related to what exactly the reform of private property has handed to government.

15. Reich (1966) does not use the term "contract state" in "The New Property," but what he is referring to corresponds to other usages of the term, in particular, Kleinberg's (1973). Titmuss (1969:231) uses the epithet "The Pressure Group State" to refer to the equivalent phenomenon in Great Britain. The empirical referent of my discussion will be the United States, although the analytic phenomenon is by no means confined to this country. Finally, I might add that Reich includes what I have called "social welfare entitlements" as well as some of the content of social rights in his generic notion of "largesse." See below for my discussion of the value of keeping these various forms of largesse analytically distinct.

16. We might presume that there is less improvisation and more adequate understanding of the government contract today than nearly a decade ago when Kleinberg wrote this. Nevertheless, the overall point stands: the rationalization of administrative law lags far behind the rationalization of the civil or statute law (see also Stewart, 1975).

17. In the formal organizational literature, this process would be equivalent to the notion of "vertical integration." Vertical integration entails bringing into the organization's explicit network of activities the earlier operations of an overall sequence, thus achieving a more predictable and controlled organizational environment. The buying of a dairy farm by a milk distributing company would be an example. In the case of administrative law Reich is similarly arguing for a more rationalized (controlled, predictable) environment for the citizen-sovereign relationship when largesse is at stake.

18. Reich's (1966) discussion of the meaning and value of property rights elaborates this point.

19. For a related discussion covering both Marx's and Weber's views, see Beirne (1979). For other treatments on Marx see Feuer (1959), Bober (1965), and Petrovic (1967).

20. Weber (1968:729–31), however, treats the conditions that might surround freedom, coercion, and law in a "socialist community."

21. See Dahrendorf (1958) and Kanter (1973).

22. See Marx's "Points on the Modern State and Civil Society" from *Notebooks of 1844–45* in Easton and Guddat, 1967:399–400.

23. This is by no means to ignore distinctions among the socialist nations of Eastern Europe or distinctions among elites within the U.S.S.R. The "successors" to which I make broad reference do not form a monolithic outlook.

Fischer-Galati's (1979) collection on the communist parties of Eastern Europe makes this patently clear, as does the collection edited by Jones (1978) on Eastern European socialist nations. Some earlier work on Eastern European stratification systems is contained in Heller (1969) and a treatment of the Yugoslavian experience appears in Denitch (1976). Finally, "Socialism: Trials and Errors" illuminates the many-faceted character of the phenomenon and its elites.

24. This was a comment made by Osnos (1980) in describing the life of Boris Pasternak, who won, and was forced to reject, the Nobel prize for his authorship of *Dr. Zhivago* (1958).

25. Epithets associated with that era and later years ("capitalist pigs," "imperialist running dogs," and the like) appear to refer more to the economic system or colonial expansion to keep the economic system functioning than to the overall relationship of the administrative state to the citizen. No term of a breadth equivalent to "absolutism," for example, describes the administrative activities of the laissez-faire state.

26. This was exactly Lester Ward's view. See his "Theory and Practice Are at War" (1881) and "The Laissez Faire Doctrine Is Suicidal" (1884) in Commager (1967:22–36 and 63–68).

27. Wolfe writes: "The blossoming of laissez faire at the end of the century rewrote history. . . . Actually its life was deceptively short. Pure laissez faire began its new popularity some time between 1870 and 1880; by World War I it was to all intents and purposes finished, never again to appear except in the nostalgic fantasies of a class in decline. Thus its total life was equal to that of one generation of jurists, politicians, and thinkers, in only two countries, and at a time when its theoretical precepts were matter of factly violated in practice; yet that one generation was able to produce a body of ideas whose influence was as deep as its underlying philosophy was shallow. Like the burst of a flash cube, the key ideas of laissez faire burned with spectacular intensity before lapsing into dark nothingness. The very brilliance of the flash blinded people to its true nature, for during its lifetime the basic nostrums of the doctrine were accepted by workers as well as employers, religious leaders as well as atheists, normal men as well as immoral societies" (1977:52).

28. In this connection Wolfe refers to the provision of direct subsidies to manufacturers practiced under mercantilism, "the Colbertian system of royal support for the makers of luxurious goods being the classic example" (1977:28).

29. Though this analysis of gratuities and rights has centered only upon those to which legal relevance is attached by virtue of the subject-ruler or citizen-sovereign relationship, it would hold similarly for social relationships whose legality is immaterial. Here is where political sociology meets social psychology, and from there, psychology. A few examples will illustrate these connections.

One of the chief effects of the women's movement has been to make couples far more conscious of the degree to which the gratuities-rights continuum characterizes household arrangements. At one extreme, under traditional male-female role definitions, it was the wife-mother's duty to attend to the myriad details of household management and childrearing. In turn, she had the "right" to her mate's economic support. Correlatively, it was the husband-father's duty to earn enough money to support his dependents. In turn, he had the "right" to his mate's attentiveness as regarded the details of management of home and children. Under these definitions of the situation, household tasks or babysitting done by the male, as well as income brought in by the female, would be considered "extra," that is, "gratuitous." Neither would have a "right" to expect this of the other as long as each was fully carrying out his or her duties.

At the other extreme, under newly idealized male-female role definitions, if both male and female bring home approximately equivalent shares of the "bacon," both would have the duty to assume approximately equivalent shares of the household management and childrearing tasks. This is popularly known as "liberation," meaining that males are liberated from the duty of providing the sole household income and females from the duty of assuming responsibility for an endless series of both diffuse and specific demands associated with home and children. "Gratuitousness" in such a household would arise in the degree that one or the other party contributed more than his or her "fair share" of domestic performance, holding income contribution constant.

At the intermediary degrees of this continuum fall a hefty portion of the households of advanced societies today. Female labor force participation rates guarantee that traditional male-female role definitions of the household situation are becoming increasingly obsolete (for the United States see the U.S. Department of Commerce's two publications, *A Statistical Portrait of Women in the United States, 1978* and *Issues in Federal Statistical Needs Relating to Women*). In turn, male-female income differentials guarantee that the idealized "liberated" household remains yet to become the norm. In the gratuities-rights framework, this means that many households, manifestly or latently, are in a state of flux and are, accordingly, characterized by an unremitting jockeying for redefinitions of the situation in the direction of transforming "favors" into "rights" to avoid the disadvantages of indebtedness. This, of course, leads back to the sociological literature of exchange and power (Blau's [1967] statement is classic) as well as reciprocity (Mauss, 1954; Gouldner, 1960). More concretely, at what point may a male expect his mate to improve the family's standard of living by earning income without incurring her debt? To what degree may a female expect her mate to assume home and child management tasks without incurring his debt? When both parties work an eight-hour day in the "outside" world, but bring home differential paychecks, the issues grow somewhat more complex: the couple become caught between the "traditional" role definitions of the past and the ideals of "fairness" that guide them toward the future.

In another vein, the gratuities-rights distinction can be applied to an analysis of the informal and formal sides of work performance in organizational settings. Hennig and Jardim (1977) analyze both formal and informal work requirements in organizations to which women aspire to rise to managerial positions. It is clear from their depiction that the "formal" organization corresponds to the realm in which relationships are impersonalized and outcomes bear the character of rights. (Pay raises based strictly upon length of time employed would be an example of a right within the organization's formal rules.) By contrast, the "informal" organization corresponds to the realm in which relationships are personalized and outcomes bear the character of favors. (Having a "godfather" who "takes you with him" as he moves up the organizational ladder would here be an example of the gratuitous side of informal organization.) The point of the authors' examination of the formal and informal sides of organization is to demonstrate the tendency for females to rely for success primarily upon the functioning of the formal organization and what should "rightfully" accrue to them from competent task performance. By contrast, they argue, females tend to be comparatively unaware of, or incapable of using, the informal realm of personalized relationships and favors that frequently mean the crucial difference between career advancement or professional stagnation.

Writings in the field of psychology touch, in varying degrees of explicitness, upon the issue of gratuities and indebtedness, on the one hand, and rights and independence, on the other. In their popular volume, *Money Madness*, Goldberg and Lewis (1979) depict a number of personality types according to the individual's orientation toward money. In turn, the authors examine the ways various types of individuals will use money to, among other things, either incur or avoid the debt of others. Of immediate interest are two of their types: "power grabbers" will give money only to the degree that they can indebt the beneficiary, never within a context that the latter has a "right." "Autonomy worshipers" use money to buy independence from indebtedness to others, preferring, instead, a lifestyle in which their freedom to do what they wish to do is "earned" and therefore, "rightful." A few questions posed by the authors to help the reader ascertain whether he or she may be involved with a power grabber highlight the relationship between the disciplines of sociology and psychology. To wit, in the degree that social structural conditions facilitate each person's capacity to provide for his or her own needs, then personalized relationships having the following distastefully indebting character are less likely to form stemming from purely economic need on the part of the beneficiary:

> "You may be involved with a power grabber if:
> "You are overly fearful of antagonizing the person.
> "You try overly hard to please the person. . . .
> "When the person owes you money, you are afraid to ask for it.
> "Even though you have earned the money, when the person pays you it
> is done in such a way as to imply it is a gift.
> "When you work for the person, you always feel underpaid but you
> also feel unneeded and are fearful of being fired if you protest.
> "Even though the person procrastinates in paying you or pays you
> less than you bargained for, you still fell humbled and grateful when
> you are finally paid" (Goldberg and Lewis, 1979:127).

Finally, the growing popular literature on "assertiveness" could only be born of an era when the "gratuity" undergoes increasingly invidious comparison with the notion of "rights." In the book that claims to have "started it all," authors Alberti and Emmons (1970) appear to have selected a title that captures the essence of the transformation that is taking place between individuals as individuals, as well as between citizens and sovereign: *Your Perfect Right: A Guide to Assertive Behavior*.

30. The same arguments have been made with regard to social insurance and public assistance in the United States. The substantive distinctions are becoming blurred while legitimation rationales and funding sources are fighting losing battles to remain distinct (see Heidenheimer, Heclo, and Adams, 1975:199 and 278ff.; Thimmesch, 1978). Steiner states that it has become increasingly obvious that "characteristics usually attributed to social insurance and public assistance respectively are really not inherent and indispensable aspects of each. . . . Extension of unemployment compensations by federal action in 1961 (and proposed by President Johnson as a permanent program in

1965), may be viewed as a dividend to those involved in the insurance program, but it is equally realistic to view it as public assistance. . . . No other insurance program has been known to provide additional months of benefits because jobs were scarce. Finally, the existence of a minimum benefits schedule and periodic increases in benefits voted by Congress in old age and survivors' insurance is another deviation from the payment-benefit relationship ordinarily associated with an insurance plan. In short, however much it pleases us to believe that social insurance is not public charity, it sometimes is" (1966:251). Steiner isolates a key to the distinction between rights and entitlements or assistance when he notes that "it pleases us. . . . " Rights do please us: they bespeak legitimacy. They are without stigma. Thus, "today's pensioners acquire benefits which far exceed the value of any contributions made during their working lives. But through the postwar period the doctrine of individualistic, earned insurance has been steadfastly maintained by both administrators and Congress" (Heidenheimer, Heclo, and Adams, 1975:203).

31. "Welfare cheating" can itself have both a formal and a substantive character. "Formal" welfare cheating would refer to the collection of benefits illegally. The letter of the law is violated in the garnering of a benefit. "Substantive" welfare cheating would refer to the collection of a benefit by adhering to the letter of the law, while simultaneously evading its intent or "spirit." The actions of the "Pentagon wordsmiths" above would epitomize the latter category of deception. In addition, what we may consider a subvariety of "formal" welfare cheating would be a case in which a benefit were enjoyed but in which the recipient did not keep his part of the bargain. For example, it regularly appears in U.S. newspapers that students are lax in repaying educational loans underwritten by the U.S. government: "The loan program is a national disgrace. . . . The default rate is 17 per cent nationally." Moreover, middle-income students are the greatest risk when it comes to repaying personal loans for their education with just a small percentage of the default rate representing loans to lower-income people ("Educator Says Loans Go To Wrong Students").

Facts such as these are rarely associated in the popular mind with welfare cheating. Rather, the more common image has now been captured in "a new game soon to hit the market" in which the players "are 'able-bodied welfare recipients' who collect money by snatching purses and having illegitimate children and who try to avoid falling into the 'working person's rut.'" The game, called "Public Assistance," was created by two businessmen who see it as a humorous lampooning of welfare cheaters and liberal government bureaucrats. In the game, "players try to accumulate money as they move back and forth between the 'able-bodied welfare recipient's promenade' and the 'working person's rut.'" To charges that there is nothing funny about the game, and that "It's a really obnoxious game and comes close to bordering on racism," the creators retorted, "We didn't invent this game—government liberals did. We just put it in a box" ("Welfare Game: 'Obnoxious' and 'Racist' or Just a Humorous Pastime?").

BIBLIOGRAPHY

Aaron, Henry. *On Social Welfare*. Cambridge, Mass.: Abt Books, 1980.
"Administrative Discretion." *Law and Contemporary Problems* 37 (1972): entire issue.
Alberti, Robert E., and Emmons, Michael L. *Your Perfect Right: A Guide to Assertive Behavior*. San Luis Obispo, Calif.: Impact Publishers, 1970.
American Enterprise Institute for Public Policy Research. *The Administration's 1979 Welfare Reform Proposal*. Washington, D.C.: American Enterprise Institute for Public Policy Research, 1979.
Anderson, Jack. "Andrus' Skeleton Rattles." *Seattle Post-Intelligencer*, 13 February 1980, p. B2.
Anderson, James, E. "Economic Regulatory and Consumer Protection Policies." In *Nationalizing Government: Public Policies in America*, edited by Theodore J. Lowi and Alan Stone, pp. 61–84. Beverly Hills and London: Sage Publications, 1978.
Baran, Paul A., and Sweezy, Paul M. *Monopoly Capital: An Essay on the American Economic and Social Order*. New York and London: Modern Reader Paperbacks, 1966.
Baum, Daniel J. *The Welfare Family and Mass Administrative Justice*. New York: Frederick A. Praeger Publishers, 1974.
Beirne, Piers. "Ideology and Rationality in Max Weber's Sociology of Law." *Research in Law and Sociology* 2 (1979):103–31.
Bell, Daniel. *The Coming of Post-Industrial Society*. New York: Basic Books, 1973.
Bendix, Reinhard. *Max Weber: An Intellectual Portrait*. Garden City, N.Y.: Doubleday Anchor Books, 1962.
_____. *Nation-Building and Citizenship*. Berkeley: University of California Press, 1977.
_____. *Kings or People: Power and the Mandate to Rule*. Berkeley: University of California Press, 1978.
Benn, S. I., and Peters, R. S. *Social Principles and the Democratic State*. London: George Allen and Unwin Ltd., 1959.
Berman, Harold J. *Justice in the U.S.S.R.: An Interpretation of Soviet Law*. Rev. ed., enlarged. Cambridge, Mass.: Harvard University Press, 1950, 1963.
Beveridge, Sir William. *Social Insurance and Allied Services*. New York: Macmillan, 1942.
Blachly, Frederick F., and Oatman, Miriam E. *Administrative Legislation and Adjudication*. Washington, D.C.: Brookings Institution, 1934.
Blau, Peter M. "Critical Remarks on Weber's Theory of Authority." *American Political Science Review* 52 (1963):305–16.
_____. *Exchange and Power in Social Life*. New York: Wiley, 1967.

Bober, M. M. *Karl Marx's Interpretation of History*. 2d ed., rev. New York: Norton, 1965.

Bottomore, T. B. *Elites and Society*. Baltimore: Penguin Books, 1964.

Bowler, M. Kenneth. *The Nixon Guaranteed Income Proposal*. Cambridge, Mass.: Ballinger, 1974.

Braybrooke, David. *Three Tests for Democracy: Personal Rights, Human Welfare, and Collective Preference*. New York: Random House, 1968.

Brecht, Arnold. *Political Theory*. Princeton: Princeton University Press, 1959.

Briggs, Asa. "The Welfare State in Historical Perspective." *Archives of European Sociology* 11 (1961):221–58.

Brinton, Crane. *The Anatomy of Revolution*. New York: Vintage Books, 1959.

Bryant, Hilda. "Paternity Quiz in Welfare Cases Halted." *Seattle Post-Intelligencer*, 26 January 1979, p. A6.

Burke, Vince J., and Burke, Vee. *Nixon's Good Deed: Welfare Reform*. New York and London: Columbia University Press, 1974.

Burns, Eveline M. *Social Security and Public Policy*. New York: McGraw-Hill, 1956.

―――. *Social Welfare in the 1980's and Beyond*. Berkeley: Institute of Governmental Studies, University of California, 1977.

Carrow, Milton M. *The Background of Administrative Law*. Newark, N.J.: Associated Lawyers Publishing Company, 1948.

"Carter, Congress, and Welfare: A Long Road." *Congressional Quarterly Almanac* 33 (1977):471–78.

Chapman, Brian. *The Profession of Government*. London: George Allen and Unwin Ltd., 1959.

Clark, Colin. *Poverty before Politics*. London: Institute of Economic Affairs, 1977.

Commager, Henry Steele. *Lester Ward and the Welfare State*. Indianapolis and New York: Bobbs-Merrill, 1967.

Cotgrove, Stephen. "Technology, Rationality, and Domination." *Social Studies of Science* 5 (1975):55–78.

Cox, Archibald. "Constitutional Adjudication and the Promotion of Human Rights." *Harvard Law Review* 80 (1966):91–122.

Crozier, Michel. *The Bureaucratic Phenomenon*. Chicago: University of Chicago Press, Phoenix Books, 1969.

Cutright, Phillips. "Political Structure, Economic Development, and National Security Programs." *American Journal of Sociology* 70 (1965):537–50.

Dahrendorf, Ralf. "Out of Utopia." *American Journal of Sociology* 64 (1958):115–27.

―――. *Society and Democracy in Germany*. Garden City, N.Y.: Doubleday, Anchor Books, 1969.

Danziger, Sheldon; Haveman, Robert; and Smolensky, Eugene. "The Program for Better Jobs and Income—A Guide and a Critique." A study prepared for the use of the Joint Economic Committee, Congress of the United States. Washington, D.C.: Government Printing Office; Madison, Wisc.: Institute for Research on Poverty Reprint Series, 1977. Reprint 259.

Danziger, Sheldon, and Plotnick, Robert. "Can Welfare Reform Eliminate Poverty?" Madison, Wisc.: University of Wisconsin, Institute for Research on Poverty Discussion Papers, no. 517–78, 1978.

Davis, Kenneth Culp. *Discretionary Justice: A Preliminary Inquiry*. Baton Rouge: Louisiana State University Press, 1969.

————, and European Associates. *Discretionary Justice in Europe and America*. Urbana: University of Illinois Press, 1976.

Deacon, Richard. *A History of the Russian Secret Service*. London: Frederick Muller, 1972.

DeJouvenel, Bertrand. *Sovereignty: An Inquiry into the Political Good*. Chicago and London: University of Chicago Press, Phoenix Books, 1963.

Delany, William. "The Development and Decline of Patrimonial and Bureaucratic Administrations." *Administrative Science Quarterly* 7 (1963):458–501.

Denitch, Bogdan Denis. *The Legitimation of a Revolution: The Yugoslav Case*. New Haven and London: Yale University Press, 1976.

Devereux, Edward D., Jr. "Parsons' Sociological Theory." In *The Social Theories of Talcott Parsons*, edited by Max Black, pp. 1–63. Englewood Cliffs, N.J.: Prentice-Hall, Inc., 1961.

Dickinson, John. *Administrative Justice and the Supremacy of Law in the United States*. Cambridge, Mass.: Harvard University Press, 1927.

Djilas, Milovan. *The New Class: An Analysis of the Communist System*. New York: Frederick A. Praeger Publishers, 1957.

Durkheim, Emile. *The Division of Labor in Society*. Glencoe, Ill.: Free Press, 1947.

Easton, Lloyd D., and Guddat, Kurt H., eds. *Writings of the Young Marx on Philosophy and Society*. Garden City, N.Y.: Doubleday, Anchor Books, 1967.

"Educator Says Loans Go to Wrong Students." *Seattle Times*, 29 October 1980, p. A17.

Eimicke, William B. "Debate over Welfare in Britain." *Social Work* 18 (1973):84–91.

Eisen, Arnold. "The Meanings and Confusions of Weberian 'Rationality.' " *British Journal of Sociology* 26 (1978):57–70.

Eisenstadt, S. N. *The Political Systems of Empires*. New York: Free Press, 1963.

————, ed. *Political Sociology*. New York: Basic Books, Inc., 1971.

Etzioni, Amitai. "The Crisis of Modernity: Deviation or Demise?" *Social Studies of Human Relations* 21 (1973):370–94.

Feagin, Joe R. *Subordinating the Poor: Welfare and American Beliefs*. Englewood Cliffs, N.J.: Prentice-Hall, 1975.

Feuer, Lewis S., ed. *Marx and Engels: Basic Writings on Politics and Philosophy*. Garden City, N.Y.: Doubleday, Anchor Books, 1959.

Fischer-Galati, Stephen, ed. *The Communist Parties of Eastern Europe*. New York: Columbia University Press, 1979.

Flora, Peter, and Heidenheimer, Arnold J., eds. *The Development of the Welfare State in Europe and America*. New Brunswick, N.J.: Transaction Books, 1980.

Fraser, Derek. *The Evolution of the British Welfare State: A History of Social Policy since the Industrial Revolution*. London: Macmillan, 1973.

————, ed. *The New Poor Law in the Nineteenth Century*. New York: St. Martin's Press, 1976.

Freeman, Roger A. *The Growth of American Government: A Morphology of the Welfare State*. Stanford: Hoover Institution Press, 1975.

Friedman, Kathi V. "Politics and Government." In *Sociology: An Introduction*, edited by Reece McGee, pp. 463–94. Hinsdale, Ill.: Dryden Press, 1977.

Friedman, Lawrence M. *The Legal System: A Social Science Perspective*. New York: Russell Sage Foundation, 1975.

Friedman, Milton. *Capitalism and Freedom*. Chicago: University of Chicago Press, 1962.

————, and Friedman, Rose. *Free to Choose: A Personal Statement*. New York and London: Harcourt, Brace, Jovanovich, 1980.

Friedrich, Carl J. *Tradition and Authority*. London: Macmillan, 1972.

Friedrichs, David O. "The Legitimacy Crisis in the United States: A Conceptual Analysis." *Social Problems* 27 (1980): 540–55.

Fromm, Erich., ed. *Socialist Humanism*. Garden City, N.Y.: Doubleday, 1965.

Fuller, Lon. "Collective Bargaining and the Arbitrator." *Wisconsin Law Review* 1 (1963):3–46.

Furniss, Norman, and Tilton, Timothy. *The Case for the Welfare State: From Social Security to Social Equality*. Bloomington: Indiana University Press, 1977.

Garvey, Gerald. "Environmentalism versus Energy Development: The Constitutional Background to Environmental Administration." *Public Administration Review* 35 (1975):328–33.

Gaylin, Willard; Glasser, Ira; Marcus, Steven; and Rothman, David. *Doing Good: The Limits of Benevolence*. New York: Pantheon Books, 1978.

"Genetic Creations Can Be Patented." *Seattle Times*, 16 June 1980, p. 1.

George, Vic, and Wilding, Paul. *Ideology and Social Welfare*. London and Boston: Routledge and Kegan Paul, 1976.

Gerth, H. W., and Mills, C. Wright, eds. *From Max Weber: Essays in Sociology*. New York: Oxford University Press, Galaxy, 1958.

Girvetz, Harry K. "Welfare State." In *International Encyclopedia of the Social Sciences*, edited by David Sills, pp. 512–21. New York: Crowell, Collier, Macmillan, 1968.

Glasser, Ira. "Prisoners of Benevolence: Power versus Liberty in the Welfare State." In *Doing Good: The Limits of Benevolence*, by Willard Gaylin, Ira Glasser, Steven Marcus, and David Rothman, pp. 97–170. New York: Pantheon Books, 1978.

Glazer, Nathan. "Should Judges Administer Social Services?" *Public Interest* 50 (1978):64–80.

Goldberg, Herb, and Lewis, Robert. *Money Madness: The Psychology of Saving, Spending, Loving, and Hating Money*. New York: Signet Books, 1979.

Goodin, Robert. *The Politics of Rational Man*. London and New York: Wiley, 1976.

Gordon, David, ed. *Problems of Political Economy*. 2d ed. Lexington, Mass: Heath, 1977.

Gouldner, Alvin W. "The Norm of Reciprocity: A Preliminary Statement." *American Sociological Review* 25 (1960):161–79.

Gregory, Roy, and Hutchesson, Peter. *The Parliamentary Ombudsman: A Study in the Control of Administrative Action*. London: George Allen and Unwin Ltd., 1975.

Grey, Thomas C. "Property and Need: The Welfare State and Theories of Distributive Justice." *Stanford Law Review* 28 (1976):877–902.

Grisham, Roy A., Jr., and McConaughy, Paul D., eds. *Encyclopedia of U.S. Government Benefits*. 2d ed. New York: Avon Books, Equinox, 1975.

Gronbjerg, Kirsten A. *Mass Society and the Extension of Welfare: 1960–1970*. Chicago and London: University of Chicago Press, 1977.

Guins, George C. *Soviet Law and Soviet Society*. The Hague: Martinus Nijhoff, 1954.

Gurr, Ted Robert. *Why Men Rebel*. Princeton: Princeton University Press, 1971.

Habermas, Jurgen. *Toward a Rational Society: Student Protest, Science and Politics*. Boston: Beacon Press, 1970.

———. *Legitimation Crisis*. Boston: Beacon Press, 1975.

Hacker, Andrew. *The End of the American Era*. New York: Atheneum, 1972.

Hancock, M. Donald, and Sjoberg, Gideon, eds. *Politics in the Post-Welfare State: Responses to the New Individualism*. New York and London: Columbia University Press, 1972.

Handler, Joel F. "Controlling Official Behavior in Welfare Administration." In *The Law of the Poor*, edited by Jacobus tenBroek and the editors of the *California Law Review*, pp. 155–86. San Francisco: Chandler Publishing Company, 1966.

———. *Protecting the Social Service Client: Legal and Structural Controls on Official Discretion*. Poverty Policy Analysis Series. New York: Academic Press, 1979.

———. *Reforming the Poor: Welfare Policy, Federalism, and Morality*. New York and London: Basic Books, 1972.

Hayek, Friedrich A. *The Road to Serfdom*. Chicago: University of Chicago Press, 1944.

Hazard, John N., and Shapiro, Isaac. *The Soviet Legal System: Post-Stalin Documentation and Historical Commentary*. Published for the Parker School of Foreign and Comparative Law, Columbia University in the City of New York. Dobbs Ferry, N.Y.: Oceana, 1962.

Heclo, Hugh. *Modern Social Policies in Britain and Sweden: From Relief to Income Maintenance*. New Haven and London: Yale University Press, 1974.

Heidenheimer, Arnold J.; Heclo, Hugh; and Adams, Carolyn Teich. *Comparative Public Policy: The Politics of Social Choice in Europe and America*. New York: St. Martin's Press, 1975.

Heilbroner, Robert L. *Marxism: For and Against*. New York and London: Norton, 1980.

Heller, Celia S. *Structured Social Inequality: A Reader in Comparative Social Stratification*. New York: Macmillan, 1969.

Hennig, Margaret, and Jardim, Anne. *The Managerial Woman*. Garden City, N.Y.: Doubleday, Anchor Press, 1977.

Hofman, Steven, and Brown, Rhonda. "Balanced Budgets and Phony Numbers." *Washington Star*, 30 July 1980, p. A13.

Horowitz, Donald. *The Courts and Social Policy*. Washington, D.C.: Brookings Institution, 1977.

"How Far Can Congress Go?" *Time*, 10 December 1979, p. 99.

Huber, Joan. "The Politics of Public Assistance: Western Europe and the United States." In *Major Social Issues: A Multidisciplinary View*, edited by J. Milton Yinger and Stephen J. Cutler, pp. 109–25. New York: Free Press, 1978.

Huntington, Samuel P. "Political Modernization: America vs. Europe." *World*

Politics 18 (1966):378–414. Reprinted in *State and Society: A Reader in Comparative Political Sociology*, edited by Reinhard Bendix, pp. 170–200. Boston: Little, Brown and Company, 1968.

Israel, Joachim. "The Welfare State—A Manifestation of Late Capitalism." *Acta Sociologica* 17 (1974):310–29.

Janowitz, Morris. "Sociological Theory and Social Control." *American Journal of Sociology* 81 (1975):82–108.

———. *Social Control of the Welfare State*. New York: Elsevier, 1976.

Jenkins, Shirley, ed. *Social Security in International Perspective: Essays in Honor of Eveline M. Burns*. New York: Columbia University Press, 1969.

Jones, Harry W. "Rule of Law and the Welfare State." *Columbia Law Review* 58 (1958):143–56.

Jones, T. Anthony, ed. "Social Change in Socialist Societies." *Social Forces* 57 (1978): Part I, pp. 361–546.

Jowell, Jeffrey L. *Law and Bureaucracy: Administrative Discretion and the Limits of Legal Action*. Port Washington, N.Y.: Dunellen Publishing Company, Inc., 1975.

Kalberg, Stephen. "Max Weber's Types of Rationality: Cornerstones for the Analysis of Rationalization Processes in History." *American Journal of Sociology* 85 (1980):1145–79.

Kanter, Rosabeth Moss. *Commitment and Community: Communes and Utopias in Sociological Perspective*. Cambridge, Mass.: Harvard University Press, 1973.

Kelsen, Hans. *Society and Nature: A Sociological Inquiry*. London: Kegan Paul, Trench, Trubner, and Co., 1946.

Kershaw, David, and Fair, Jerilyn. *The New Jersey Income-Maintenance Experiment*. Institute for Research on Poverty Monograph Series, vol. 3. New York: Academic Press, 1976–77.

King, Anthony. "Ideas, Institutions and the Policies of Governments: A Comparative Analysis." *British Journal of Political Science* 3 (1973):409–23.

Kleinberg, Benjamin S. *American Society in the Postindustrial Age: Technocracy, Power, and the End of Ideology*. Columbus, Ohio: Charles E. Merrill Publishing Company, 1973.

Landis, James M. *The Administrative Process*. New Haven and London: Yale University Press, 1966.

Lasswell, Harold D., and Kaplan, Abraham. *Power and Society: A Framework for Political Inquiry*. New Haven and London: Yale University Press, 1963.

Law, Sylvia. *An American Civil Liberties Union Handbook: The Rights of the Poor*. New York: Avon, Discus Books, 1974.

Leichter, Howard M. *A Comparative Approach to Policy Analysis: Health Care Policy in Four Nations*. Cambridge: Cambridge University Press, 1979.

Lenski, Gerhard E. *Power and Privilege: A Theory of Social Stratification*. New York: McGraw-Hill, 1966.

Leys, Wayne A. R. "Ethics and Administrative Discretion." *Public Administration Review* 3 (1943):10–23.

Lindenfeld, Frank, ed. *Reader in Political Sociology*. New York: Funk and Wagnalls, 1968.

Lipset, Seymour M. *Political Man: The Social Bases of Politics*. Garden City, N.Y.: Doubleday, 1960.

Lowi, Theodore J. *American Government: Incomplete Conquest*. Hinsdale, Ill.: Dryden Press, 1976.
_____. *The End of Liberalism: Ideology, Policy, and the Crisis of Public Authority*. New York: Norton, 1969.
_____. *The End of Liberalism: The Second Republic of the United States*. 2d ed. New York: Norton, 1979.
_____. "Europeanization of America? From United States to United State." In *Nationalizing Government: Public Policies in America*, edited by Theodore J. Lowi and Alan Stone, pp. 15–29. Beverly Hills and London: Sage Publications, 1978.
_____, and Stone, Alan, eds. *Nationalizing Government: Public Policies in America*. Beverly Hills and London: Sage Publications, 1978.
Lurie, Irene. "Integrating Income Maintenance Programs: Problems and Solutions." In *Integrating Income Maintenance Programs*, edited by Irene Lurie, pp. 1–38. Institute for Research on Poverty Monograph Series. New York: Academic Press, 1975.
MacRae, Duncan, Jr. *The Social Function of Social Science*. New Haven and London: Yale University Press, 1976.
_____. Written Communication, 1979.
Mandell, Betty Reid. *Welfare in America*. Englewood Cliffs, N.J.: Prentice-Hall, 1975.
Marmor, Theodore R. *Poverty Policy: A Compendium of Cash Transfer Proposals*. Chicago: Aldine-Atherton, 1971.
Marris, Peter, and Rein, Martin. *Dilemmas of Social Reform: Poverty and Community Action in the United States*. 2d ed. Chicago: Aldine, 1973.
Marshall, Thomas H. *Sociology at the Crossroads*. London: Heinemann, 1963.
_____. *Social Policy*. 3d ed., rev. London: Hutchinson University Library, 1970.
_____. "Value Problems of Welfare-Capitalism." *Journal of Social Policy* 1 (1972):15–32.
Marx, Karl. *Economic and Philosophic Manuscripts of 1844*. Moscow: Foreign Languages Publishing House, 1961.
_____, and Engels, Friedrich. *Basic Writings on Politics and Philosophy*. Edited by Lewis S. Feuer. Garden City, N.Y.: Doubleday, Anchor Books, 1959.
_____. *The Communist Manifesto*. New York: Washington Square Press, 1971.
Mashaw, Jerry L.; Goetz, Charles J.; Goodman, Frank I.; Schwartz, Warren F.; Verkuil, Paul R.; and Carrow, Milton M. *Social Security Hearings and Appeals*. Toronto and Lexington: D. C. Heath and Company, Lexington Books, 1978.
Mauss, Marcel. *The Gift: Forms and Functions of Exchange in Archaic Societies*. Translated by J. Cunnison. Glencoe, Ill.: Free Press, 1954.
Mayers, Lewis. *The American Legal System*. Rev. ed. New York, Evanston, and London: Harper and Row Publishers, 1955, 1964.
McIntosh, Donald. "Weber and Freud: On the Nature and Sources of Authority." *American Sociological Review* 35 (1970):901–11.
Meenaghan, Thomas M., and Washington, Robert O. *Social Policy and Social Welfare*. New York: Free Press, 1980.
Michelman, Frank I. "Property, Utility, and Fairness: Comments on the Ethi-

cal Foundations of 'Just Compensation' Law." *Harvard Law Review* 80 (1967):1165–1258.

Milius, Peter. "Federal Welfare: More and More It's Aid for Housing." *Seattle Times*, 2 September 1979, p. K3.

Mishra, Ramesh. "Welfare and Industrial Man: A Study of Welfare in Western Industrial Societies in Relation to a Hypothesis of Convergence." *Sociological Review* 21 (1973):535–66.

Mommsen, Wolfgang. "Max Weber's Political Sociology and His Philosophy of World History." *International Social Science Journal* 17 (1965):23–45.

Moore, Barrington, Jr. *Social Origins of Dictatorship and Democracy: Lord and Peasant in the Making of the Modern World*. Boston: Beacon Press, 1967.

Mosca, Gaetano. *The Ruling Class*. New York: McGraw-Hill, 1939.

Moynihan, Daniel Patrick. *The Politics of a Guaranteed Income: The Nixon Administration and the FAP*. New York: Random House, 1973.

Müller-Armack, Alfred. *Wirtschaftslenkung und Marktwirtschaft*. Hamburg: Verlag für Wirtschaft und Sozialpolitik, 1947.

Myrdal, Gunnar. *Beyond the Welfare State*. New Haven and London: Yale University Press, 1969.

————. "The Place of Values in Social Policy." *Journal of Social Policy* 1 (1972):1–14.

Neumann, Franz. *The Democratic and the Authoritarian State*. New York: Free Press, 1966.

Nonet, Philippe, and Selznick, Philip. *Law and Society in Transition: Toward Responsive Law*. New York: Harper and Row Publishers, Harper Colophon Books, 1978.

Nozick, Robert. *Anarchy, State, and Utopia*. New York: Basic Books, 1974.

"1 Million May Lose Jobless Benefits." *Seattle Times*, 11 February 1980, p. 1.

Organization for Economic Cooperation and Development. *Negative Income Tax: An Approach to the Co-ordination of Taxation and Social Welfare Policies*. Paris: Organization for Economic Cooperation and Development, 1974.

Osnos, Peter. "The Last Year in the Life of Boris Pasternak." *Washington Post, Bookworld*, 13 July 1980, p. 11.

Pareto, Vilfredo. *The Mind and Society*. Translated by A. Bongiorno and Arthur Livingston. New York: Harcourt, Brace, and World, 1935.

————. *Sociological Writings*. Selected and introduced by S. E. Finer. Translated by Derick Mirfin. New York: Frederick A. Praeger Publishers, 1966.

Parsons, Talcott. *The Structure of Social Action*. New York: McGraw-Hill, 1937.

————. *The Social System*. Glencoe, Ill.: Free Press, 1951.

————. *Structure and Process in Modern Societies*. Glencoe, Ill.: Free Press, 1961.

Pechman, Joseph A., and Timpane, P. Michael, eds. *Work Incentives and Income Guarantees: The New Jersey Negative Income Tax Experiment*. Washington, D.C.: Brookings Institution, 1975.

Petrovic, Gajo. *Marx in the Mid-Twentieth Century: A Yugoslavian Philosopher Reconsiders Karl Marx's Writings*. Garden City, N.Y.: Doubleday, Anchor Books, 1967.

Phillips, Derek L. *Equality, Justice, and Rectification: An Exploration in*

Normative Sociology. London, New York, and San Francisco: Academic Press, 1979.

Piven, Frances Fox, and Cloward, Richard A. *Regulating the Poor: The Functions of Public Welfare.* New York: Vintage Books, 1972.

Pound, Roscoe. *Administrative Law: Its Growth, Procedure, and Significance.* Pittsburgh: University of Pittsburgh Press, 1942.

Prettyman, E. Barrett. *Trial by Agency.* Charlottesville, Va.: Virginia Law Review Association, 1959.

Pritchard, Joel. *Your Congressman Reports,* April 1980.

Pryor, Frederic L. *Public Expenditures in Communist and Capitalist Nations.* Homewood, Ill.: Irwin, 1968.

Rawls, John. *A Theory of Justice.* Cambridge, Mass.: Harvard University Press, Belknap Press, 1971.

"Recession: It's Enough to Make You Sick." *Seattle Post-Intelligencer,* 17 June 1980, p. 1.

Reich, Charles. "The New Property." *Public Interest* 3 (1966):57–89.

Rein, Martin, and Heclo, Hugh. "What Welfare Crisis?—A Comparison of Britain, Sweden, and the United States." *Public Interest* 33 (1973):61–83.

Rheinstein, Max, ed. *Max Weber On Law in Economy and Society.* New York: Clarion, 1967.

Rimlinger, Gaston V. "Social Security, Incentives, and Controls in the U.S. and U.S.S.R." *Comparative Studies in Society and History* 4 (1961):104–24. Reprinted in *Social Welfare Institutions: A Sociological Reader,* edited by Mayer N. Zald, pp. 102–22. New York: Wiley, 1965.

———. *Welfare Policy and Industrialization in Europe, America, and Russia.* New York: Wiley, 1971.

Ritti, R. Richard, and Hyman, Drew W. "The Administration of Poverty: Lessons from the Welfare Explosion, 1967–1973." *Social Problems* 25 (1977):157–75.

Rohrbough, Malcolm J. *The Land Office Business: The Settlement and Administration of American Public Lands, 1789–1837.* New York: Oxford University Press, 1968.

Rose, Michael E. "Settlement, Removal and the New Poor Law." In *The New Poor Law in the Nineteenth Century,* edited by Derek Fraser, pp. 25–44. New York: St. Martin's Press, 1976.

Rosen, Michael B. "Tenants' Rights in Public Housing." In *Housing for the Poor: Rights and Remedies,* edited by Project on Social Welfare Law, Supplement 1, pp. 154–261. New York: New York University School of Law, 1967.

Rossi, Peter H., and Lyall, Katharine C. *Reforming Public Welfare: A Critique of the Negative Income Tax Experiment.* New York: Russell Sage Foundation, 1976.

Roth, Guenther, "Socio-Historical Model and Developmental Theory: Charismatic Community, Charisma of Reason and the Counterculture." *American Sociological Review* 40 (1975):148–57.

———, and Wittich, Claus, eds. *Economy and Society by Max Weber.* New York: Bedminster Press, 1968. 2d ed. Berkeley: University of California Press, 1979.

Rothman, David J. "The State as Parent: Social Policy in the Progressive Era." In *Doing Good: The Limits of Benevolence,* by Willard Gaylin, Ira

Glasser, Steven Marcus, and David Rothman, pp. 67–96. New York: Pantheon Books, 1978.

Rowat, Donald C., ed. *The Ombudsman: Citizen's Defender*. London: George Allen and Unwin Ltd., 1965.

Rowley, Charles K., and Peacock, Alan. *Welfare Economics: A Liberal Restatement*. New York: Wiley, 1975.

Sabine, George H. *A History of Political Theory*. New York: Henry Holt and Company, 1937.

———. "The Two Democratic Traditions." *The Philosophical Review* 61 (1952):451–74.

Sanger, S. L. "260,000 in State May Lose Food Stamps." *Seattle Post-Intelligencer*, 17 April 1980, p. 1.

Scandinavian Sociological Association. "The Nordic Welfare States." *Acta Sociologica* 21 (1978):Supplement.

Scates, Shelby. "Soviet Bureaucracy Metes Out Tractors, Words and Terror." *Seattle Post-Intelligencer*, 18 May 1980, p. B3.

Schaar, John H. *Legitimacy in the Modern State*. New Brunswick, N.J.: Transaction Books, 1980.

Schwartz, Bernard. *French Administrative Law and the Common-Law World*. New York: New York University Press, 1954.

———. *An Introduction to American Administrative Law*. 2d ed. Dobbs Ferry, N.Y.: Oceana, 1962.

———. *Legal Control of Government: Administrative Law in Britain and the United States*. Oxford: Clarendon Press, 1972.

Selznick, Philip. *Law, Society, and Industrial Justice*. New York: Russell Sage Foundation, 1969.

Shapiro, Martin. *The Supreme Court and Administrative Agencies*. New York: Free Press, 1968.

Shils, E. A. "Charisma, Order and Status." *American Sociological Review* 30 (1965):199–213.

Shipler, David K. "In Russia, A Pair of Jeans Is the Mark of Success." *Seattle Times*, 11 March 1979, section K, pp. 1 and 3.

Sleeman, J. F. *The Welfare State: Its Aims, Benefits and Costs*. London: George Allen and Unwin Ltd., 1973.

"Socialism: Trials and Errors." *Time*, 13 March 1978, pp. 24–36.

Spencer, Martin E. "Weber on Legitimate Norms and Authority." *British Journal of Sociology* 21 (1970):123–34.

Spindler, Arthur. *Public Welfare*. New York: Human Sciences Press, 1979.

"State Welfare Cut Illegal, Court Rules." *Seattle Post-Intelligencer*, 29 October 1980, p. A9.

Stein, Bruno. *Social Security and Pensions in Transition: Understanding the American Retirement System*. New York: Free Press, 1980.

Steiner, Gilbert Y. *Social Insecurity: The Politics of Welfare*. Chicago: Rand McNally, 1966.

———. *The State of Welfare*. Washington, D.C.: Brookings Institution, 1971.

Stewart, Richard B. "The Reformation of American Administrative Law." *Harvard Law Review* 88 (1975):1669–1813.

Stone, Alan. "Planning, Public Policy and Capitalism." In *Nationalizing Government: Public Policies in America*, edited by Theodore J. Lowi and Alan Stone, pp. 427–42. Beverly Hills and London: Sage Publications, 1978.

Storey, James R.; Harris, Robert; Levy, Frank; Fechter, Alan; and Nichel, Richard C. *The Better Jobs and Income Plan*. Welfare Reform Policy

Analysis Series, 1. Washington, D.C.: Urban Institute, 1978.

Street, Harry. *Justice in the Welfare State*. 2d ed. London: Stevens and Sons, 1975.

Strong, Douglas H., and Rosenfield, Elizabeth S. "Ethics or Expediency: An Environmental Question." *Environmental Affairs* 5 (1976):255–70.

Svitak, Ivan. "The Sources of Socialist Humanism." In *Socialist Humanism*, edited by Erich Fromm, pp. 16–28. Garden City, N.Y.: Doubleday, Anchor Books, 1966.

Swidler, Ann. "The Concept of Rationality in the Work of Max Weber." *Sociological Inquiry* 43 (1973):35–42.

tenBroek, Jacobus, and Wilson, Richard B. "Public Assistance and Social Insurance: A Normative Evaluation." *UCLA Law Review* 1 (1954):237–302.

Theobald, Robert. *Free Men and Free Markets, Proposed: A Guaranteed Income*. New York: Clarkson N. Potter, 1963.

Thimmesch, Nick. "The Fraud in Social Security 'Reform.'" *Seattle Times*, 7 November 1978, editorial page.

Thompson, Victor A. *Modern Organization*. New York: Alfred A. Knopf, 1961.

Titmuss, Richard M. *Essays on the Welfare State*. Boston: Beacon Press, 1969.

———. *Social Policy: An Introduction*. London: George Allen and Unwin, 1974.

Tonsor, Steven J. "The Conservative Elements in American Liberalism." *Review of Politics* 35 (1973):489–500.

Trilling, Lionel. "Manners, Morals, and the Novel." In *The Liberal Imagination: Essays on Literature and Society*, pp. 199–215. Garden City, N.Y.: Doubleday Anchor Books, 1950.

Tuchman, Barbara. *A Distant Mirror: The Calamitous Fourteenth Century*. New York: Alfred A. Knopf, 1978.

Tucker, Robert C. *The Marxian Revolutionary Idea*. New York: Norton, 1970.

Tussman, Joseph. *Obligation and the Body Politic*. New York: Oxford University Press, 1960.

U.S. Department of Commerce. Bureau of the Census. *Census Bureau Conference on Issues in Federal Statistical Needs Relating to Women, 1978*. Current Population Reports: Special Studies, Series P-23, no. 83. Washington, D.C.: Government Printing Office, 1978.

———. *A Statistical Portrait of Women in the United States: 1978*. Current Population Reports: Special Studies, Series P-23, no. 100. Washington, D.C.: Government Printing Office, 1978.

Viner, Jacob. "The U.S. As a 'Welfare State.'" In *Man, Science, Learning and Education*, edited by S. W. Higginbotham, pp. 213–19. Houston: Rice University, 1963.

Ward, Lester. "Theory and Practice Are at War." *The Penn Monthly* 12 (1881):321–36. Reprinted in *Lester Ward and the Welfare State*, edited by Henry Steele Commager, pp. 22–36. Indianapolis and New York: Bobbs-Merrill, 1967.

Weaver, Paul H. "Regulation, Social Policy, and Class Conflict." *Public Interest* 50 (1978):45–63.

Weber, Max. *On Law in Economy and Society*. Edited by Max Rheinstein. New York: Clarion, 1967.

———. *Economy and Society*. Edited by Guenther Roth and Claus Wittich.

New York: Bedminster Press, 1968. 2d ed. Berkeley: University of California Press, 1979.

Webster, Noah. *Webster's New Twentieth Century Dictionary of the English Language, Unabridged.* 2d ed. Cleveland and New York: World Publishing Company, 1970.

Weed, Frank J. "Industrialization and Welfare Systems: A Critical Evaluation of the Convergence Hypothesis." *International Journal of Comparative Sociology* 20 (1979):282–91.

Welch, Claude E., Jr., and Taintor, Mavis Bunker, eds. *Revolution and Political Change.* North Scituate, Mass., and Belmont, Calif.: Duxbury Press, 1972.

"Welfare Game: 'Obnoxious' and 'Racist' or Just a Humorous Pastime?" *Seattle Times,* 9 October 1980, p. A10.

Wheeler, Harvey. *The Restoration of Politics.* Santa Barbara, Calif.: Center for the Study of Democratic Institutions, 1965.

Wilensky, Harold L. *The Welfare State and Equality: Structural and Ideological Roots of Public Expenditures.* Berkeley: University of California Press, 1975.

————. *The 'New Corporatism,' Centralization, and the Welfare State.* Contemporary Political Sociology Series, vol. 2. London and Beverly Hills: Sage Publications, 1976.

————, and Lebeaux, Charles N. *Industrial Society and Social Welfare.* New York: Free Press, 1965.

Willer, David E. "Max Weber's Missing Authority Type." *Sociological Inquiry* 37 (1967):231–39.

Williams, Robin M., Jr. *American Society: A Sociological Interpretation.* 2d ed., rev. New York: Alfred A. Knopf, 1960.

Williams, Walter. *The Case for the Negative Income Tax: The Second Time Around.* Seattle: Institute for Governmental Research, University of Washington, 1972.

Wittfogel, Karl. *Oriental Despotism: A Comparative Study of Total Power.* New Haven: Yale University Press, 1957.

Wolfe, Alan. *The Limits of Legitimacy: Political Contradictions of Contemporary Capitalism.* New York: Free Press, 1977.

Woll, Peter. *Administrative Law: The Informal Process.* Berkeley and Los Angeles: University of California Press, 1963.

"Worker's Right to Refuse Dangerous Task Upheld." *Seattle Times,* 26 February 1980, p. 1.

Zald, Mayer N. "Demographics, Politics, and the Future of the Welfare State." *Social Service Review* 50 (1977):110–24.

————, ed. *Social Welfare Institutions: A Sociological Reader.* New York: Wiley, 1965.

INDEX

Absolutist state, 168; transition to liberal state, 200

Adams, Carolyn Teich, 119, 202

Adjudication: defined, 4, 5; "pure," 29; particularistic, and special law, 31; relationship to adversarial procedures, 105; and the rule of law, 169; primitive, 183; contrasted with administration, 166–70, 183–86; and the masking of administrative disbursement of largesse, 196–99; "irrational" and "primitive formalism," 219 (chap. 2, n. 2). *See also* Adjudicative principle; Administration; Administrative adjudication

Adjudicative principle, 9; progressive rationalization of, 168, 169; and avenues of appeal, 169; and regime legitimacy, 169; absorption of by administration, 182; emergence of within legal order, 183; as analogue of social control, 210–12; highest expression of, 212

Adjudicator vs. administrator: differences in objectives, 98–99

Administration: contrasted with adjudication, 4, 17, 26–27, 30–31, 87, 113, 166–70, 169, 183–86, 196–99; defined, 5; basis of indispensability of welfare state, 5, 102; two usages of, 6–7, 88, 90, 97, 104, 115; bureaucratic, 7, 88, 90; absorption of private society into the ambit of, 20, 174–82, 190; "pure," 28, 199; postwar intentions to unify, 77; rationalization of, 88, 90, 91; arbitrary nature of, 88, 105–10; patriarchal or patrimonial, 90, 91, 93; for-

mally rationalized, 91; substantively rationalized, 91; purposes of, 91–92; as antithetical to supremacy of the law, 97; comparative novelty of, 101; need to reconcile with older functions of rule, 102, 150; of social welfare, costs associated with, 137–39, 226 (n. 5); and regime effectiveness, 167–69; as oldest form of government, 183; tyranny of, 184; privileges of, 190–92; primeval, 199

Administrative adjudication, 89; defined, 10, 94; indispensability of in modern state, 12, 95–97; need to synchronize with regular adjudication, 13, 97–102; and due process, 95; volume of, 95–96. *See also* Administrative law; Entitlements

Administrative agencies or staffs, 6–7; and decision-making biases, 11–12, 92–93; and demand for expertness, 102; prerogatives of and unreviewable orders, 149; proliferation of, 153; parallels between regulatory and redistributive, 153–54. *See also* Administrative law

"Administrative imperative," 95–97

Administrative law: defined, 8; need for articulation with rule of law, 13, 89, 97–101, 176; and congruity with statute objectives, 90–91; rationalization of, 92, 165, 166–67, 168; and absence of counterpart to substantive rationalization of, 98–99, 137–38, 178; circumstances surrounding the rise of, 150; and the public